THE $7 A MEAL SLOW COOKER COOKBOOK

FEED A FAMILY FOR $7 OR LESS

301 INEXPENSIVE MEALS THE WHOLE FAMILY WILL LOVE!

Linda Larsen

Pillsbury Bake-Off® recipe tester

Contains material adapted and abridged from *The Everything® Meals on a Budget Cookbook* by Linda Larsen, copyright © 2008 by F+W Publications, Inc., ISBN 10: 1-59869-508-8, ISBN 13: 978-1-59869-508-3; *The Everything® Slow Cooker Cookbook* by Margaret Kaeter, copyright © 2002 by F+W Publications, Inc., ISBN 10: 1-58062-667-X, ISBN 13: 978-1-58062-667-5; *The Everything® Slow Cooking for a Crowd Cookbook* by Katie Thompson, copyright © 2005 by F+W Publications, Inc., ISBN 10: 1-59337-391-0, ISBN 13: 978-1-59337-391-7; *The Everything® Quick and Easy 30-Minute, 5-Ingredient Cookbook* by Linda Larsen, copyright © 2006 by F+W Publications, Inc., ISBN 10: 1-59337-692-8, ISBN 13: 978-1-59337-692-5; *The Everything® Tex-Mex Cookbook* by Linda Larsen, copyright © 2006 by F+W Publications, Inc., ISBN 10: 1-59337-580-8, ISBN 13: 978-1-59337-580-5; *The Everything® No Trans Fat Cookbook* by Linda Larsen, copyright © 2007 by F+W Publications, Inc., ISBN 10: 1-59869-533-9, ISBN 13: 978-1-59869-533-5; *The Everything® Low Cholesterol Cookbook* by Linda Larsen, copyright © 2008 by F+W Publications, Inc., ISBN 10: 1-59869-401-4, ISBN 13: 978-1-59869-401-7; *The Everything® Meals for a Month Cookbook* by Linda Larsen, copyright © 2005 by F+W Publications, Inc., ISBN 10: 1-59337-323-6, ISBN 13: 978-1-59337-323-8; and *The About.com Guide to Shortcut Cooking* by Linda Larsen, copyright © 2007 by F+W Publications, Inc., ISBN 10: 1-59869-273-9, ISBN 13: 978-1-59869-273-0.

Published by
Adams Media, a division of F+W Media, Inc.
57 Littlefield Street, Avon, MA 02322. U.S.A.
www.adamsmedia.com

ISBN 10: 1-60550-118-2
ISBN 13: 978-1-60550-118-5

Printed in the United States of America.

J I H G F E D C B A

Library of Congress Cataloging-in-Publication Data
is available from the publisher.

This publication is designed to provide accurate and authoritative information with regard to the subject matter covered. It is sold with the understanding that the publisher is not engaged in rendering legal, accounting, or other professional advice. If legal advice or other expert assistance is required, the services of a competent professional person should be sought.

—From a *Declaration of Principles* jointly adopted by a Committee of the American Bar Association and a Committee of Publishers and Associations

This book is available at quantity discounts for bulk purchases.

For information, please call 1-800-289-0963.

CONTENTS

iv   INTRODUCTION

1   CHAPTER 1: SLOW COOKING ON A BUDGET

10   CHAPTER 2: APPETIZERS AND SNACKS

34   CHAPTER 3: BREAKFAST

57   CHAPTER 4: BEEF

81   CHAPTER 5: PORK AND HAM

102   CHAPTER 6: CHICKEN—LIGHT MEAT

124   CHAPTER 7: CHICKEN—DARK MEAT

143   CHAPTER 8: SEAFOOD

162   CHAPTER 9: VEGETARIAN

183   CHAPTER 10: SIDE DISHES

209   CHAPTER 11: SANDWICHES

230   CHAPTER 12: SOUPS

257   CHAPTER 13: SALADS

275   CHAPTER 14: STEWS, CHILIS, AND CHOWDERS

302   CHAPTER 15: DESSERT

325   APPENDIX A: GLOSSARY

328   APPENDIX B: SUGGESTED MENUS

330   INDEX

INTRODUCTION

The slow cooker is really a wonderful appliance. Get in the habit of using it and you will save money and time. Just add food to the slow cooker and turn it on, and several hours later you'll come back to perfectly prepared breakfast, lunch, or dinner.

However, there is one common complaint about this appliance: all the foods cooked in it tend to taste the same. That's not the case with these recipes. You'll learn how to make sandwich fillings, cold salads, breakfast stratas, and delicious desserts in your slow cooker, along with the traditional roasts, stews, and soups.

As always, to cook successfully on a budget, you must follow a few rules. Starting to cook at home, from scratch, is really the most important. You will automatically spend less money when you buy simple foods and prepare them at home. Just think of all the people who have to make money in a restaurant: the owners, suppliers, cooks, wait staff, and cleaners. You are paying their salaries when you eat out. So of course that food is more expensive.

Making and abiding by a grocery list is another important rule. Having a list in hand will keep you focused, and helps reduce all the temptation grocers build into their stores. When you're comparing the prices of two kinds of onions, you'll be less likely to think about the warm and gooey filled doughnuts beckoning you from the bakery.

My first budget book, *The Everything® Meals on a Budget Book*, included some slow cooker recipes, but not many. This book was a wonderful challenge to write, and these recipes really fit the way we live today. The price of every single food has risen dramatically since I wrote the first book, and there's really no end in sight. To survive, we'll have to change the way we eat, and that starts at home, in our kitchens.

The cost for each recipe was figured using NutriBase Clinical Version 7.0. To get the best representative cost for each ingredient, price lists at SimonDelivers.com, YourGrocery.com, and Peapod.com were used. Sale prices, discounts, and coupons were not included in the calculations, so you may find that prices in your area are higher or lower than those stated here.

And don't worry—these recipes are delicious and inviting as well as being inexpensive to make. Get your whole family involved in preparing food, and you'll be teaching them a valuable life skill, as well as taking care of them.

CHAPTER 1

SLOW COOKING ON A BUDGET

Once considered a throwback to the 1960s, slow cookers have come into their own. A slow cooker is one of the easiest and most cost-effective ways to cook food. They can turn inexpensive cuts of meat into a feast and they cook all day while you are busy with your life. You can control your budget, save time, and eat very well by using a slow cooker for every meal of the day.

WHAT'S A SLOW COOKER?

A slow cooker, or Crock-Pot, is a metal, electric appliance with its heat sources on the sides and bottom. A crockery or glass insert is usually used. The food heats up slowly and evenly from the consistent heat. Some appliances you may think are a slow cooker actually are not. Those appliances just heat from the bottom: they are not considered true slow cookers.

The slow cooker uses consistent, low heat to cook food through conduction. On low, the temperature is around 180°F, and on high, the temperature is about 280°F. These temperatures are high enough to get the food past the danger zone of 40°F to 140°F and cook the food thoroughly, but keep it moist and tender.

When you buy a slow cooker, look for one with a removable liner. This makes cleaning the slow cooker much easier. The liner is usually made of stoneware or ceramic material, and is thick and heavy to trap and conduct heat.

Types of Slow Cookers

Today, you can find slow cookers in just about every shape and size. Tiny 1-cup slow cookers are great for making dips, compotes, and sauces. Slow cookers with a 2-cup capacity are ideal for appetizers and for two-person households. The most common slow cookers hold 3½ to 4-quarts, and feed families of 4–6 easily.

And then there are the giants: 7-quart slow cookers to serve a crowd.

SLOW COOKER CAPACITY

SLOW COOKER SIZE	SERVINGS	FOODS TO COOK
1-quart	1–2	Appetizers, dips
2-quart	2–3	Sauces, 2 servings
3½-quart	4	Family meals
4-quart	5–6	Family meals
5-quart	6–8	Large family meals
6-quart	8–10	Roasts, hams
7-quart	10–12	Whole chicken, turkey

The controls have changed too in the past 10 years. Once there were only three settings: off, low, and high. Now sophisticated electronic controls let you delay cooking time, keep the food warm after it's cooked, and program the cooking times for specific dishes that you make often.

SAVE MONEY COOKING

You will save money if you cook at home rather than spend your money in restaurants. The Crock-Pot helps save money and time because it cuts down on the work, and the simpler, more basic foods that work best in the appliance are cheaper.

Keep your slow cookers on the counter, and once you get into the habit of using them, it will take you less and less time to prepare the food. The skill will become second nature. Choose to make your own meals and you will control what's in the food you feed your family.

The slow cooker has other advantages over an oven. It won't heat up the kitchen like an oven or a boiling pot on the stovetop will, which saves money on cooling costs in the summer. Also, opening an oven door lets out heat which means the oven has to heat up again. The slow cooker stays closed during its cooking cycle, so it maintains heat and a proper cooking temperature.

BEST SLOW COOKER FOODS

The foods that cook best in the slow cooker are inexpensive cuts of lean meat, hard root vegetables, brown rice, and processed cheeses. The long, slow heat is the best environment for these foods. And the bonus? These are the most inexpensive foods in the supermarket.

The cheapest beef cuts at the butcher counter are top and bottom round, sirloin tip, and stew meat. These cuts require long, slow cooking to break down fibers; just the type of heat and cooking environment provided by the slow cooker.

Stews and soups are made for the slow cooker. And because they cook all together in a closed environment, the flavors develop, blend, and mingle far better than simmering in a pot on the stove.

CHEAPEST SLOW COOKER FOODS

FOOD	COST PER POUND	SERVINGS
Round steak	$3.50	4
Potatoes	60¢	3
Cabbage	80¢	4
Onions	$1.00	4
Brown rice	$2.50	10
Chicken thighs	$2.60	4
Legumes	$1.20	12
Barley	$1.50	8
Carrots	99¢	12

You can even make salads and sandwiches in the slow cooker. Sandwich fillings are a no-brainer, but when you want to make a potato or chicken salad, cook the main ingredients in the slow cooker. Then combine with a dressing and chill; the salad's done!

What's Cheaper?

A lot of your grocery savings will depend on what you buy. It's important to know that while boneless, skinless chicken breasts and bone-in breasts cost about the same amount, buying whole chicken breasts and deboning them yourself will give you more for your money. The bones and skin can be saved to make chicken stock.

In fact, for all of the recipes in this book I recommend buying bone-in, skin-on chicken breasts and removing the large breast muscle yourself. If you do this, a boneless, skinless chicken breast will cost you about a dollar, plus you can make free stock. Buying them already boned and skinned will cost about $1.20 apiece, but with no extra goodies for stock.

Frozen and canned vegetables will usually be cheaper than fresh, except when they are in season. And don't worry about the nutrition of these products. Processed produce has just as many vitamins as fresh; in many cases, even more because it's processed within a few hours of harvest. Fresh vegetables and fruits, especially when they come from other countries or spend days on a truck, take a long time to get to the market. And every day they lose vitamin content.

Buying a cheaper top round steak and cooking it for hours in the slow cooker will result in a tender and flavorful cut of beef that just takes a bit more work than plopping a tenderloin or ribeye on the grill. A stew made in the slow cooker will cost less and offer better nutrition than those sodium-packed cans of food you just reheat. You get the idea!

Unit pricing is one of the best tools to budget shopping. Look at the price per ounce to see if that huge box of pasta is a better buy than the smaller one. Most grocery stores have unit pricing tags on the shelves right under the product. You can also bring a calculator to the store to figure it out for yourself. Just divide the price by the number of ounces in the product and compare.

The general rule is: the more work you do in the kitchen, the more money you will save. Cook "lower on the food chain" with simple foods that you prepare from scratch. This will save you money and make your meals healthier too.

THE PLAN

Begin your budget savings by planning. Plan every meal. Plan for snacks and for the occasional evening out. Plan to use leftovers, and budget for special occasions. When you have meals planned for the week, you won't spend time thinking about every meal, what you'll serve, if the food is in the house or a shopping trip is necessary, and what to do with leftovers.

It's an initial expense, but think about buying more than one size and shape of slow cooker. If you have three slow cookers, you can cook a main dish, a side dish, and a dessert all at the same time. Or cook two parts of one meal, like a Beef Carbonnade and a rice pilaf to serve it over. Plan to use your Crock-Pots efficiently to make preparing a meal even easier.

SAVE TIME COOKING

The slow cooker also saves time in cooking. Preparation for foods is quite minimal. Often you just peel and cube vegetables, top them with meat, then add a liquid and turn it on. Many times you can prep foods the night before, then just combine everything in the slow cooker in the morning, turn it on, and dinner will be waiting for you.

Even if a recipe calls for browning meats or cooking onions, you don't have to. Browning large cuts of meat before they are added to the slow cooker is done for the sake of appearance and a slightly enhanced taste. Onions are often sautéed before being added to the slow cooker to deglaze a pan after a meat has been browned. But ground meats do have to be cooked before they are added to the slow cooker, both for appearance and to reduce fat.

FLEXIBILITY

Believe it or not, the slow cooker offers great flexibility, both in the types of food you cook and the recipes you can make. You can make a cold salad in a slow cooker, or make a hot chili topping you can spoon over toasted sourdough buns. Breakfast is easy in the slow cooker, and desserts are a welcome treat. And you can flavor the food any way you'd like.

If you're like most Americans, you spend a lot of money eating out; in fact, almost 50 percent of our food budget is currently spent on food not prepared at home. While it's fun to eat out, you can do the same thing at home for less than half the cost. Slow cooker Mexican, Chinese, Greek, and even French cuisine can easily be made in your own kitchen for a fraction of restaurant food. It's just as authentic, you don't have to worry about food safety or the nutrition, and you can come home to a delicious meal every night.

THE INDISPENSABLE LIST

To start cooking on a budget, first you need to know what you have in the house, what your family likes to eat, and what you know you can cook. The slow cooker makes it easy because really all you do is prep the food and let it cook. Then you have to make a list every time you go grocery shopping.

Get Organized

To get started, go through your pantry, fridge, and freezer and take stock. Pick a couple of recipes for your slow cooker and make a list of the ingredients you need. Cook those foods for the week.

If your family likes the food, add the recipes and the ingredients to two lists: your recipe file and your master shopping list. Then do the same for the next week.

After two or three weeks, you'll see a pattern emerge. You may notice you buy carrots and onions every week, or garlic and potatoes. Ground beef or round steak, chicken thighs or pork loin may make frequent appearances. You can then make up a master list that you use every week. The rest of the list should come from other ingredients you'll need, like lettuce for salads, breakfast cereals, milk, and juice.

When you go shopping, abide by the list. But at the same time, be open to change! You may find that there are in-store specials on certain foods, especially meats, which may change your meal plan. Be flexible and look for good buys.

USING COUPONS

You've seen those news stories where a woman buys a full cart of groceries for $2.18. While that is possible, saving that much money on groceries with coupons is practically a full-time job and requires double-couponing as well as buying many prepackaged and processed foods. By using these tips and shopping wisely, you can use coupons to save 10 to 20 percent from your grocery bill.

When you are looking for a coupon, think about these things:

- Will the coupon make that item the cheapest in unit pricing?
- Will you be able to use all of the food before the expiration date?
- Does your family like this food, and will they eat it?
- Is the food nutritious or junk food?
- Can you easily use the food in your regular meal planning?

To get organized, purchase a loose-leaf notebook and a file folder to hold menus and coupons. You can arrange the folder in several ways: according to the layout of your grocery store, according to the categories of food, or according to expiration date. Be sure you understand what food the coupon applies to, and buy that exact product. And go through the folder often, making a note of which coupons you want to use and which ones are close to their expiration date.

Make sure to read the fine print on the coupons carefully. Sometimes you can use more than one coupon on a product, and if that product happens to be on sale, the savings can really add up. More often, you need to purchase a specific size and brand of product that matches the coupon exactly.

If a store runs out of an item you have a coupon for, or that is on sale, ask for a rain check, then keep that rain check in the coupon folder. When the item is restocked, the grocery store will mail you a notice, and you can buy it at the sale price.

CARING FOR YOUR SLOW COOKER

Slow cookers will last for many years as long as you care for them properly. As with any kitchen appliance, read the manufacturer's booklet carefully and follow all safety rules and instructions. Slow cookers are easy to clean and maintain if you follow a few rules.

Don't Submerge the Unit

The external, or heating, unit should never be submerged in water. This will ruin the electric and electronic parts. To clean the external unit, unplug it, make sure it's cool, and wipe down with a damp soapy sponge or cloth. Rinse with a plain cloth and dry thoroughly before storing.

The stone or ceramic insert is usually dishwasher-safe, but check with the manufacturer. As soon as the food is removed, add warm water and soap and let the insert soak for awhile. The food should come off easily.

Never use stainless steel or steel scrubbing pads to clean a sealed ceramic insert; you will scratch the finish. Once the finish is scratched, the insert may crack. Not only that, but cracks can harbor food over time, which can lead to food poisoning.

Cooking Bags

Cooking bags are heavy-duty plastic bags that are made to withstand heat. They are relatively inexpensive, and save you time cleaning. They lift right out of the slow cooker insert, and then you just throw them away.

Never use an ordinary plastic bag or food storage bag to line the slow cooker; it will melt right onto the insert or unit. Then you'll have to buy a new slow cooker!

SHOP ONCE A WEEK

Most budget books tell you to shop only once a week. If you are organized and know that you'll use the food you buy within that time, this is a smart idea, not only for your food budget, but your gasoline budget as well.

But if you let food go to waste, if you throw a frozen pizza into the oven instead of slicing the vegetables and making that quiche you had planned, it's better to shop more often and buy less at one time.

This works best if a grocery store with good prices is on your route home from work or school. Combine errands to save on gas, but make sure to shop for groceries last. Perishable and frozen foods should go directly from the grocery store to your fridge and freezer, as quickly as possible.

The number of times you shop in a week also depends on how far you are from a grocery store. If there is one with reasonable prices and good stock within walking distance, you can shop more often, look for buys, and take advantage of coupons and sales.

WASTE: THE BUDGET BUSTER

The biggest budget buster isn't that $7.00 salmon or $3.00 bag of chips. It's waste! Americans throw away almost 45 percent of the food they buy. If you spend $900 a month on food, you may be throwing away more than $400 a month. Whether it's a head of lettuce that languishes in the fridge until it wilts, or a bag of chicken breasts imperfectly wrapped so it develops freezer burn, food is easy to waste.

When you buy foods, be sure that you keep track of expiration dates. If anything that you buy fresh can be frozen, try your best to freeze that food before it slips past the expiration or use-by date.

Wrap meats in freezer wrap, label, and freeze. Many fruits can be individually flash-frozen, then packed into hard-sided containers. Cheeses and butter also freeze well, packaged into freezer bags. Thaw these foods in the refrigerator, never at room temperature.

How Long Do Foods Last?

How long should perishable products be kept on the counter or in the fridge until they're no longer safe or wholesome? There are some fairly rigid rules about how soon food should be used before it must be frozen or thrown away. On manufactured and dairy products, and on some meat products, be sure to scrupulously follow the expiration dates stamped on the package.

Never let perishable food stand outside of refrigeration or freezing longer than two hours; one hour if the ambient temperature is above 80°F. Do not let frozen foods thaw on the counter; they must thaw slowly in the refrigerator.

Leftovers have to be planned into your budget to make another meal. Spend a little money to get reusable good quality food containers that will hold the food until you're ready to use it. Always refrigerate food promptly, know what's in your fridge and freezer, and plan your weekly meals with leftovers in mind.

Food Savers

There are some products you can buy that can help reduce waste. Green Bags made by Evert Fresh do work, although some sources say the food doesn't stay fresh as long as claimed. The bag should keep your peppers and asparagus fresh and wholesome for 5–7 days, which is 3–4 days longer than produce.

You can also look into vacuum sealers, which remove the air from food containers to help prevent freezer burn. Of course, you can get close to the same result this way: use a heavy-duty freezer bag, seal it almost to the end, then insert a straw and suck out as much air as possible. Seal the bag, label, and freeze immediately.

SLOW COOKER SAFETY

There are some rules you need to follow to make sure the food you prepare in the slow cooker is safe. Some are basic kitchen safety rules, but others are particular to the slow cooker.

Before you use it, inspect the insert for cracks or chips. This can weaken the insert, and the container may leak when the appliance heats, creating a fire hazard. Make sure the cord is free of cracks or splits. Always place the slow cooker on a heatproof surface when it's in use.

Don't cook frozen meat in the slow cooker. These foods will stay in the danger zone of 40°F to 140°F for too long a time in the low and slow heat.

Always use a meat thermometer to check the final temperature of chicken, pork, and beef. Chicken breasts should be cooked to 165°F, thighs to 170°F. Pork is cooked to 150°F, while beef should reach 145°F.

Always remove the food from the slow cooker after it's done cooking. Do not place the food in the crockery insert in the fridge to cool. The thick walls of the insert, designed to hold heat during cooking, will slow down the cooling process and, once again, keep the food in the danger zone too long.

If you follow these rules, your slow cooker will last for years and you'll prepare safe, healthy meals for your family. Now let's get started in the kitchen with these delicious and easy recipes that cost less than $7.00 to prepare, and feed at least four people.

CHAPTER 2

APPETIZERS AND SNACKS

11   The Dip Olé!

12   Sweet-and-Sour Mini Sausages

13   Slow Cooker Caponata

14   Three-Cheese Dip

15   Zorba's Hummus

16   Apple Chutney

17   Spicy Shrimp and Cheese Dip

18   Cheesy Taco Dip

19   Creamy Refried Bean Dip

20   Roasted Garlic

21   Onion Chutney

22   Honey Pineapple Chicken Wings

23   Spicy Empanadas

24   Eggplant Caviar

25   Buffalo Wings

26   Slow Cooker Reuben Dip

27   Bean Nachos

28   Queso con Chile

29   Sweet 'n Crisp Curried Nuts

30   Best-Ever Snack Mix

31   Suave Cooked Salsa

32   Peanut Caramel Corn

33   Double Blueberry Chutney

The Dip Olé!

 Serves 8

Total Cost: $5.55
Calories: 220.81
Fat: 11.93 grams
Protein: 10.45 grams
Cholesterol: 32.85 mg
Sodium: 282.79 mg

1 cup dried pinto beans
1 onion, chopped
½ teaspoon salt
1 tablespoon chili powder
1 (3-ounce) package cream cheese, softened

½ cup sour cream
2 jalapeño peppers, minced
2 cups chopped iceberg lettuce
1 tomato, chopped
1 cup shredded Cheddar cheese

Make sure that you thoroughly cook dried beans for best texture. For a splurge, add a layer of guacamole between the bean and cream cheese layer.

1. Two days before you serve the dip, sort the pinto beans, removing any foreign objects. Rinse the beans thoroughly and cover with 10 cups cold water. Cover and let stand overnight. In the morning, drain the beans and place in a 2-quart slow cooker with the onion. Add 3 cups water, cover, and cook on low for 8–9 hours until tender.
2. Test to see whether the beans are tender. If necessary, drain the pinto beans, reserving ¼ cup of the cooking liquid. Place the beans and onions in large bowl with the salt and chili powder. Using a potato masher, mash the beans, leaving some whole. Add reserved cooking liquid as needed until a spreading consistency is reached.
3. In another medium bowl, beat cream cheese until softened. Add sour cream and chiles; mix until blended.
4. On a large platter, spread the pinto bean mixture. Top with the sour cream mixture, leaving a 1-inch border of the bean mixture showing around the edges. Top with lettuce, tomato, and cheese. Serve immediately or cover and chill up to 2 days. Serve with taco or tortilla chips.

Sweet-and-Sour Mini Sausages

Serves 6

Total Cost: $6.98
Calories: 325.53
Fat: 15.60 grams
Protein: 11.12 grams
Cholesterol: 50.65 mg
Sodium: 854.32 mg

1 (8-ounce) can pineapple tidbits in juice

1 pound small fully cooked sausages

1 onion, chopped

2 tablespoons honey

2 tablespoons brown sugar

¼ cup apple cider vinegar

¼ cup applesauce

¼ cup ketchup

2 tablespoons mustard

1 green bell pepper, chopped

The sausages you want for this recipe are called "Little Smokies." Kids and adults alike will gobble up this excellent appetizer.

1. Drain pineapple, reserving juice. In 3-quart slow cooker, combine pineapple, sausages, and onion, and mix gently.
2. In medium bowl, combine 2 tablespoons reserved pineapple juice, honey, brown sugar, vinegar, applesauce, ketchup, and mustard, and mix well. Pour into slow cooker and stir.
3. Cover and cook on low for 4–5 hours until sausages are hot. Add green peppers. Cover and cook on low for 30 minutes longer, until peppers are tender. Stir and serve.

Mini Sausages
Mini sausages are one of the least expensive types of pork sausage. They come in many varieties and flavors. Choose the mildest for this recipe, since the other ingredients add lots of flavor. If you use uncooked sausages, cook them in a pan until browned before you add them to the slow cooker.

Slow Cooker Caponata

 Serves 6

$ Total Cost: $4.87
Calories: 87.34
Fat: 3.34 grams
Protein: 2.13 grams
Cholesterol: 0.0 mg
Sodium: 382.43 mg

1 tablespoon olive oil

1 onion, chopped

3 cloves garlic, minced

½ pound plum tomatoes, chopped

1 eggplant, peeled and chopped

½ cup chopped celery

½ (6-ounce) can tomato paste

1 teaspoon dried basil

½ teaspoon dried oregano

1 tablespoon sugar

1 tablespoon lemon juice

½ teaspoon salt

⅛ teaspoon pepper

1 tablespoon vinegar

⅓ cup chopped black olives

Caponata is an eggplant-based mixture that can be served as an appetizer with crackers and vegetables, as a sandwich spread, or as a side dish.

1. In 4- or 5-quart slow cooker, combine all ingredients except olives; mix well.
2. Cover and cook on low for 7–8 hours until vegetables are tender and mixture blends. Stir in olives and place in serving dish. Let cool for 30 minutes. Serve warm or cold.

Three-Cheese Dip

 Serves 8

$ Total Cost: $6.06
Calories: 306.32
Fat: 25.05 grams
Protein: 14.10 grams
Cholesterol: 76.26 mg
Sodium: 623.04 mg

¾ pound processed cheese, cubed

1 (8-ounce) package cream cheese, cubed

1 cup shredded Muenster cheese

1 tablespoon cornstarch

⅓ cup mayonnaise

½ cup sliced green onions, white and green parts

This creamy, melty cheese dip is delicious with crisp fresh vegetables. You could add meatballs, cooked chicken, or artichoke hearts for more interest.

1. In 2-quart slow cooker, combine processed cheese and cream cheese. Toss Muenster cheese with cornstarch and add to slow cooker along with mayonnaise; mix gently.
2. Cover and cook on low for 2–3 hours or until cheeses are melted, stirring twice during cooking time. Top with green onions and serve with fresh vegetables, crackers, and tortilla chips.

Processed Cheese

Processed cheese, usually found in American flavor, is made from real cheese but has ingredients like colors, flavoring, and emulsifiers added. The emulsifiers make the cheese melt very smoothly and protect it from heat, which makes this type of cheese a good choice for the slow cooker.

Zorba's Hummus

 Serves 6

$ Total Cost: $1.81
Calories: 188.34
Fat: 10.12 grams
Protein: 7.13 grams
Cholesterol: 0.0 mg
Sodium: 239.20 mg

¾ cup dried garbanzo beans (chickpeas)

1 onion, chopped

4 cloves garlic

2 cups water

3 tablespoons lemon juice

2 tablespoons olive oil

3 tablespoons peanut butter

½ teaspoon salt

⅛ teaspoon pepper

Hummus is usually made with tahini, or sesame seed paste. It's quite expensive, so peanut butter is an inexpensive alternative; use the real thing for a splurge.

1. Sort through the garbanzo beans and rinse well. Cover with cold water and let stand overnight. The next day, drain the beans, rinse well, and place in 2-quart slow cooker with onion, whole garlic cloves, and water. Cover, and cook on low for 8 to 10 hours until beans are tender.
2. Drain beans. Place beans, onion, and garlic in food processor along with lemon juice, half of the olive oil, peanut butter, salt, and pepper. Process until smooth. Place in serving dish and drizzle with remaining olive oil. Serve with tortilla or pita chips.

Apple Chutney

Serves 6

Total Cost: $2.95
Calories: 62.65
Fat: 0.07 grams
Protein: 0.33 grams
Cholesterol: 0.0 mg
Sodium: 194.94 mg

2 apples, peeled and chopped

1 onion, chopped

3 cloves minced garlic

¼ cup sugar

¼ cup apple cider vinegar

1 teaspoon ground ginger

½ teaspoon salt

⅛ teaspoon pepper

Chutney is very expensive; a bottle of mango chutney can cost $4.00. Make your own in your slow cooker; it's easy and fun.

1. Combine all ingredients in a 2-quart slow cooker and mix well. Cover and cook on low for 5–6 hours, stirring twice during cooking time, until the apples and onions are tender and mixture is blended.
2. Spoon into 1-cup containers and refrigerate up to 1 week. Chutney may be frozen up to 3 months. Thaw in refrigerator before use.

Use Chutney

You can use chutney in many ways. It can be combined with sour cream, mayonnaise, or cream cheese to make an appetizer dip or sandwich spread. It's delicious as a sauce for grilled fish or chicken, and can be added to salad dressings for a green or pasta salad. Use your imagination!

Spicy Shrimp and Cheese Dip

 Serves 6

$ Total Cost: $6.47
Calories: 165.87
Fat: 12.05 grams
Protein: 11.41 grams
Cholesterol: 89.09 mg
Sodium: 374.20 mg

2 slices bacon

1 (4-ounce) can small shrimp, drained

1 onion, chopped

2 cloves garlic, minced

1 tomato, chopped

1 (3-ounce) package cream cheese, cubed

1 cup shredded Monterey jack cheese

1 tablespoon cornstarch

⅛ teaspoon Tabasco sauce

⅛ teaspoon pepper

Shrimp combined with bacon is always delicious. Add creamy melted cheese and you'll have a hit on your hands.

1. Cook bacon in saucepan until crisp. Drain bacon on paper towels and crumble; set aside.
2. Add onion and garlic to drippings in saucepan; cook and stir for 1–2 minutes. Combine with remaining ingredients in 2-quart slow cooker.
3. Cover and cook on low for 1½ to 2 hours, or until cheese is melted and dip is blended, stirring twice during cooking time. Serve with crackers and apple slices.

Cheesy Taco Dip

 Serves 6

$ Total Cost: $6.44

Calories: 319.52

Fat: 17.76 grams

Protein: 15.93 grams

Cholesterol: 60.61 mg

Sodium: 850.16 mg

½ pound pork sausage

1 onion, chopped

2 cloves garlic, minced

1 jalapeño pepper, minced

1 cup mild salsa

⅓ pound processed
American cheese, cubed

1 tomato, chopped

1 tablespoon chili powder

2 tablespoons cornstarch

¼ cup tomato juice

2 cups shredded lettuce

1 cup shredded CoJack
cheese

Place bowls of chopped tomatoes, sour cream, and olives around so people can build their own nachos. You could add chopped avocados, too; sprinkle them with some lemon juice to slow down browning.

1. In large skillet, cook pork sausage until partially done. Add onions, garlic, and jalapeño pepper; continue cooking until sausage is thoroughly cooked. Drain well.
2. Place in 2-quart slow cooker along with salsa, cheese, tomato, and chili powder. Mix well. Cover and cook on low for 6–7 hours, stirring once during cooking time.
3. In small bowl, combine cornstarch and tomato juice. Add to slow cooker; cover and cook on high for 30 minutes. Sprinkle with lettuce and cheese. Serve with tortilla chips and the fresh topping ingredients, if desired.

Using Taco Dip

If you layer this taco dip in a shallow serving bowl, you can use it as a topping bar for tacos. Just tell people to scoop their spoon down through the dip and it contains just about everything you'd like to put on your taco. Make this dip ahead of time and refrigerate it until you're ready to serve for an easy idea.

The $7 a Meal Slow Cooker Cookbook

Creamy Refried Bean Dip

 Serves 6

$ Total Cost: $4.30

Calories: 255.37

Fat: 17.12 grams

Protein: 12.50 grams

Cholesterol: 54.29 mg

Sodium: 543.26 mg

1 (15-ounce) can refried beans

½ cup salsa

¼ cup sour cream

1 cup shredded Cheddar
   cheese

½ cup shredded Muenster
   cheese

3 ounces cream cheese,
   cubed

2 teaspoons chili powder

⅛ teaspoon pepper

Refried beans are rich and creamy, and are inexpensive too. Look for vegetarian refried beans made without lard.

1. Combine all ingredients in 2-quart slow cooker and mix gently to combine. Cover and cook on low for 2 to 2½ hours, stirring every 20 minutes, until dip is hot and cheese is melted.
2. Serve with taco chips, tortilla chips, carrot sticks, and celery sticks.

Roasted Garlic

Serves 6

$ Total Cost: $2.60
Calories: 69.56
Fat: 4.60 grams
Protein: 1.27 grams
Cholesterol: 0.0 mg
Sodium: 197.28 mg

3 full heads garlic

2 tablespoons olive oil

½ teaspoon salt

⅛ teaspoon pepper

When garlic is roasted it becomes nutty, creamy, and sweet. Stir it into soups or sandwich spreads, or serve it plain on water crackers.

1. Cut tops from garlic bulbs and discard. Remove some of the papery skins from the garlic heads.
2. Tear off sheet of heavy duty foil and line 1-quart slow cooker and top with the garlic heads, cut side up. Sprinkle with salt and pepper and drizzle with remaining oil.
3. Cover and cook on low for 4–5 hours, or until garlic is tender when pierced with knife. To serve, squeeze garlic out of skins into a small bowl and spread on toasted bread or crackers.

Roasted Garlic

Roasted garlic has so many uses. You can spread it under the skin of a chicken to be roasted, mix it into butter to serve with a grilled steak, or added it to cream cheese and chopped green pepper to make a sandwich spread. It freezes well too; squeeze it out of the skins and freeze in ice cube trays up to 3 months.

Onion Chutney

Serves 12

Total Cost: $6.99
Calories: 116.13
Fat: 3.93 grams
Protein: 1.05 grams
Cholesterol: 10.16 mg
Sodium: 131.52 mg

8 yellow onions
2 cloves garlic, chopped
¼ cup butter
1 teaspoon seasoned salt
¼ teaspoon white pepper

½ cup brown sugar
½ cup apple cider vinegar
2 tablespoons minced fresh gingerroot

This chutney can be served warm or cold. If you let it cool for an hour or so, and then spoon it over any type of soft cheese, it will slightly melt the cheese. Yum.

1. Peel onions and coarsely chop. Combine in 2-quart slow cooker with garlic and butter.
2. Cover and cook on low for 8–10 hours, stirring once during cooking time, until onions are browned and caramelized.
3. Stir in seasoned salt, pepper, brown sugar, vinegar, and gingerroot. Cover and cook on high for 1–2 hours or until mixture is blended and hot.
4. Remove mixture from slow cooker to a large bowl. Cover loosely and let cool for 1–2 hours before serving over Brie or Camembert cheese. Serve with crackers and toasts for spreading.

Honey Pineapple Chicken Wings

 Serves 6

💲 Total Cost: $5.89

Calories: 188.93

Fat: 4.97 grams

Protein: 17.29 grams

Cholesterol: 43.09 mg

Sodium: 362.93 mg

1 pound chicken wings

2 cloves garlic, minced

1 (5-ounce) can crushed pineapple

⅛ teaspoon pepper

⅓ cup honey

3 tablespoons low-sodium soy sauce

1 tablespoon vegetable oil

Chicken wings are inexpensive and surprisingly full of meat. Because the meat is close to the bone, it's sweet and tender.

1. Cut the wing tip off each chicken wing and discard tips. Place wings on a broiler rack and broil 6-inches from heat for 3–4 minutes until wings start to brown.
2. Combine all of the remaining ingredients in a 2–3-quart slow cooker and mix well. Add wings and stir.
3. Cover and cook on low for 6–7 hours or until wings are tender, thoroughly cooked, and glazed.

Chicken Wings vs. Drummies

This varies with the grocery store, but often chicken wings are the complete wing, with three parts: the drummie, or section with the most meat, the wing itself, which has less meat, and the tip, which is clipped off and used to make stock. Drummies are cut apart for you, and are more expensive, plus you don't get the tips for stock.

Spicy Empanadas

 Yields 36 Empanadas; serves 12

Total Cost: $4.70
Calories: 150.38
Fat: 5.55 grams
Protein: 4.93 grams
Cholesterol: 9.79 mg
Sodium: 350.93 mg

1 tablespoon olive oil

½ cup finely chopped onion

1 tablespoon curry powder

1 cup frozen vegetarian
burger crumbles, thawed

2 russet potatoes, peeled
and cubed

½ teaspoon salt

⅛ teaspoon cayenne pepper

36 (3 to 4-inch) wonton
wrappers

3 tablespoons butter, melted

This is a two-part recipe; you make the filling in the slow cooker, then fill and bake the empanadas when you want to eat.

1. In heavy saucepan, heat olive oil over medium heat. Add onion; cook and stir for 3 minutes. Combine in 2-quart slow cooker with curry powder, crumbles, potatoes, salt, and pepper. Cover and cook on low for 6–7 hours or until vegetables are tender. Remove from slow cooker and cool for 30 minutes.

2. Preheat oven to 375°F. Place 6 wonton wrappers on work surface. Place 1 rounded tablespoon filling in center of wrapper. Brush edges of wrapper with water. Fold wrapper over filling, forming a triangle. Press edges to seal. Place filled empanadas on ungreased cookie sheet and brush with butter. Bake for 8 to 12 minutes or until empanadas are light golden brown. Cool for 15 minutes, then serve.

Eggplant Caviar

 Serves 6

$ Total Cost: $3.27
Calories: 112.21
Fat: 8.58 grams
Protein: 3.55 grams
Cholesterol: 0.0 mg
Sodium: 197.36 mg

1 medium eggplant

1 teaspoon salt, divided

2 tablespoons olive oil

½ cup finely chopped onion

4 cloves garlic, minced

2 tablespoons lemon juice

⅛ teaspoon cayenne pepper

½ cup toasted chopped walnuts

When cooked and combined with onion and lemon juice eggplant does taste a bit like caviar—only it's better for you!

1. Preheat oven to 375°F. Peel eggplant and slice into ½-inch rounds. Sprinkle with ½ teaspoon salt; let stand for 10 minutes, then rinse and pat dry.
2. Combine in 3-quart slow cooker with olive oil, onion, garlic, lemon juice, ½ teaspoon salt, and pepper. Cover and cook on low for 6–7 hours or until vegetables are tender.
3. Turn slow cooker off and mash eggplant mixture with a fork until partially smooth. Stir in walnuts and serve immediately, or place in bowl, cover, and refrigerate for up to 24 hours before serving.

Toasting Nuts

Toasting nuts brings out their flavor and makes a little go a long way. To toast nuts, preheat an oven (or the toaster oven) to 350°F. Spread nuts in a single layer on a baking sheet. Toast for 8–12 minutes, shaking pan once during cooking time, until the nuts are fragrant and a bit darker in color. Let cool completely before chopping.

Buffalo Wings

 Serves 8

$ Total Cost: $6.52
Calories: 176.01
Fat: 8.18 grams
Protein: 14.07 grams
Cholesterol: 44.97 mg
Sodium: 479.68 mg

1 pound chicken wings

3 tablespoons low-sodium soy sauce

¼ cup apple cider vinegar

2 tablespoons Dijon mustard

2 tablespoons honey

2 tablespoons brown sugar

½ teaspoon salt

1 teaspoon hot sauce

4 cloves garlic, minced

½ cup minced onion

1 cup low fat sour cream

This spicy and savory sauce is perfect with tender chicken. Serve this appetizer with plenty of napkins.

1. Cut wings into three pieces; reserve tips for Chicken Stock (page 234). In heavy duty food storage bag, combine remaining ingredients except sour cream; mix well. Add chicken wings and seal bag. Place bag in baking dish; refrigerate for at least 8 hours, up to 24 hours.
2. When ready to prepare, pour chicken and half of marinade into 3-quart slow cooker. Cover and cook on low for 6–7 hours or until chicken is tender.
3. While wings are cooking, place remaining marinade in small saucepan. Bring to a simmer over high heat, then reduce heat to low and cook for 10–15 minutes, stirring frequently, until mixture is syrupy. Let cool for 15–20 minutes, then combine with sour cream and chill; serve as a dipping sauce.

Slow Cooker Reuben Dip

 Serves 6

$ Total Cost: $5.02
Calories: 242.45
Fat: 17.20 grams
Protein: 9.10 grams
Cholesterol: 47.14 mg
Sodium: 544.43 mg

3 cups chopped red cabbage

1 onion, chopped

2 cloves garlic, minced

2 tablespoons apple cider vinegar

2 tablespoons honey

½ teaspoon salt

½ (8-ounce) package cream cheese, cubed

1 cup shredded Swiss cheese

⅓ cup Thousand Island dressing

1 (3-ounce) package thinly sliced corned beef, chopped

Reuben sandwiches and dip are usually made with sauerkraut. This one is different; red cabbage is cooked until tender, then combined with the dip ingredients.

1. In a 2-quart slow cooker, combine cabbage, onion, garlic, vinegar, honey, and salt. Stir to combine, then cover and cook on low for 7 hours or until cabbage and onions are tender.
2. Drain the cabbage mixture; then return it to the slow cooker. Add remaining ingredients; stir to combine. Cover and cook on low for 2–3 hours longer or until cheeses melt. Stir to blend, and serve.

Make it Vegetarian

This dip can easily be made vegetarian by just omitting the corned beef. For vegans, use dairy-free cream cheese and Swiss cheese. For texture, you could stir in some uncooked cabbage at the end; about ½ cup will do. Serve this dip with crackers, breadsticks, carrot and celery sticks, and toasted French bread slices.

Bean Nachos

 Serves 8

$ Total Cost: $6.35
Calories: 283.20
Fat: 12.30 grams
Protein: 10.64 grams
Cholesterol: 18.45 mg
Sodium: 614.55 mg

1 (15-ounce) can refried beans

1 cup canned pinto beans

1 tablespoon chili powder

1 cup chunky salsa

1 tomato, seeded and chopped

1 jalapeño chile, seeded and chopped

4 cups tortilla chips

½ cup shredded Cheddar cheese

½ cup shredded Muenster cheese

¼ cup chopped cilantro

The combination of smooth refried beans along with chunky whole beans is really nice in these nachos. They can be topped with just about anything you like.

1. In 2-quart slow cooker, combine refried beans, pinto beans, chili powder, and salsa. Cover and cook on low for 3–4 hours or until mixture is hot and blended.
2. Preheat oven to 400°F. Place tortilla chips on a large rimmed baking sheet and set aside. Pour bean mixture evenly over chips. Sprinkle with tomato, chile, and cheeses. Bake for 15–20 minutes until cheeses melt and begin to bubble. Sprinkle with cilantro and serve.

Queso con Chile

 Serves 6

$ Total Cost: $3.17
Calories: 237.27
Fat: 18.97 grams
Protein: 12.69 grams
Cholesterol: 49.39 mg
Sodium: 486.34 mg

1 (8-ounce) package processed
  American cheese food

1 cup shredded pepper jack
  cheese

1 (14-ounce) can tomatoes
  with green chiles, undrained

½ cup sour cream

The only secret to this recipe is to use processed cheese food, simply because it melts perfectly and there's no danger that the recipe can be overcooked.

Cube cheese food and place in 2-quart slow cooker along with pepper jack cheese and undrained tomatoes. Cover and cook on low for 1½ to 2 hours, stirring twice during cooking time, until mixture is melted and smooth. Stir in sour cream and serve with lots of tortilla chips.

Cheese with Something Extra

You may be able to find Mexican processed cheese food in the grocery store. It contains the usual blend of cheeses, emulsifiers, and seasonings, but also adds spicy ingredients such as chili powder, ground dried chiles, and onion powder, along with chopped fresh or dried chiles.

Sweet 'n Crisp Curried Nuts

Serves 8

$ Total Cost: $6.67
Calories: 359.34
Fat: 31.59 grams
Protein: 9.00 grams
Cholesterol: 15.26 mg
Sodium: 244.87 mg

2 cups walnut halves

1 cup peanuts

¼ cup butter, melted

⅓ cup powdered sugar

2 tablespoons honey

2 teaspoons curry powder

½ teaspoon salt

⅛ teaspoon cayenne pepper

Curry has a sweet and hot flavor. You can find inexpensive curry blends in the spice aisle of the supermarket.

1. Combine all ingredients in a 1-quart slow cooker. Cover and cook on low for 3–4 hours or until nuts are glazed, stirring twice during cooking time.
2. Uncover slow cooker and cook on high for 1 hour, stirring every 15 minutes, until nuts are toasted. Place on wire rack to cool, then store covered in airtight container.

Best-Ever Snack Mix

Yields 6 cups; serves 12

$ Total Cost: $6.99
Calories: 258.39
Fat: 20.38 grams
Protein: 7.95 grams
Cholesterol: 15.53 mg
Sodium: 325.15 mg

2 cups small square cheese crackers

2 cups square corn cereal

1 cup walnut pieces

1 cup peanuts

⅓ cup butter

2 tablespoons Worcestershire sauce

½ teaspoon onion salt

⅛ teaspoon pepper

¼ cup finely grated Romano cheese

Put out small bowls of this snack mix and replace them every hour to keep the mix fresh and crisp. You might want to make another batch of this delicious recipe.

1. In 3-quart slow cooker, combine crackers, cereal, walnuts, and peanuts; toss to mix.
2. In small saucepan, melt butter over medium heat. Remove from heat and stir in remaining ingredients except cheese. Drizzle over mixture in slow cooker. Stir gently to coat, then cover and cook on low for 2 hours.
3. Uncover slow cooker and cook for 1 hour, stirring occasionally. Then sprinkle with cheese, turn heat to high, and cook for 15–20 minutes longer, stirring once during cooking time. Place mixture on cookie sheet to cool. Store covered in airtight container.

Snack Mixes

Use your imagination when making your own snack mixes. There are lots of fun ingredients that would work in any recipe. Bagel chips, other nuts like soy nuts, pecans, or almonds, would be delicious. And you can season them any way you'd like. A sweet version would use honey instead of Worcestershire sauce, plain salt, and powdered sugar instead of cheese.

Suave Cooked Salsa

Yields 3 cups; serving size ¼ cup

$ Total Cost: $5.36
Calories: 51.15
Fat: 2.52 grams
Protein: 1.29 grams
Cholesterol: 0.0 mg
Sodium: 200.34 mg

4 red tomatoes, chopped

1 green bell pepper, chopped

2 jalapeño peppers, minced

1 chopped onion

4 cloves garlic, minced

2 tablespoons lemon juice

½ teaspoon salt

⅛ teaspoon cayenne pepper

1 tablespoon olive oil

Salsa is one of the easiest recipes to make, although it can be very expensive to buy. If you have fresh tomatoes from your garden, all the better!

1. Combine all ingredients in 2-quart slow cooker. Cover and cook on low for 2½ to 3 hours or until peppers and onion are tender.
2. At this point you can make a smooth salsa by using an immersion blender or processing the salsa in a blender or food processor. Place in large bowl, cover, and chill until cold.

Peanut Caramel Corn

Serves 8

$ Total Cost: $3.25
Calories: 347.82
Fat: 19.24 grams
Protein: 8.27 grams
Cholesterol: 15.26 mg
Sodium: 176.34 mg

½ cup corn syrup

½ cup brown sugar

1 teaspoon vanilla

¼ cup butter

¼ cup peanut butter

8 cups dry popped popcorn

1 cup Spanish peanuts

Peanut butter adds an unusual touch and richness to classic Caramel Corn. You could leave out the peanuts if you'd like; just use 9 cups of popcorn.

1. Combine corn syrup, brown sugar, vanilla, butter, and peanut butter in the slow cooker. Cook uncovered on high until the butter melts and sugar is dissolved, about 1 hour, stirring every 15 minutes.
2. Be sure to remove any unpopped kernels from the popcorn. Add popcorn and peanuts to mixture in slow cooker and stir well to coat. Cover and cook on high for 1 hour, stirring every 15 minutes. Then uncover and cook on low for 30 minutes, stirring every 15 minutes.
3. Spread mixture on lightly greased cookie sheet and let cool completely. Break into pieces and store in airtight container.

Popcorn

For recipes using popcorn, don't use the microwave variety. The popcorn should be plain and popped in an air popper or on the stove. To pop on the stove, put 1 tablespoon vegetable oil in a large saucepan with a lid. Add ¼ cup popcorn, cover, and place over medium-high heat. When popping starts, shake pan until popping slows.

Double Blueberry Chutney

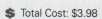 Serves 8

$ Total Cost: $3.98

Calories: 141.42

Fat: 5.28 grams

Protein: 2.21 grams

Cholesterol: 4.20 mg

Sodium: 126.47 mg

4 cups fresh blueberries

½ cup dried blueberries

1 onion, minced

1 small tart apple, cored, peeled, and chopped

2 cloves garlic, minced

¼ cup orange juice

⅓ cup brown sugar

2 teaspoons curry powder

½ teaspoon salt

⅛ teaspoon pepper

1 tablespoon butter

2 tablespoons cornstarch

¼ cup water

Serve this chutney hot or cold, plain or poured over cream cheese, along with fruit for dipping. It's also excellent as a sandwich spread or filling.

1. Combine all ingredients except cornstarch and water in 2-quart slow cooker. Stir to blend. Cover and cook on low for 5–7 hours or until blueberries pop and apple is very tender.
2. In small bowl combine cornstarch and water; stir to blend. Stir into chutney mixture. Cover and cook on high for 20–30 minutes or until chutney has thickened. Serve hot or cold.

CHAPTER 3

BREAKFAST

35   Apple Walnut Strata

36   Fruit Compote

37   Nutty Slow Cooker Oatmeal

38   Bacon and Waffle Strata

39   Honey Apple Bread Pudding

40   Hash Brown Casserole

41   Slow-Cooker Fruity Oatmeal

42   Spinach, Cheese, and Egg Casserole

43   Bacon Sweet Potato Hash

44   Sausage Rolls

45   Breakfast Pitas

46   Breakfast Casserole

47   Egg Muffin Sandwiches

48   Sausage Breakfast Casserole

49   Hash Brown Potato Bake

50   Slow-Cooker Scrambled Eggs

51   Breakfast Granola Bake

52   Cornbread Sausage Strata

53   Ham and Corn Casserole

54   Monte Cristo Sandwich Strata

55   Potato Frittata

56   Apple Butter

Apple Walnut Strata

 Serves 6

Total Cost: $5.28
Calories: 357.67
Fat: 16.56 grams
Protein: 11.97 grams
Cholesterol: 112.35 mg
Sodium: 238.72 mg

¼ cup light cream

¼ cup orange juice

3 eggs, beaten

3 tablespoons sugar

½ teaspoon cinnamon

1 teaspoon vanilla

4 cups cubed French bread

1 cup granola

½ cup chopped toasted walnuts

2 Granny Smith apples, peeled and cubed

This delicious strata is great for brunch. The combination of flavors is perfect; serve with cold applesauce and heavy cream for a nice contrast.

1. Spray a 3 or 4-quart slow cooker with nonstick cooking spray. In medium bowl, combine cream, orange juice, eggs, sugar, cinnamon, and vanilla and blend well with whisk. Set aside.
2. Place ⅓ of the bread in the bottom of prepared slow cooker and sprinkle with ⅓ of the granola, walnuts, and apples. Repeat layers. Pour egg mixture over all.
3. Cover and cook on high for 1½ to 2 hours or until just set. Do not cook on low.

Toasting Nuts

To toast almonds or other nuts, place them in a dry skillet over medium heat and toss until fragrant and golden brown. You can also microwave them for 3–4 minutes on low power until fragrant. Finally, bake the nuts in a 350°F oven for 8–9 minutes, shaking the pan occasionally, until the nuts are golden.

Fruit Compote

Serves 10

$ Total Cost: $6.84
Calories: 190.29
Fat: 3.64 grams
Protein: 0.50 grams
Cholesterol: 9.16 mg
Sodium: 115.46 mg

1 (16-ounce) can pineapple tidbits

1 (21-ounce) can apple pie filling

1 cup frozen peach slices, chopped

½ cup brown sugar

2 teaspoons curry powder

¼ teaspoon salt

3 tablespoons butter

1 tablespoon cornstarch

2 tablespoons water

Fruit compote can be served as-is on a cold winter morning. Or use it to top French toast or waffles, or as a nice topping for hot oatmeal.

1. Drain canned pineapple, reserving juice. Combine all ingredients except cornstarch and water, plus ⅓ cup reserved pineapple juice in a 2-quart slow cooker.
2. Cover and cook on low for 5–6 hours, stirring twice during cooking time, until fruit is hot and mixture is bubbling. In small bowl, combine cornstarch and water; stir into slow cooker. Cover and cook on high for 10–15 minutes until thickened. Serve over pancakes, or as a cereal topping.

Nutty Slow Cooker Oatmeal

Serves 6

$ Total Cost: $3.47
Calories: 310.57
Fat: 17.42 grams
Protein: 8.31 grams
Cholesterol: 10.18 mg
Sodium: 423.32 mg

1½ cups steel-cut oatmeal

2 tablespoons butter

1 cup chopped walnuts

6 cups water

½ cup brown sugar

1 teaspoon salt

1 teaspoon cinnamon

⅛ teaspoon nutmeg

Steel-cut oats are the only kind that will not cook to mush in the slow cooker. Toasting them and the nuts brings out the best flavor in this simple recipe.

1. Place oatmeal in large skillet over medium high heat. Toast, stirring constantly, for 8–9 minutes or until oatmeal is fragrant and begins to brown around the edges. Remove to 3½-quart slow cooker.
2. In same pan, melt butter and add chopped walnuts. Toast over medium heat, stirring constantly, until nuts are toasted. Combine with all remaining ingredients except spices in 3–4-quart slow cooker. Cover and cook on low for 7–9 hours, until oatmeal is tender. Stir in spices, cover, and let stand for 10 minutes. Serve topped with a bit of butter, maple syrup, brown sugar, and more chopped nuts.

Leftover Oatmeal

You can use leftover oatmeal in several recipes. Stir a spoonful into oatmeal cookie batter, or chill it, cut it into squares, and fry it in butter for another breakfast treat. Or stir it into a combination of ground beef and pork to make meatloaf or meatballs (use about ½ cup oatmeal per pound of meat). There's no reason to let anything go to waste!

Bacon and Waffle Strata

 Serves 5

 Total Cost: $5.48
Calories: 408.10
Fat: 25.33 grams
Protein: 19.48 grams
Cholesterol: 238.44 mg
Sodium: 684.81 mg

4 slices bacon

5 frozen waffles, toasted

1 cup shredded Colby cheese

¼ cup chopped green onions

1 (5-ounce) can evaporated milk

½ (8-ounce) package cream cheese, softened

4 eggs

½ teaspoon dry mustard

This version of strata uses crisp waffles, which bake into a wonderfully textured casserole in the slow cooker.

1. In large skillet, cook bacon until crisp. Drain on paper towels, crumble, and set aside. Cut toasted waffles into cubes. Layer bacon and waffle cubes with cheese and green onions in 3½-quart slow cooker.
2. Drain skillet, discarding bacon fat; do not wipe out. Add milk and cream cheese to skillet; cook over low heat, stirring frequently, until cheese melts and mixture is smooth.
3. Remove skillet from heat and beat in eggs, one at a time, until smooth. Stir in dry mustard and pour into slow cooker. Cover and cook on low for about 4–5 hours, until eggs are set. Serve with warmed maple syrup, if desired.

Honey Apple Bread Pudding

 Serves 6

2 apples, chopped

¼ cup apple juice

⅓ cup brown sugar

¼ cup honey

2 tablespoons butter, melted

4 eggs, beaten

⅓ cup whole milk

1 teaspoon vanilla

½ teaspoon cinnamon

8 slices raisin swirl bread

½ cup raisins

This fabulous recipe is almost like a dessert. Serve it along with some fresh fruit and scrambled eggs for the perfect brunch.

1. In medium saucepan, combine apples with apple juice. Bring to a simmer; simmer for 5 minutes, stirring frequently. Remove from heat and set aside for 10 minutes. Drain apples, reserving juice.
2. In small bowl, combine brown sugar, honey, and butter; mix well and set aside. In large bowl, combine reserved apple juice, eggs, milk, vanilla, and cinnamon; beat well and set aside.
3. Cut bread slices into cubes. In 3½-quart slow cooker, layer ⅓ of the bread cubes, raisins, apples, and the brown sugar mixture. Repeat layers. Pour egg mixture over all.
4. Cover and cook on high for 3½ to 4½ hours, until pudding is set. Turn off slow cooker and let cool for 30 minutes, then serve.

Apples for Slow Cooking

For slow cooking, choose apples that hold their shape well in baking. Good choices include Red Delicious, Granny Smith, Jonathan, McIntosh, and Winesap. Red Delicious and Granny Smith apples are usually the most inexpensive. For more texture and color, leave the peel on; just core the apples and cut into cubes.

Hash Brown Casserole

 Serves 6

$ Total Cost: $5.89
Calories: 626.74
Fat: 30.37 grams
Protein: 18.98 grams
Cholesterol: 241.72 mg
Sodium: 972.39 mg

1 tablespoon butter

1 onion, chopped

2 cloves garlic, minced

6 cups frozen hash brown potatoes

¾ cup shredded mozzarella cheese

6 eggs

½ teaspoon dried thyme leaves

½ teaspoon salt

⅛ teaspoon pepper

1 (5-ounce) can evaporated milk

½ cup shredded Cheddar cheese

2 tablespoons chopped parsley

You could add cooked bacon or breakfast sausage to this excellent casserole if you'd like.

1. Spray inside of 3½-quart slow cooker with nonstick cooking spray. In skillet, melt butter over medium heat. Add onion and garlic; cook and stir until crisp-tender. Let cool about 10 minutes.
2. Place ⅓ of the frozen hash brown potatoes in the slow cooker. Add ⅓ of onion mixture and ⅓ of the mozzarella cheese. Repeat layers, ending with the cheese.
3. In medium bowl, beat eggs, seasonings, and milk until blended. Pour over the ingredients in the slow cooker, cover and turn on low. Cook for 10–12 hours, until set. Sprinkle with Cheddar cheese and parsley; let stand until cheese melts, then serve.

Slow-Cooker Fruity Oatmeal

 Serves 8

$ Total Cost: $6.00
Calories: 304.12
Fat: 8.11 grams
Protein: 6.62 grams
Cholesterol: 9.90 mg
Sodium: 163.17 mg

2 cups steel-cut oats

5 cups water

1½ cups orange juice

½ teaspoon salt

½ teaspoon cinnamon

2 apples, peeled and chopped

½ cup dried fruit bits

½ cup brown sugar

½ cup half-and-half

1 cup granola

You can warm leftover oatmeal in the microwave to serve it again. Substitute your favorite dried fruit, like raisins or dried cranberries, for the dried fruit bits if you'd like.

1. The night before you want to eat, toast oats over low heat in small saucepan for 5–8 minutes, stirring frequently until light golden brown. Place in 3-quart slow cooker.
2. Add remaining ingredients except half-and-half and granola. Stir well. Cover and cook on low for 7–9 hours.
3. In the morning, stir in the half-and-half and cook for 10 minutes longer. Sprinkle with granola and serve.

Steel-Cut Oats

Steel-cut oats are whole oat grains, or groats, that have been sliced into pieces. They stand up very well to the long cooking time of the slow cooker. You can also cook them on the stovetop. Use 4 cups liquid for 1 cup of oats, and simmer over medium-low heat for 40–50 minutes, stirring occasionally.

Spinach, Cheese, and Egg Casserole

 Serves 6

$ Total Cost: $6.74

Calories: 303.72

Fat: 19.12 grams

Protein: 22.88 grams

Cholesterol: 187.16 mg

Sodium: 961.43 mg

1 (16-ounce) bag frozen cut leaf spinach

2 cups cottage cheese

1 (3-ounce) package cream cheese

1 cup shredded Cheddar cheese, divided

4 eggs, beaten

¼ cup flour

½ teaspoon salt

½ teaspoon dried basil leaves

⅛ teaspoon pepper

4 tablespoons butter, melted

1 tablespoon chopped parsley

Cottage cheese and cream cheese make a creamy filling for this delicious breakfast casserole.

1. Thaw spinach and drain well; place in large bowl. In food processor, combine cottage cheese with cream cheese; process or blend until smooth. Add to spinach along with ¾ cup Cheddar cheese.
2. In small bowl, beat eggs, flour, salt, basil, pepper, and butter and mix well. Stir into spinach mixture.
3. Pour into 3-quart slow cooker. Cover and cook on low for 5–6 hours or until mixture is set. Sprinkle with ¼ cup Cheddar cheese and parsley; cover, and let stand until cheese is melted. Serve immediately.

Bacon Sweet Potato Hash

Serves 4

Total Cost: $5.67
Calories: 338.52
Fat: 14.92 grams
Protein: 5.80 grams
Cholesterol: 31.82 mg
Sodium: 733.14 mg

4 slices bacon

1 onion, chopped

3 sweet potatoes, peeled

⅓ cup brown sugar

¼ cup orange juice

¼ cup applesauce

3 tablespoons butter, melted

½ teaspoon salt

⅛ teaspoon pepper

¼ cup chopped pecans

Hash recipes usually use leftover russet potatoes, but this one is different. Sweet potatoes add great flavor and nutrition to the recipe.

1. In large skillet, cook bacon until crisp; drain on paper towels, crumble, cover, and refrigerate. Drain all but 2 tablespoons drippings from skillet. Add onion; cook and stir for 5 minutes, until onion softens, stirring to loosen brown bits from skillet.
2. Cut sweet potatoes into 1-inch cubes. Combine potatoes and onions in 4-quart slow cooker; stir to mix.
3. In small bowl, combine all remaining ingredients except pecans and stir well. Pour into slow cooker. Cover and cook on low for 8–9 hours or until potatoes are tender.
4. Stir in reserved bacon and the pecans; cover and cook for 30 minutes longer. If desired, you can place a fried egg on top of each serving of hash.

Sweet Potatoes

Sweet potatoes aren't yams, and yams aren't sweet potatoes. The orange potatoes we buy in the supermarket are related to morning glories, while the larger yams, with white starchy flesh, are related to lilies. Sweet potatoes are full of Vitamin A and have a wonderful soft, tender texture when slow cooked.

Sausage Rolls

Serves 8

$ Total Cost: $6.45

Calories: 360.90

Fat: 20.91 grams

Protein: 14.35 grams

Cholesterol: 81.71 mg

Sodium: 761.44 mg

¾ cup soft bread crumbs

1 egg, beaten

¼ cup brown sugar

¼ cup applesauce

½ teaspoon salt

⅛ teaspoon pepper

½ teaspoon dried marjoram leaves

1½-pounds mild bulk pork sausage

2 tablespoons butter

¼ cup honey

¼ cup chicken broth

These sausage rolls are like meatballs, but shaped like sausages, and flavored for breakfast. They are slightly spicy and very pleasing.

1. In large bowl, combine crumbs, egg, brown sugar, apple-sauce, salt, pepper, and marjoram. Mix well. Stir in sausage.
2. Shape into rolls 3" × 1". In large skillet, melt butter over medium heat. Add sausage rolls, about 8 at a time, and cook until browned on all sides, about 5–6 minutes. As rolls cook, drain on paper towels, then place into 3-quart slow cooker.
3. In small bowl, combine honey and chicken broth and mix well. Pour over sausage rolls in slow cooker.
4. Cover slow cooker and cook on low for 8–9 hours or until sausage rolls are thoroughly cooked, to 165°F on a meat thermometer. Remove from slow cooker with slotted spoon to serve.

Breakfast Pitas

Serves 4

$ Total Cost: $4.26
Calories: 399.31
Fat: 24.71 grams
Protein: 22.75 grams
Cholesterol: 463.41 mg
Sodium: 923.64 mg

2 tablespoons butter

1 onion, chopped

2 cloves garlic, chopped

8 eggs, beaten

½ teaspoon salt

⅛ teaspoon pepper

½ cup salsa

1 cup shredded pepper jack cheese

4 pita breads

2 tablespoons chopped parsley

The spicy filling for these pitas cooks all night in the slow cooker, so when you get up, just fill pita breads and go!

1. The night before, spray 2-quart slow cooker with nonstick cooking spray. In small skillet, melt butter over medium heat. Add onion and garlic; cook and stir until tender, about 5 minutes. Remove from heat.
2. In large bowl, combine eggs, salt, and pepper and beat well. Stir in onion mixture, salsa, and cheese. Pour into slow cooker. Cover and cook on low for 7–8 hours.
3. In the morning, stir mixture in slow cooker. Split pita breads and fill with egg mixture; top with parsley and serve immediately.

Pita Breads

Pita breads are available in plain and whole wheat. The whole wheat pitas are usually a bit more expensive, but you get more fiber and B vitamins. Either type will work in just about any recipe. Pita breads freeze really well, so when they go on sale, buy some, repackage, and freeze up to 3 months.

Breakfast Casserole

$ Total Cost: $7.00

Calories: 398.48

Fat: 22.18 grams

Protein: 25.21 grams

Cholesterol: 228.29 mg

Sodium: 903.12 mg

½ pound breakfast link sausage

5 slices cracked wheat bread, cubed

1 red bell pepper, chopped

½ cup shredded Swiss cheese

½ cup shredded Muenster cheese

4 eggs

½ cup whole milk

½ cup small-curd cottage cheese

1 tablespoon yellow mustard

½ teaspoon salt

⅛ teaspoon white pepper

¼ cup shredded Romano cheese

The combination of textures, flavors, and colors in this rich and hearty casserole is just wonderful. Serve with some fresh fruit for a complete breakfast.

1. Cook the link sausage until done in large skillet over medium heat. Drain on paper towels, then cut into 1-inch pieces. Spray a 3½-quart slow cooker with nonstick cooking spray.

2. Layer sausage pieces, bread, bell pepper, and Swiss and Muenster cheeses in slow cooker.

3. In food processor or blender, combine eggs, milk, cottage cheese, mustard, salt, and white pepper. Process or blend until smooth. Pour into slow cooker. Let stand for 20 minutes.

4. Sprinkle with Romano cheese; cover. Cook on high for 2 hours, then reduce heat to low and cook for another 1 to 1½ hours or until casserole is set.

Egg Muffin Sandwiches

Serves 4

4 slices bacon

8 eggs

⅓ cup evaporated milk

¼ teaspoon salt

⅛ teaspoon white pepper

½ teaspoon dried thyme leaves

2 tablespoons butter

6 English muffins, split

6 slices American cheese, unwrapped

You could substitute homemade biscuits or pita breads for the English muffins if you'd like.

1. In heavy skillet, cook bacon until crisp; remove from skillet and drain on paper towels. Crumble bacon and set aside.
2. In large bowl, beat eggs with milk and seasonings. Grease a 2-quart slow cooker with nonstick cooking spray. Stir cheese and crumbled bacon into eggs and pour into slow cooker.
3. Cover and cook on low for 6–8 hours or until eggs are set and thoroughly cooked.
4. Spread butter on split sides of English muffins and toast in toaster oven until light golden brown. Place one slice American cheese on half of each English muffin. Top with egg mixture, dividing evenly among muffins. Top egg mixture with remaining cheese slices and cover with remaining English muffin halves. Serve immediately.

Fast-Food Breakfast Sandwiches

This recipe is similar to fast-food breakfast sandwiches, but it costs a lot less and it's better for you. You could add tomato, green bell pepper, or different kinds of cheese to make the sandwich your own. Or cook some pork sausage and use that instead of bacon. They're perfect for breakfast on the run.

Sausage Breakfast Casserole

Serves 6

Total Cost: $6.76
Calories: 345.17
Fat: 22.58 grams
Protein: 21.39 grams
Cholesterol: 404.38 mg
Sodium: 673.54 mg

1 tablespoon butter

1 onion, chopped

2 cloves garlic, minced

8 ounces skinless breakfast sausages

1 cup shredded Cheddar cheese, divided

1 jalapeño, minced

10 eggs

½ teaspoon salt

⅛ teaspoon pepper

1 red bell pepper, chopped

This hearty casserole is slightly spicy with the jalapeño pepper. If you don't like spicy foods in the morning, just leave it out.

1. Grease inside of slow cooker with ½ tablespoon butter. In medium skillet, melt ½ tablespoon butter over medium heat. Add onion and garlic; cook and stir until tender, about 5 minutes.
2. Remove onion and garlic to 3-quart slow cooker. Add sausages to skillet; cook and stir until browned. Drain well and add to slow cooker; top with half of cheese.
3. In large bowl, combine jalapeño, eggs, salt, and pepper and beat well. Stir in red bell pepper and pour into slow cooker. Top with rest of cheese.
4. Cover and cook on low for 7–8 hours or until eggs are set and casserole is bubbly. Serve immediately.

Hash Brown Potato Bake

 Serves 4

💲 Total Cost: $3.60
Calories: 495.33
Fat: 25.23 grams
Protein: 9.69 grams
Cholesterol: 29.01 mg
Sodium: 763.54 mg

1 tablespoon vegetable oil

1 clove garlic, chopped

1 green chile, chopped

½ cup milk

1 (3-ounce) package cream cheese

½ teaspoon salt

⅛ teaspoon white pepper

1 tablespoon flour

3 cups frozen hash brown potatoes

1 cup frozen corn

¼ cup grated Parmesan cheese

This delicious breakfast bake doesn't use any eggs. A cream cheese sauce binds and flavors the potato and vegetable mixture.

1. In heavy skillet, heat oil and cook garlic until crisp-tender, about 2 minutes. Add green chile, cook and stir for 1 minute, then add milk, cream cheese, salt, pepper, and flour. Cook and stir over medium heat until cream cheese is melted and sauce is blended. Remove from heat and let cool for 10 minutes.
2. Fold in frozen potatoes and frozen corn. Place in 2-quart slow cooker and top with Parmesan cheese. Cover and cook on low for 7–8 hours or until set and browned on top. Serve immediately.

Frozen Hash Brown Potatoes

Look for different types of hash brown potatoes; some come packaged with vegetables like onions and peppers. Regular hash potatoes are shredded, while Southern potatoes are cut into small cubes. Most slow cooker recipes using hash potatoes call for frozen potatoes, right out of the bag.

Slow-Cooker Scrambled Eggs

Serves 6

2 tablespoons butter

9 eggs

2 tablespoons flour

½ cup heavy cream

½ teaspoon salt

⅛ teaspoon white pepper

1 cup shredded Swiss cheese

3 tablespoons grated Parmesan cheese

Scrambled eggs can be made at your leisure in the slow cooker. Keep them warm for only 1 hour after cooking time is done. If any are left over at that point (doubtful!), discard them.

1. Using 1 tablespoon of the butter, grease a 2-quart slow cooker. Melt the rest of the butter and pour into slow cooker.
2. In large bowl, beat eggs with flour, cream, salt, and pepper. Stir in Swiss cheese and pour into slow cooker.
3. Sprinkle with Parmesan cheese, cover, and cook on high for about 2 to 2½ hours, stirring twice during cooking time, until eggs are creamy and reach a temperature of 145°F.

Breakfast Granola Bake

 Serves 5

Total Cost: $6.43
Calories: 450.72
Fat: 22.98 grams
Protein: 10.65 grams
Cholesterol: 12.21 mg
Sodium: 104.56 mg

1 apple, peeled and chopped

1 pear, peeled and chopped

2 tablespoons lemon juice

2 cups granola

½ cup chopped walnuts

¼ cup honey

1 (4-ounce) jar puréed pears

½ teaspoon cinnamon

⅛ teaspoon salt

2 tablespoons butter, melted

Apples, pears, and granola are a wonderful combination in this casserole. It's a little like hot cereal, but with more texture.

1. Place apples and pears in bottom of a 2-quart slow cooker. Sprinkle with lemon juice. Top with granola and walnuts.
2. In medium bowl, combine remaining ingredients and mix well. Pour into slow cooker. Cover and cook on low for 7–9 hours or until apples and pears are tender. Serve with cold honey and heavy cream, if desired.

Inexpensive Granola

Granola prices vary widely, depending on which brand you buy. The least expensive is usually bulk granola you can find in health food stores. The most expensive is the brand name cereals with lots of nuts and special ingredients. Use your favorite granola in this and other recipes.

Cornbread Sausage Strata

Serves 5

Total Cost: $3.49
Calories: 500.30
Fat: 28.12 grams
Protein: 16.87 grams
Cholesterol: 156.58 mg
Sodium: 1093.32 mg

½ pound hot bulk Italian sausage

1 onion, chopped

1 cup flour

½ cup yellow cornmeal

2 tablespoons sugar

1 teaspoon baking powder

½ teaspoon baking soda

½ teaspoon salt

2 eggs

½ cup whole milk

¼ cup butter, melted

½ cup shredded Colby cheese

A bit of cornbread and sausage in the morning is a great way to start the day. This rich strata is delicious served with a fresh fruit salad.

1. In large skillet, cook sausage with onions over medium heat, stirring to break up sausage, until sausage is cooked. Drain well and remove from heat.
2. In large bowl, combine flour, cornmeal, sugar, baking powder, baking soda, and salt. In medium bowl, combine eggs, milk, and butter. Mix well. Add egg mixture to dry ingredients, stirring just until combined.
3. Spray a 2-quart slow cooker with nonstick baking spray containing flour. Place half of the batter in the slow cooker; top with half of the sausage and half of the cheese. Repeat layers.
4. Cover and cook on high for 2½ to 3½ hours or until cornbread tests done when tested with a toothpick. Serve immediately by spooning out of the slow cooker as in spoon bread.

Ham and Corn Casserole

 Serves 6

💲 Total Cost: $6.74
🥄 Calories: 369.83
Fat: 20.12 grams
Protein: 23.80 grams
Cholesterol: 300.52 mg
Sodium: 388.39 mg

1 onion, chopped	1 tablespoon sugar
1 tablespoon olive oil	⅛ teaspoon pepper
5 eggs	1 (10-ounce) package frozen corn, thawed
¾ cup milk	
2 tablespoons flour	1 cup chopped smoked ham
1 cup shredded Swiss cheese	¼ cup grated Parmesan cheese

Like a crustless quiche, corn and ham bake in the slow cooker in an egg-and-cheese filling. Drizzle with warmed maple syrup if desired.

1. Preheat oven to 350°F. In heavy skillet, sauté onion in olive oil until crisp-tender. Remove from heat and cool 10 minutes.
2. In large bowl, beat eggs until foamy and blended. Add milk and beat well. Add flour, Swiss cheese, sugar, pepper, corn, and ham and mix to blend. Stir in cooled sautéed onions.
3. Pour into greased 3-quart slow cooker and top with Parmesan cheese. Cover and cook on high for 3–4 hours or until casserole is set. Serve immediately.

Ham in the Slow Cooker

The ham you buy in the grocery store is fully cooked, unless you're purchasing a pork shoulder. Since it's pre-cooked, all you're doing in the slow cooker is reheating it. These recipes only need to cook for 3–4 hours to fully reheat the ham and bring out its best flavor.

Monte Cristo Sandwich Strata

Serves 6

Total Cost: $6.97
Calories: 452.94
Fat: 19.82 grams
Protein: 24.92 grams
Cholesterol: 102.93 mg
Sodium: 304.13 mg

8 slices sourdough bread, cubed

1 (12-ounce) can chicken, drained

1 cup shredded Swiss cheese

½ cup chopped cooked ham

6 eggs

½ cup heavy cream

½ teaspoon salt

⅛ teaspoon pepper

½ teaspoon dried oregano leaves

3 tablespoons cider vinegar

¼ cup currant jelly

3 tablespoons water

2 tablespoons honey

½ teaspoon paprika

2 tablespoons butter

¼ cup powdered sugar

½ cup crisp rice cereal crumbs

Monte Cristo sandwiches are layered chicken and ham sandwiches that traditionally are deep-fried. This method, in a slow cooker, is much easier.

1. Spray a 3-quart slow cooker with nonstick cooking spray. Layer cubed bread, chicken, cheese, and ham in slow cooker.
2. In large bowl, combine eggs, cream, salt, pepper, and oregano; beat well. Pour into slow cooker. Let mixture stand for 20 minutes, pushing bread back down into the egg mixture as necessary. Cover and cook on low for 4–5 hours or until egg mixture is set.
3. In small saucepan, combine vinegar, jelly, water, honey, paprika, and butter. Bring to a simmer, then reduce heat and simmer, stirring frequently, for 8–9 minutes until sauce is blended and slightly thickened.
4. To serve strata, scoop out of slow cooker and drizzle with currant jelly sauce. Sprinkle with powdered sugar and cereal crumbs, and serve immediately.

Potato Frittata

 Serves 5

$ Total Cost: $4.52
Calories: 329.18
Fat: 10.19 grams
Protein: 21.17 grams
Cholesterol: 122.90 mg
Sodium: 317.33 mg

1 (16-ounce) package frozen hash brown potatoes

1 onion, diced

2 cloves garlic, minced

¾ cup shredded Cheddar cheese

¼ cup shredded Muenster cheese

6 eggs

½ cup sour cream

½ teaspoon salt

⅛ teaspoon pepper

1 cup chopped canned apricots

2 tablespoons honey

2 teaspoons fresh thyme leaves

Topping a moist and hearty potato frittata with an herb-and-apricot mixture really perks up the flavor and wakes up your taste buds.

1. Spray a 3-quart slow cooker with nonstick cooking spray. Layer potatoes, onions, garlic, and cheeses in slow cooker.
2. In large bowl, combine eggs with sour cream and beat until blended. Stir in salt and pepper and mix well. Pour into slow cooker.
3. Cover and cook on high for 4–5 hours or until eggs are set. In medium bowl, combine apricots, honey, and thyme; mix gently. Serve apricot topping with frittata.

About Frittatas

Frittatas are heavier, sturdier omelettes. Because they are cooked over lower, slower heat, the end result isn't as puffy or light as an omelette; perfect for the slow cooker. Check the consistency of the frittata at the shortest cooking time. The temperature should reach 145°F, and the eggs will be set and firm.

Apple Butter

Yields 4 cups; serving size ¼ cup

$ Total Cost: $4.39
Calories: 197.18
Fat: 0.12 grams
Protein: 1.28 grams
Cholesterol: 0.0 mg
Sodium: 44.57 mg

8 large tart apples, peeled

1½ cups brown sugar

1½ cups sugar

¼ cup apple cider vinegar

2 teaspoons cinnamon

½ teaspoon ground ginger

½ teaspoon salt

Apple butter is delicious as a spread on toasted bread, and it's a good substitute for half of the oil in some simple baked recipes.

1. Core apples and cut into pieces. In a 4-quart slow cooker, combine all ingredients; mix well. Cover and cook on low 10–12 hours, stirring occasionally, until apple butter is thick and deep golden brown. Remove lid after 8 hours for a thicker apple butter.
2. As the apple butter cooks, you'll need to stir more often to prevent burning. Be sure to thoroughly scrape sides and bottom of slow cooker each time you stir. If desired, use an immersion blender to make apple butter smoother.
3. Spoon apple butter into 1-cup jars or freezer containers. Refrigerate up to 2 weeks or freeze up to 2 months.

CHAPTER 4

BEEF

58   Crock-Pot Fajitas

59   Beef Chimichangas

60   Beef with Broccoli

61   Shredded Beef Soft Tacos

62   Crock-Pot Beef Stroganoff

63   Crock-Pot Spaghetti and Meat Sauce

64   Swiss Steak

65   Fork Tender Pot Roast

66   Sweet and Sour Beef

67   Garlic and Onion Pot Roast

68   Slow-Cooker Beef Rouladen

69   Tex-Mex Meatloaf

70   Beef Carbonnade

71   Mexicali Rice and Beef

72   Beefy Baked Beans

73   Tangy Apricot Cube Steaks

74   Beans and Meatballs

75   Picadillo

76   Porcupine Meatballs

77   Chili Mac

78   Beef and Potato Casserole

79   Smoky Beans and Beef Dinner

80   Beef and Bean Potpie

Crock-Pot Fajitas

 Serves 4

1 onion, chopped

4 cloves garlic, minced

¾ pound bottom round steak

1 tablespoon chili powder

½ teaspoon salt

¼ teaspoon pepper

½ cup salsa

1 green bell pepper

1 yellow summer squash

4 flour tortillas

½ cup sour cream

Fajitas are Mexican sandwiches, using tortillas as the bread. Cook the meat first until tender, then add the tender vegetables later to preserve their texture and flavor.

1. Place onions and garlic in a 4-quart slow cooker. Cut steak into 2-inch pieces and toss with chili powder, salt, and pepper; put in slow cooker. Top with salsa, cover, and cook on low for 8–9 hours or until steak is tender.
2. Remove meat from slow cooker and shred. Return to slow cooker with bell pepper and sliced summer squash. Cook on high for 30–40 minutes or until pepper is tender. Serve with flour tortillas, sour cream, and your favorite garnishes.

Beef Chimichangas

 Serves 6

💲 Total Cost: $6.69
🍴 Calories: 398.23
Fat: 14.08 grams
Protein: 29.55 grams
Cholesterol: 63.91 mg
Sodium: 884.23 mg

¾ pound beef top round steak

1 onion, chopped

3 cloves garlic, minced

½ cup Beef Stock (page 233)

1 tablespoon chili powder

½ teaspoon salt

¾ cup salsa

½ (16-ounce) can refried beans

1 cup shredded Cheddar cheese

6 (8-inch) flour tortillas

Vegetable oil

The filling for these excellent little deep-fried filled tortillas is cooked in the Crock-Pot, making it tender and succulent. It cooks all day; when you get home, just form the chimichangas and fry until crisp.

1. Cut beef into 2-inch cubes and place in a 3-quart Crock-Pot along with onion, garlic, and stock. Cover and cook on low for 7–9 hours until beef is very tender. Using slotted spoon, remove beef and vegetables from stock. Shred meat, using 2 forks.

2. In large bowl, combine shredded beef and vegetables with chili powder, salt, and salsa. Open can of refried beans and mash slightly.

3. Spread refried beans onto each tortilla. Top each with about ¼ cup of beef mixture, then 1 tablespoon of cheese. Fold tortillas around filling, tucking in sides; use toothpicks if necessary to hold together. Freeze any remaining filling.

4. Heat 1-inch of vegetable oil in heavy deep skillet to 375°F. Fry chimichangas, two at a time, for 2–4 minutes on each side, removing from oil when brown and crisp. Drain well on paper towels before serving. If necessary, keep warm in 250°F oven until all are cooked.

Serving Suggestions

Serve these spicy and crisp chimichangas with sour cream, tomatillo salsa, red tomato salsa, and fresh guacamole for dipping. Be sure to let them cool on paper towels or kitchen towels for at least five minutes before serving; they're very hot! You can use the filling to make enchiladas or burritos too.

Beef

Beef with Broccoli

 Serves 4

$ Total Cost: $6.77
Calories: 378.92
Fat: 8.12 grams
Protein: 35.99 grams
Cholesterol: 84.15 mg
Sodium: 849.32 mg

¾ pound beef bottom round steak

1 teaspoon ground ginger

¼ teaspoon salt

⅛ teaspoon cayenne pepper

2 cloves garlic, minced

1 onion, minced

3 tablespoons low-sodium soy sauce

½ (8-ounce) can water chestnuts, drained

2 cups Beef Stock (page 233), divided

1 (16-ounce) package frozen broccoli florets

3 tablespoons cornstarch

1 cup rice

This classic Asian dish is usually stir-fried in a wok. The slow cooker method is easier, and the dish is just as delicious.

1. Cut beef into 1-inch cubes. In shallow bowl, combine ginger, salt, pepper, garlic, onion, and soy sauce and blend. Add beef cubes and stir to coat. Cover and refrigerate for 1–2 hours.

2. Pour beef mixture into 3 to 4-quart slow cooker along with drained water chestnuts, ½ cup water, and half of the Stock. Cover and cook on low for 7 to 8 hours until beef is tender, adding thawed broccoli during last hour of cooking time. During last 30 minutes of cooking time, combine cornstarch with ½ cup water and add to slow cooker; stir well, cover, and cook until thickened.

3. Combine remaining stock with enough water to make 2 cups. Cook rice in this mixture, covered, over medium heat for 15 to 20 minutes, until tender. Serve Beef with Broccoli over rice.

Shredded Beef Soft Tacos

Serves 4

¾ pound beef top round steak

1 onion, chopped

3 cloves garlic, minced

½ cup water

¾ cup salsa

2 cups torn lettuce

1 tomato, seeded and chopped

½ cup shredded Cheddar cheese

½ cup sour cream

4 (10-inch) flour tortillas

The meat for these delicious tacos cooks in the Crock-Pot, so when you come home from work or school, all you have to do is assemble the tacos and eat them!

1. Place beef, onion, and garlic in 4-quart Crock-Pot and pour water over all. Cover and cook on low for 8–10 hours until beef is very tender. Remove meat and vegetables from Crock-Pot. Using 2 forks, shred meat, mixing with onion and garlic.
2. Combine meat mixture and salsa in a large bowl. In another large bowl, combine cheese and sour cream. Soften tortillas by wrapping in microwave-safe paper towels and heating on medium for 2–3 minutes.
3. Place ¼ cup beef filling on a flour tortilla and top with lettuce, tomatoes, and sour cream mixture. Serve immediately.

Another Method

You can also make these tacos in the usual way: heat purchased crisp taco shells and serve with meat mixture, lettuce mixture, sour cream mixture, and any other condiments you'd like. The combination of hot crisp taco shell, tender, hot meat filling, and cold vegetables and sour cream is fabulous.

Crock-Pot Beef Stroganoff

 Serves 4

$ Total Cost: $5.46

Calories: 326.14

Fat: 13.88 grams

Protein: 31.88 grams

Cholesterol: 96.80 mg

Sodium: 513.23 mg

¾ pound beef top round steak

2 tablespoons flour

½ teaspoon salt

⅛ teaspoon pepper

1 onion, chopped

4 cloves garlic, chopped

2 carrots, sliced

1 tablespoon mustard

1 cup Beef Stock (page 233)

2 tablespoons Worcestershire sauce

½ teaspoon dried marjoram

½ cup sour cream

1 tablespoon cornstarch

This elegant dish is a variation on traditional Beef Stroganoff. It's an excellent dish for company. You can double it if you'd like; use a 4-quart slow cooker.

1. Cut steak into 1-inch pieces and toss with flour, salt, and pepper. Place onion, garlic, and carrots in 3½-quart slow cooker and top with beef.
2. In small bowl, combine mustard, Beef Stock, Worcestershire sauce, and marjoram; mix well and pour into slow cooker. Cover and cook on low for 8–9 hours or until beef and vegetables are tender.
3. In medium bowl, combine sour cream and cornstarch with 1 cup of the hot liquid from the Crock-Pot and mix well with wire whisk. Stir into Crock-Pot until blended; cook on high for 25 to 30 minutes, until mixture is thickened. Serve over hot cooked noodles or rice.

Crock-Pot Spaghetti and Meat Sauce

Serves 6

💲 Total Cost: $6.64

Calories: 539.73

Fat: 15.53 grams

Protein: 24.03 grams

Cholesterol: 44.16 mg

Sodium: 809.32 mg

¾ pound 80% lean ground beef

1 onion, chopped

3 cloves garlic, chopped

1 carrot, coarsely grated

1 teaspoon dried basil leaves

¼ teaspoon dried red pepper flakes

½ cup Beef Stock (page 233)

1 (26-ounce) jar pasta sauce

1 (16-ounce) package spaghetti pasta

⅓ cup grated Parmesan cheese

This rich and well-flavored spaghetti sauce can be made with ground turkey, ground pork sausage, or ground chicken if you'd like.

1. In large saucepan, brown ground beef with onion and garlic until beef is cooked, stirring to break up meat. Drain well and pour into a 3–4-quart slow cooker.
2. Add carrot, basil, red pepper flakes, Stock, and pasta sauce. Cover and cook on low for 7 to 8 hours, until sauce is bubbling and vegetables are tender.
3. Cook pasta according to package directions; drain, and serve with spaghetti sauce and meatballs. Top with Parmesan cheese.

Spaghetti Sauce

Packaged spaghetti sauce varies wildly in price, depending on your priorities. Canned sauce is cheaper than bottled, and you can find the sauce with meat, without, in organic forms, with and without cheese, and full of vegetables. Look for whatever is important to you.

Swiss Steak

Serves 4

Total Cost: $5.53
Calories: 411.32
Fat: 22.12 grams
Protein: 35.42 grams
Cholesterol: 108.00 mg
Sodium: 724.69 mg

1 pound round steak

½ teaspoon salt

⅛ teaspoon pepper

3 tablespoons flour

3 carrots, sliced

1 onion, chopped

2 cloves garlic, chopped

1 (8-ounce) can tomato sauce

2 tablespoons olive oil

1 tablespoon Dijon mustard

½ teaspoon dried thyme leaves

Traditionally, Swiss Steak is made from tougher meat that must be cooked slowly to tenderize. Your slow cooker is the perfect appliance for this homey meal.

1. Cut steak into serving-size pieces and place on waxed paper. In small bowl, combine salt, pepper, and flour and mix well. Sprinkle half of this mixture over steak pieces and, using meat mallet or rolling pin, pound flour mixture into steak. Turn meat over and repeat process on second side with remaining mixture.
2. Heat olive oil in medium saucepan and brown steaks on both sides, about 4 minutes total; remove from saucepan. Place carrots, onions, and garlic in 3–4-quart slow cooker and top with steak. Pour tomato sauce into saucepan and bring to a boil, stirring to release pan drippings.
3. Remove saucepan from heat and stir in mustard and thyme; pour over steak in slow cooker. Cover and cook on low for 8 to 10 hours, until meat and vegetables are very tender.

Fork Tender Pot Roast

 Serves 6

💲 Total Cost: $6.98
Calories: 580.40
Fat: 19.66 grams
Protein: 30.94 grams
Cholesterol: 77.62 mg
Sodium: 644.23 mg

1 (1¼-pound) bottom round
   or chuck roast

3 tablespoons all-purpose
   flour

1 teaspoon salt

1 teaspoon paprika

¼ teaspoon pepper

1 tablespoon olive oil

1 tablespoon butter

1 onion, chopped

2 potatoes, cubed

2 carrots, sliced

1 (10-ounce) can condensed
   tomato soup

2 tablespoons cornstarch

⅓ cup water

This really is an entire meal in one; all you need to do is add a salad and some bread if you'd like.

1. Trim excess fat from roast. On shallow plate, combine flour, salt, paprika, and pepper. Dredge roast in this mixture. Heat olive oil and butter in large saucepan over medium heat. Add roast; brown on both sides, turning once, 5–8 minutes.

2. Meanwhile, place onions, potatoes, and carrots in a 5–6-quart slow cooker. Top with the browned roast. Pour ¼ cup water and tomato soup into saucepan and bring to a boil, scraping the pan to loosen drippings. Pour over roast.

3. Cover and cook on low for 8–10 hours until meat and vegetables are very tender. If necessary, you can thicken the gravy. Remove the roast and cover with foil. Then combine cornstarch and ⅓ cup water in small bowl and stir into the gravy; cover and cook on high for 20–30 minutes until thickened.

Beef Choices for Pot Roast

Pot roast is best made from inexpensive cuts of meat because the slow cooker's moist environment helps break down fibers and melt the fat so the meat becomes meltingly tender. Top and bottom round, chuck steak, and brisket are all good choices. Top and bottom round are the least expensive of the group.

Sweet and Sour Beef

 Serves 4

💲 Total Cost: $6.70
🥄 Calories: 492.56
Fat: 18.28 grams
Protein: 36.64 grams
Cholesterol: 97.04 mg
Sodium: 736.89 mg

1 pound bottom round steak, cubed

3 tablespoons all-purpose flour

½ teaspoon salt

⅛ teaspoon pepper

1 onion, chopped

1 (8-ounce) can pineapple tidbits

¼ cup apple cider vinegar

3 tablespoons sugar

2 tablespoons low-sodium soy sauce

2 cups sliced carrots

1 cup frozen green beans

1 cup Beef Stock (page 233)

2 tablespoons cornstarch

The acidic ingredients make the beef meltingly tender. For a splurge, double the amount of meat.

1. Toss cubed meat with flour, salt, and pepper. Combine in 3–4-quart slow cooker with onions. Drain pineapple, reserving liquid. Add pineapple to slow cooker along with vinegar, sugar, and soy sauce; stir until blended.
2. Add carrots, green beans, and Stock. Cover and cook on low for 8–10 hours until beef is very tender.
3. In small bowl, combine cornstarch with ½ cup reserved pineapple liquid. Add to slow cooker, stir, cover, and cook on high for 30 minutes or until sauce is thickened. Serve over hot cooked rice.

Garlic and Onion Pot Roast

Serves 5

$ Total Cost: $6.79

Calories: 407.24

Fat: 22.17 grams

Protein: 37.58 grams

Cholesterol: 119.47 mg

Sodium: 402.61 mg

8 cloves garlic, divided

½ teaspoon salt

2 tablespoons mustard

1 tablespoon horseradish

⅛ teaspoon pepper

1 (1¼-pound) bottom round beef roast

1 onion, chopped

3 carrots, sliced

½ cup Beef Stock (page 233)

Serve this fabulous old fashioned dinner with a fruit salad and some crusty rolls.

1. Finely mince 4 cloves of garlic and place on work surface. Sprinkle with salt. With side of knife, work garlic and salt together into a paste. Place in small bowl and mix with mustard, horseradish, and pepper.
2. Rub this mixture over the roast. Place a skillet over medium high heat. Sear roast on both sides until browned, about 5 minutes total.
3. Place remaining garlic, onions, and carrots, in a 4-quart slow cooker. Top with beef. Pour Beef Stock over. Cover and cook on low for 8–9 hours, or until vegetables and beef are very tender.

Beef and the Slow Cooker

Your slow cooker is the ideal appliance to cook a pot roast. Smaller roasts should be cooked in a smaller slow cooker. Choose a slow cooker that just fits the meat, leaving about an-inch or two around the sides to allow for heat conduction and circulation. For larger roasts, an oval slow cooker is the better choice.

Slow-Cooker Beef Rouladen

 Serves 4

1 tablespoon butter

1 onion, chopped

2 cloves garlic, minced

2 carrots, diced

1¼-pounds bottom round steak

3 tablespoons flour

½ teaspoon salt

⅛ teaspoon pepper

1 tablespoon vegetable oil

⅓ cup Beef Stock (page 233)

1 (8-ounce) can tomato sauce

1 tablespoon mustard

1 tablespoon Worcestershire sauce

Beef, thinly pounded and stuffed with vegetables, makes an excellent main dish for entertaining.

1. In large skillet, melt 1 tablespoon butter over medium heat. Add onion, garlic, and carrots; cook and stir until tender, about 7 minutes. Remove from heat and place in medium bowl; let cool for 15 minutes.
2. Meanwhile, cut round steak into 4 equal portions. Trim excess fat, then place between sheets of waxed paper and pound until ¼-inch thick. Divide onion mixture on beef. Roll up, enclosing filling; secure with toothpicks.
3. On plate, combine flour, salt, and pepper and mix. Dredge beef rolls in flour mixture. In same skillet, heat vegetable oil. Brown beef rolls on all sides. Place beef rolls in 4-quart slow cooker.
4. Deglaze skillet with Stock; add tomato sauce, mustard, and Worcestershire sauce and bring to a simmer. Pour into slow cooker. Cover and cook on low for 7–8 hours or until beef is tender. Serve Rouladen with sauce.

Tex-Mex Meatloaf

 Serves 5

$ Total Cost: $4.51
🌶 Calories: 365.54
Fat: 20.45 grams
Protein: 17.79 grams
Cholesterol: 107.26 mg
Sodium: 528.71 mg

½ cup finely crushed tortilla chips

1 tablespoon chili powder

½ teaspoon dried oregano

⅛ teaspoon pepper

2 tablespoons buttermilk

1 egg

¼ cup salsa

½ pound ground beef

½ pound pork sausage

2 tablespoons ketchup

1 tablespoon mustard

¼ teaspoon Tabasco sauce

You can use plain or flavored tortilla chips in this easy meatloaf as you'd like. If you don't have a meat thermometer, cook until the juices run clear and the meatloaf is no longer pink in the center.

1. In large bowl, combine tortilla chips, chili powder, oregano, pepper, buttermilk, egg, and salsa; mix well.
2. Stir in beef and sausage until just mixed. Form into an 8-inch ball. Tear off two 24-inch sheets of heavy-duty foil and fold into thirds lengthwise. Place crosswise in bottom of 4-quart slow cooker. Place meatloaf on top.
3. In small bowl, combine ketchup, mustard, and Tabasco. Spread over meatloaf. Cover slow cooker. Cook on low for 7–8 hours or until meat thermometer registers 165°F.
4. Using the foil, carefully lift the meatloaf out of the slow cooker. Drain on paper towels for 10 minutes, then slice to serve.

Meatloaf Tips

The critical steps to making meatloaf are to make sure you do not overwork the meat, as this compacts the mixture and makes the meatloaf tough. Remove the meatloaf from the slow cooker, place on serving platter, and let the meatloaf stand, covered with foil, for about 10 minutes so the juices can redistribute.

Beef

Beef Carbonnade

 Serves 6

$ Total Cost: $6.98
Calories: 365.32
Fat: 9.63 grams
Protein: 32.19 grams
Cholesterol: 81.07 mg
Sodium: 511.76 mg

1 pound beef top round steak

3 tablespoons flour

½ teaspoon salt

⅛ teaspoon pepper

1 tablespoon olive oil

1 tablespoon butter

2 onions, chopped

4 cloves garlic, chopped

1 cup beer

1 teaspoon dried thyme

3 carrots, sliced

3 cups Beef Stock (page 233)

⅓ cup dried potato flakes

1½ cups egg noodles

Beer adds great depth of flavor to this rich beef stew. To serve without freezing, keep simmering stew while you cook the noodles. Drain noodles and serve with the stew.

1. Cut steak into 1-inch pieces. Toss with flour, salt, and pepper. Heat olive oil and butter in large saucepan and cook steak, in batches, until browned, about 5 to 6 minutes per batch. When all the beef is browned, remove from pan and set aside. Cook onions and garlic in the drippings remaining in saucepan, stirring to scrape up drippings, about 3 minutes.
2. Place onion mixture in 4-quart slow cooker along with beef, beer, thyme, carrots, and Stock. Cover and cook on low for 8–9 hours or until vegetables are tender.
3. Add potato flakes and egg noodles, turn heat to high, and cook for 10–12 minutes or until noodles are tender and stew is thick. Stir and serve.

Mexicali Rice and Beef

 Serves 5

$ Total Cost: $7.00
Calories: 406.32
Fat: 15.93 grams
Protein: 19.62 grams
Cholesterol: 59.58 mg
Sodium: 504.22 mg

¾ pound ground beef

1 onion, chopped

2 cloves garlic, minced

1 cup long grain brown rice

1 cup Beef Stock (page 233)

½ cup water

2 teaspoons chili powder

1 green bell pepper, chopped

1 jalapeño pepper, minced

1 (8-ounce) can tomato sauce

2 tablespoons taco sauce

¼ teaspoon pepper

½ cup shredded Colby cheese

This hearty and rich casserole is perfect for a cold winter night. Serve it with some warmed flour tortillas, a green salad with a mild Ranch salad dressing, and a bakery cake for dessert.

1. In heavy saucepan, cook ground beef with onion and garlic until beef is browned. Place in 4-quart slow cooker and add rice, bell peppers, and jalapeño.

2. Pour Stock, water, chili powder, tomato sauce, pepper, and taco sauce into saucepan and bring to a simmer, scraping up pan drippings. Pour into slow cooker, cover, and cook on low for 7–8 hours or until rice is tender.

3. Sprinkle with cheese, cover and let stand for 10 minutes, then serve immediately.

Rice in the Slow Cooker

White rice of any type doesn't cook very well in the slow cooker, unless it's mixed in with meat, like Porcupine Meatballs (page 76). Brown rice and wild rice, which both take about 40–50 minutes to cook on the stovetop, do work well in the slow cooker. Follow directions carefully and cook just until the rice is tender.

Beefy Baked Beans

 Serves 5

$ Total Cost: $6.79
Calories: 477.46
Fat: 14.55 grams
Protein: 25.68 grams
Cholesterol: 58.82 mg
Sodium: 920.13 mg

¾ pound 80% lean ground beef

1 onion, chopped

3 cloves garlic, minced

2 (16-ounce) cans baked beans, drained

1 (15-ounce) can black beans, drained

¼ cup brown sugar

2 tablespoons apple cider vinegar

⅓ cup ketchup

⅓ cup barbecue sauce

Canned beans are an inexpensive and nutritious way to feed a crowd. Serve this over hot cooked rice for a hearty and filling dinner.

1. In large skillet, brown ground beef, stirring to break up meat. Drain well and place in 4-quart slow cooker.
2. Add all remaining ingredients and stir gently. Cover and cook on low for 8–9 hours. If sauce needs thickening, remove cover and cook on high for 20–30 minutes.

Tangy Apricot Cube Steaks

Serves 4

1 pound cube steak	1 tablespoon oil
½ teaspoon salt	1 tablespoon butter
⅛ teaspoon pepper	1 onion, chopped
¼ cup flour	½ cup beef broth
1 teaspoon paprika	⅓ cup apricot preserves

Sweet fruit and tangy onions are always a good combination. Add that to tender cube steaks and you have a feast!

1. Cut steak into serving-sized pieces. On shallow plate, combine salt, pepper, flour, and paprika; stir to blend. Dredge steaks in this mixture.
2. In large skillet, combine oil and butter over medium heat. Brown steaks on both sides, turning once, about 3–4 minutes.
3. As steaks brown, place in 3-quart slow cooker. When all the steaks are cooked, add onion and beef broth to skillet. Cook and stir over medium heat to loosen drippings. Remove from heat and add apricot preserves to skillet.
4. Pour contents of skillet into slow cooker. Cover and cook on low for 7–8 hours or until meat is very tender. Serve meat with sauce.

Cube Steak

Cube steaks are usually made of round steak, cut about ½-inch thick and run through a machine which pierces the steak with lots of needles. This helps break the fibers of the meat, resulting in a tender finish. You can also make cube steaks by cutting your own steaks and pounding them with a meat mallet. Or cook them in the slow cooker.

Beans and Meatballs

 Serves 5

 Total Cost: $5.80
Calories: 398.27
Fat: 13.54 grams
Protein: 21.88 grams
Cholesterol: 67.76 mg
Sodium: 1089.23 mg

1 tablespoon olive oil

1 onion, chopped

2 cloves garlic, minced

½ cup ketchup

2 tablespoons brown sugar

2 tablespoons mustard

1 (15-ounce) can kidney beans

1 (15-ounce) can pork and beans

12 Porcupine Meatballs (page 76)

You can use any kind of canned beans you'd like in this easy recipe. You do need one can of pork and beans, though.

1. In large saucepan, warm olive oil over medium heat. Add onion and garlic; cook and stir until tender, about 5 minutes. Add ketchup, brown sugar, and mustard and bring to a simmer.
2. Drain kidney beans and add with pork and beans to 3–4-quart slow cooker. Add onion mixture and stir.
3. Prepare Porcupine Meatballs and freeze all but 12 of them. Brown the 12 meatballs in the saucepan, about 4–5 minutes total, then add to bean mixture. Cover and cook on low for 7–8 hours or until meatballs are thoroughly cooked and tender. Serve immediately.

Picadillo

 Serves 4

💲 Total Cost: $5.97
🍴 Calories: 361.67
   Fat: 18.43 grams
   Protein: 19.25 grams
   Cholesterol: 55.94 mg
   Sodium: 704.34 mg

¾ pound ground beef

1 onion, chopped

3 cloves garlic, minced

1 (14-ounce) can diced tomatoes with green chiles, undrained

3 tablespoons tomato paste

½ cup Beef Stock (page 233)

⅓ cup raisins

2 teaspoons chili powder

½ teaspoon salt

⅛ teaspoon cayenne pepper

1 tablespoon vinegar

⅛ teaspoon cinnamon

¼ cup sliced pimento-stuffed green olives

¼ cup slivered almonds

Picadillo is a spicy beef mixture made with ground beef, raisins, olives, and almonds. Use it as a filling for tacos or enchiladas or stuffed peppers, or as an appetizer dip with tortilla chips.

1. In heavy skillet, brown ground beef with onion and garlic until beef is no longer pink, stirring frequently to break up meat. Drain well.
2. Place in 4-quart slow cooker along with remaining ingredients. Cover and cook on low for 7–8 hours or until mixture is blended. Serve with soft tacos, warmed tortillas, or hot cooked rice.

Ingredient Substitutions

Substitute golden raisins or currants for the regular raisins in this rich main dish. You could also use just about any type of olive, including kalamata and garlic-stuffed, and any kind of nut: walnuts or pine nuts would be a good choice. And you could use ground chicken or turkey instead of ground beef.

Porcupine Meatballs

 Serves 4

💲 Total Cost: $5.29
Calories: 420.59
Fat: 19.53 grams
Protein: 30.36 grams
Cholesterol: 153.66 mg
Sodium: 947.34 mg

1 tablespoon butter

¼ cup minced onion

¼ cup minced green bell pepper

¼ cup uncooked long grain white rice

1 egg

½ teaspoon salt

⅛ teaspoon pepper

1 pound 80% lean ground beef

1 (8-ounce) can tomato sauce

½ cup ketchup

½ teaspoon dried oregano leaves

Rice adds moisture and texture to these tender meatballs. The rice cooks in the meatballs in the moist slow cooker environment.

1. In large skillet, melt butter over medium heat. Add onion and green pepper; cook and stir until crisp-tender, about 5 minutes. Remove from saucepan and place in large bowl; let cool for 15 minutes.
2. Add rice, egg, salt, and pepper and mix well. Add beef and mix just until combined. Form into 20 meatballs.
3. In same skillet, brown meatballs on all sides, about 4–5 minutes total. Place in 3–4-quart slow cooker. Place tomato sauce, ketchup, and oregano into skillet; bring to a simmer, scraping up drippings. Pour over meatballs.
4. Cover and cook on low for 7–8 hours or until meatballs are thoroughly cooked. Serve over mashed potatoes or rice.

Chili Mac

 Serves 4

💲 Total Cost: $6.91
🌶 Calories: 451.53
Fat: 18.32 grams
Protein: 24.95 grams
Cholesterol: 74.43 mg
Sodium: 804.32 mg

¾ pound ground beef

1 onion, chopped

2 cloves garlic, minced

1 green bell pepper, chopped

2 tablespoons flour

½ cup taco sauce

1 (10-ounce) can condensed tomato soup

2 teaspoons chili powder

⅛ teaspoon pepper

⅛ teaspoon cayenne pepper

½ (15-ounce) can kidney beans, drained

½ cup water

½ cup grated Cheddar cheese

½ cup uncooked elbow macaroni

Chili Mac is a definite Mexican-American hybrid. Ground beef, kidney beans, and macaroni are all simmered together in a spicy tomato sauce to make a hearty and easy dinner.

1. In large skillet, brown ground beef with onion and garlic; drain well if necessary. Add green pepper and cook for another 2–3 minutes. Sprinkle with flour and cook for 2 minutes. Pour into 4-quart slow cooker.

2. Pour taco sauce and soup into skillet; bring to a simmer, stirring to scrape up drippings. Add to slow cooker along with remaining ingredients except cheese and macaroni. Cover and cook on low for 7–8 hours.

3. Add macaroni to slow cooker and turn heat to high. Cover and cook for 10–15 minutes until macaroni is tender. Sprinkle with cheese and serve.

Tone It Down for Kids

If you're serving this recipe to kids, you may want to cut down on the amount of chili powder and pepper. You could also used plain diced tomatoes, not those with added green chiles. Serve some crushed red pepper flakes or ground red chili powder on the side for those who want to make their dinner spicier.

Beef and Potato Casserole

 Serves 4

$ Total Cost: $4.63
Calories: 343.19
Fat: 13.94 grams
Protein: 19.04 grams
Cholesterol: 53.52 mg
Sodium: 623.05 mg

¾ pound ground beef

2 potatoes, sliced

3 carrots, sliced

1 onion, chopped

2 cloves garlic, minced

½ cup tomato juice

½ teaspoon salt

⅛ teaspoon pepper

½ teaspoon dried marjoram leaves

1 cup frozen baby peas

¾ cup shredded Swiss cheese

A simple layered casserole is full of flavor when it's cooked in the slow cooker. Serve this with a green salad and some crisp breadsticks.

1. In medium skillet, cook beef, stirring to break up meat, until done. Drain well if necessary. Prepare vegetables.
2. Layer beef and vegetables in a 3½-quart slow cooker, sprinkling each layer with salt, pepper, and marjoram. Pour tomato juice into slow cooker. Cover and cook on low for 7–8 hours or until vegetables are tender.
3. Turn slow cooker to high. Stir in peas and cheese, cover, and cook on high for 15–20 minutes until hot. Serve immediately.

Smoky Beans and Beef Dinner

Serves 4

3 slices smoked bacon

¾ pound ground beef

1 onion, chopped

2 cloves garlic, minced

2 carrots, sliced

1 (22-ounce) can pork and beans

1 (15-ounce) can kidney beans, drained

½ cup ketchup

¼ cup brown sugar

⅛ teaspoon pepper

You can substitute browned pork sausage or plain ground pork for the beef in this easy recipe.

1. In medium skillet, cook bacon until crisp; drain on paper towels and crumble. Drain fat from skillet; do not wipe out. Add beef, stirring to break up meat, until done. Drain well if necessary. Prepare vegetables.
2. Combine all ingredients in 4-quart slow cooker. Cover and cook on low for 8–9 hours or until vegetables are tender. Stir well and serve immediately.

Smoked Bacon

Read labels to find out if the bacon you're buying is smoked or not. All bacon is cured and some is dried, but not all is smoked. Bacon is smoked over hickory or apple wood, or smoke flavoring is added to the curing mixture. It brings a smoky flavor to any recipe.

Beef and Bean Potpie

Serves 5

$ Total Cost: $6.99
Calories: 400.23
Fat: 14.23 grams
Protein: 22.78 grams
Cholesterol: 50.63 mg
Sodium: 670.48 mg

¾ pound ground beef

1 onion, chopped

3 cloves garlic, minced

½ teaspoon salt

⅛ teaspoon pepper

½ teaspoon dried marjoram

1 (15-ounce) can kidney
   beans, drained

3 carrots, sliced

1 (10-ounce) can condensed
   tomato soup

1 (8-ounce) package corn
   muffin mix

1 egg

½ cup sour cream

2 tablespoons oil

⅓ cup grated Parmesan
   cheese

This mild pie is comforting and rich. The corn bread topping stays moist and tender when cooked in the slow cooker.

1. In large skillet, cook ground beef with onions and garlic until ground beef is done, stirring to break up meat. Drain well. Add salt, pepper, and marjoram; stir.
2. Stir in kidney beans, carrots, and soup; bring to a simmer.
3. Spray a 3½-quart slow cooker with nonstick cooking spray. Pour beef mixture into slow cooker.
4. In medium bowl, combine remaining ingredients and stir just until combined. Spoon by tablespoonsful over beef mixture in slow cooker.
5. Cover and cook on low for 6–8 hours or until corn bread is set and toothpick inserted in center of topping comes out clean.

CHAPTER 5

PORK AND HAM

82 Teriyaki Pork Chops

83 Slow Cooker BBQ Shredded Pork

84 Slow Cooker Pork and Beans

85 Caramelized Onion Apple Pork Chops

86 Slow-Cooker Lasagna

87 Pork Chops with Cabbage

88 Slow-Cooker Apricot Pork Chops

89 Carnitas

90 Slow-Cooker Braised Pork with Fruit

91 Pork Fajitas

92 Slow-Cooker Sausage and Cabbage

93 Tex-Mex Pork Casserole

94 Mexican Pork and Beans

95 Pork Sausage Spaghetti

96 Pork Adobo

97 Slow-Cooker BBQ Shredded Pork

98 Creamy Mustard Pork Chops

99 Ham and Cheese Potatoes

100 Sausage Sweet Potato Supper

101 Ham with Wild Rice

Teriyaki Pork Chops

Serves 4

4 boneless center-cut pork
chops

2 tablespoons soy sauce

½ cup pineapple juice

3 tablespoons apple cider
vinegar

2 tablespoons sugar

1 tablespoon grated
gingerroot

2 cups frozen broccoli florets

1 cup long grain rice

2 cups Chicken Stock
(page 234)

This delicious dish has the flavors of the Orient with very
little work. It's so wonderful to come home to this dish
ready and waiting for you.

1. Place pork chops in zipper-lock bag and add remaining ingredients except broccoli, rice, and stock. Seal bag and knead it
   to mix thoroughly. Refrigerate for 1–2 hours.
2. Place meat and marinade in 3 to 4-quart slow cooker, cover,
   and cook on low for 7 hours. Add broccoli and cook for 1
   hour longer or until broccoli and chops are hot and tender.
3. During last half hour of cooking, combine rice and stock in
   heavy saucepan, bring to a boil, then cover pan, reduce heat
   to low, and simmer for 15 to 20 minutes, until rice is tender
   and liquid is absorbed. Serve pork chops and broccoli over
   rice.

Slow Cooker BBQ Shredded Pork

Serves 4

$ Total Cost: $6.90
Calories: 302.81
Fat: 11.10 grams
Protein: 32.86 grams
Cholesterol: 89.53 mg
Sodium: 765.56 mg

2 onions, chopped

4 cloves garlic, minced

1 jalapeño pepper, minced

½ cup taco sauce

⅓ cup barbecue sauce

2 teaspoons chili powder

1 pound boneless pork loin roast

½ teaspoon salt

⅛ teaspoon pepper

Use this easy recipe as a filling for sandwiches or tacos, or to fill enchiladas. It's versatile and delicious.

1. In a 3-quart Crock-Pot, combine all ingredients except roast, salt, and pepper. Sprinkle roast with salt and pepper and place in Crock-Pot. Cover and cook on low for 8–10 hours or until pork is very tender.
2. Remove pork and shred with 2 forks; return to Crock-Pot and cook on high for another 30 minutes. Serve over rice, or with warmed corn or flour tortillas and guacamole.

Make-Ahead Tip

This shredded pork mixture freezes very well. Cool it completely, then pack into hard-sided freezer containers, label well, cover, and freeze up to 3 months. To thaw, let stand in the refrigerator overnight, and then reheat in saucepan over low heat, stirring gently, until hot.

Slow Cooker Pork and Beans

Serves 4

Total Cost: $6.13

Calories: 341.33

Fat: 11.71 grams

Protein: 23.61 grams

Cholesterol: 57.62 mg

Sodium: 934.23 mg

¾ pound boneless pork loin, cubed

½ teaspoon salt

½ teaspoon paprika

⅛ teaspoon pepper

1 (16-ounce) can pork and beans

1 onion, chopped

¼ cup ketchup

3 tablespoons mustard

2 tablespoons honey

Cubes of pork loin and beans are a delicious, classic, and inexpensive combination that makes a hearty meal.

1. Sprinkle pork with salt, paprika, and pepper; rub into meat. Open pork and beans and drain off half of the thick liquid. Pour half of the can of pork and beans into 3 to 4-quart slow cooker and add onions, ketchup, mustard, and honey; mix well.
2. Place half of the pork in slow cooker and top with remaining can of slightly drained pork and beans, then top with remaining pork. Cover slow cooker and cook on low for 8 to 9 hours, until meat is thoroughly cooked and tender.

Caramelized Onion Apple Pork Chops

Serves 4

$ Total Cost: $6.99
Calories: 394.97
Fat: 12.32 grams
Protein: 50.65 grams
Cholesterol: 135.55 mg
Sodium: 643.24 mg

2 tablespoons butter, divided

2 onions, chopped

1 clove garlic, minced

1 Granny Smith apple, chopped

½ teaspoon salt

⅛ teaspoon pepper

¼ cup brown sugar

4 (6-ounce) thick boneless pork chops

¼ cup flour

¼ cup chicken broth

¼ cup apple juice

1 tablespoon Dijon mustard

Caramelized onions become very sweet and tender. They are the perfect accompaniment to pork chops.

1. Melt 1 tablespoon butter in large skillet over medium heat. Add onion and garlic; cook and stir until tender, about 6 minutes. Then lower heat and cook, stirring frequently, until onions are deep golden brown, about another 30 minutes.
2. Spoon onion mixture into medium bowl; stir in apples, salt, pepper, and sugar. Let cool for 15 minutes. Meanwhile, cut a pocket into the side of each pork chop.
3. Stuff some of the onion mixture into each pork chop. Dredge chops in flour. Melt remaining 1 tablespoon butter in skillet; brown pork chops on both sides.
4. Place remaining onion mixture into 4-quart slow cooker; top with pork chops. Deglaze pan with chicken broth and apple juice; stir in mustard and pour over chops. Cover and cook on low for 8–9 hours until pork is tender.

Onions

Frequently eating onions can help reduce cholesterol and lower blood pressure. The sulfur compounds that make you cry when you cut them also work their magic on your body. Onions also have quercetin, which has been found to have anti-tumor properties. In fact, eating lots of onions can reduce the risk of cancers up to 80 percent.

Slow-Cooker Lasagna

 Serves 5

 Total Cost: $6.98
Calories: 523.94
Fat: 26.71 grams
Protein: 26.51 grams
Cholesterol: 120.32 mg
Sodium: 1042.12 mg

¾ pound bulk Italian sausage

1 onion, chopped

3 cloves garlic, minced

1 (8-ounce) can tomato
sauce

¼ cup tomato paste

1 teaspoon dried Italian
seasoning

1 cup Chicken Stock
(page 234)

1 (3-ounce) package cream
cheese, softened

¾ cup part-skim ricotta
cheese

1 egg

1 cup shredded part-skim
mozzarella cheese

⅛ teaspoon pepper

1 tablespoon dried parsley
flakes

6 uncooked lasagna noodles

That's right—lasagna in the Crock-Pot! This rich and delicious recipe is close to
authentic lasagna, but adds cream cheese for more creaminess.

1. In heavy skillet, sauté sausage until almost cooked. Drain off excess fat and add onion and
   garlic. Cook and stir until sausage is cooked and vegetables are crisp-tender. Add tomato
   sauce, paste, Italian seasoning, and Stock. Simmer sauce, stirring frequently, for 5 to 10
   minutes to blend flavors.
2. Meanwhile, in large bowl, beat cream cheese and ricotta cheese until blended. Add egg,
   then stir in mozzarella cheese, pepper, and parsley.
3. Place ⅓ of the sauce in the bottom of a 3–4-quart slow cooker. Top with 2 lasagna noodles, breaking them as necessary to fit. Top with ½ of the cheese mixture, then ⅓ of meat
   mixture. Top with 2 more lasagna noodles, then remaining cheese mixture. Finally, add
   remaining lasagna noodles and remaining meat mixture.
4. Cover slow cooker and cook on low for 6 to 8 hours until noodles are tender. Serve by
   scooping up a large spoonful from the bottom of the slow cooker.

Pork Chops with Cabbage

Serves 4

1 onion, chopped

2 cloves garlic, minced

4 cups chopped green cabbage

1 apple, chopped

4 (3.5-ounce) boneless pork chops

⅛ teaspoon white pepper

1 tablespoon olive oil

¼ cup brown sugar

¼ cup apple cider vinegar

1 tablespoon mustard

Cabbage is the ideal accompaniment to pork. It's tangy and sweet and becomes very tender when cooked in the slow cooker.

1. In 3 to 4-quart slow cooker, combine onion, garlic, cabbage, and apple and mix well.
2. Trim pork chops of any excess fat and sprinkle with pepper. Heat olive oil in large saucepan over medium heat. Brown chops on just one side, about 3 minutes. Add to slow cooker with vegetables.
3. In small bowl, combine brown sugar, vinegar, and mustard and mix well. Pour into slow cooker. Cover and cook on low for 7–8 hours or until pork and cabbage are tender. Serve immediately.

Cabbage and Nutrition

Cabbage is a member of the cruciferous vegetable family, which also includes cauliflower and broccoli. These vegetables have phytochemicals called indoles which may help protect heart health. Cabbage is high in vitamin C, fiber, and folate. Red cabbage has more vitamin C and fiber than green cabbage.

Slow-Cooker Apricot Pork Chops

Serves 4

4 center-cut boneless pork chops

½ cup dried apricots, chopped

½ cup apricot nectar

¼ cup apricot preserves

2 cloves garlic, minced

1 tablespoon Dijon mustard

3 tablespoons honey

½ teaspoon salt

⅛ teaspoon white pepper

2 carrots, sliced

The combination of sweet apricots with mustard and garlic is really delicious with pork.

Place all ingredients in 3- to 4-quart slow cooker, cover, and cook on low for 8 hours or until pork chops and carrots are tender. Serve with hot cooked rice, couscous, or pasta.

Carnitas

 Serves 6

💲 Total Cost: $6.68
🥄 Calories: 289.43
Fat: 13.21 grams
Protein: 33.38 grams
Cholesterol: 89.00 mg
Sodium: 272.91 mg

1½-pound pork roast

½ teaspoon salt

¼ teaspoon pepper

1 teaspoon cumin

1 onion, chopped

3 cloves garlic, chopped

½ cup Chicken Stock (page 234)

Carnitas is slowly roasted pork that is then cooked in dry heat until crisp. Serve with heated flour tortillas, chopped vegetables, and let everyone make their own sandwiches.

1. Sprinkle roast with salt, pepper, and cumin, and place in a 3-quart Crock-Pot. Surround with onions and garlic and pour Chicken Stock over all. Cover and cook on low for 8–9 hours until pork is very tender.
2. Preheat oven to 400°F. Remove pork from Crock-Pot and place in large baking pan. Using 2 forks, shred meat. Take 1 cup of pan juices from the Crock-Pot and mix into pork.
3. Bake at 400°F for 15–20 minutes or until pork is crisp on top. Stir pork mixture thoroughly and bake for 15–20 minutes longer or until pork is again crisp on top. Serve with crisp tacos, flour or corn tortillas, and lots of salsa.

Make It Spicy

Traditionally, carnitas is cooked without chili powder or fresh or dried chiles. However, you can certainly add some to the Crock-Pot to help flavor the pork as it cooks. A chipotle pepper packed in adobo sauce, or a couple of fresh jalapeño peppers, minced, would be delicious.

Slow-Cooker Braised Pork with Fruit

 Serves 4

1 (1¼-pound) boneless pork shoulder roast

½ teaspoon salt

¼ teaspoon pepper

3 tablespoons flour

1 tablespoon butter

1 onion, chopped

2 cloves garlic, minced

½ cup dark raisins

½ cup golden raisins

⅓ cup apple juice

3 tablespoons apple cider vinegar

2 tablespoons cornstarch

⅓ cup water

½ cup chicken broth

½ teaspoon dried marjoram leaves

1 bay leaf

The slow cooker is a wonderful choice for entertaining, because the food cooks happily all by itself while you do other things.

1. Cut roast into 2-inch pieces and sprinkle with salt, pepper, and flour. In large saucepan, heat butter over medium heat. Brown the pork cubes about 2–3 minutes total. Remove to a 4-quart slow cooker.
2. Add onion and garlic to saucepan; cook and stir for 4–5 minutes to loosen pan drippings. Add to slow cooker along with all remaining ingredients except cornstarch and water.
3. Cover and cook on low for 7–8 hours, or until pork registers 160°F. Remove bay leaf. In small bowl combine cornstarch and water; stir into slow cooker and cook on high for 10–15 minutes until sauce is thickened. Serve over hot cooked rice.

Pork Fajitas

 Serves 4

$ Total Cost: $6.53
Calories: 448.49
Fat: 17.42 grams
Protein: 24.12 grams
Cholesterol: 56.78 mg
Sodium: 940.25 mg

2 boneless pork chops

1 tablespoon chili powder

½ teaspoon salt

⅛ teaspoon cayenne pepper

1 onion, sliced

2 cloves garlic

½ cup Chicken Stock (page 234)

1 green bell pepper, sliced

1 cup shredded Cheddar cheese

4 (10-inch) flour tortillas

¼ cup chopped cilantro

Instead of being grilled or stir-fried, the pork in this recipe is slowly cooked so the meat is very tender.

1. Cut pork chops into thin strips and place in medium bowl. Sprinkle with chili powder, salt, and cayenne pepper; let stand for 15 minutes.
2. Combine in 3-quart slow cooker with onion, garlic, and Chicken Stock. Cover and cook on low for 7–8 hours or until pork is tender.
3. Shred pork using two forks. Stir mixture in slow cooker. Make fajitas with green bell pepper, cheese, tortillas, and cilantro.

How to Warm Tortillas
Serve any dish that has a lot of sauce with a bunch of warmed flour or corn tortillas. To warm tortillas, wrap them in foil and place them in a 350°F oven for about 10 minutes. Or wrap in microwave-safe paper towels and microwave on high for 20–30 seconds. Place them in a tortilla warmer and serve.

Slow-Cooker Sausage and Cabbage

 Serves 4

$ Total Cost: $5.40

**** Calories: 459.76
Fat: 25.93 grams
Protein: 17.82 grams
Cholesterol: 83.92 mg
Sodium: 1297.25 mg

1 pound bratwurst

1 onion, chopped

4 cloves garlic, minced

3 cups chopped green cabbage

3 tablespoons sugar

¼ cup red wine vinegar

½ teaspoon salt

⅛ teaspoon pepper

3 tablespoons English mustard

This hearty recipe is satisfying on a cold winter night. Serve it with dark crusty bread, toasted and spread with butter.

1. In large skillet, cook bratwurst over medium heat until it begins to brown. Remove from heat. Add onion and garlic; cook and stir until onion is crisp-tender, about 4 minutes.
2. In 3½-quart slow cooker, combine onion, garlic, cabbage, sugar, wine vinegar, salt, and pepper and mix. Top with bratwurst and spread bratwurst with mustard. Cover and cook on low for 7–8 hours or until cabbage is tender and sausage is thoroughly cooked.

Tex-Mex Pork Casserole

 Serves 4

$ Total Cost: $6.93
Calories: 420.14
Fat: 15.00 grams
Protein: 40.83 grams
Cholesterol: 96.93 mg
Sodium: 930.45 mg

1 pound pork loin

1 tablespoon chili powder

½ teaspoon cumin

½ teaspoon salt

⅛ teaspoon cayenne pepper

1 tablespoon butter

1 onion, chopped

2 cloves garlic, minced

1 jalapeño pepper, minced

½ cup Chicken Stock (page 234)

½ cup taco sauce

1 (15-ounce) can black beans

Serve this spicy casserole with warmed flour or corn tortillas, hot cooked rice, guacamole, and sour cream.

1. Cut pork into 1-inch cubes. In small bowl, combine chili powder, cumin, salt, and cayenne pepper and mix well. Add to pork cubes and toss to coat well. In heavy skillet, cook coated pork cubes in butter until browned, about 4 minutes.

2. Meanwhile, place onion, garlic, and jalapeño pepper in a 3½ to 4-quart Crock-Pot. Add browned pork cubes and pour Stock over all. Top with taco sauce and rinsed and drained black beans; mix well. Cover and cook on low for 8–10 hours or until pork is very tender.

Peppers

Peppers vary in spice and heat level. In general, the larger the pepper, the sweeter. Green bell peppers are sweet with no heat, while habanero peppers, which are very tiny, are fiery hot. Jalapeños are spicy, but not too hot. Choose the peppers you'd like to use in your recipes.

Mexican Pork and Beans

 Serves 4

$ Total Cost: $3.81

Calories: 351.84

Fat: 8.88 grams

Protein: 20.40 grams

Cholesterol: 21.45 mg

Sodium: 793.42 mg

1 cup dried pinto beans

4 slices thick bacon

2 cups Chicken Stock (page 234)

1 cup water

3 cloves garlic, minced

1 onion, chopped

½ cup taco sauce

1 tablespoon chili powder

2 tablespoons brown sugar

½ teaspoon dried oregano leaves

½ teaspoon salt

⅛ teaspoon cayenne pepper

Thick-cut bacon adds lots of flavor to this hearty bean dish. You could substitute the same amount of ham if you'd like.

1. Cover pinto beans with water, bring to a boil, and boil for 2 minutes. Remove from heat, cover, and let stand for 1 hour. Meanwhile, cube bacon and cook over medium heat until crisp. Drain on paper towels.
2. Drain beans, rinse, and place in 3½-quart slow cooker. Add bacon along with Stock and water, garlic, and onion. Cover and cook on low for 6 hours until beans are almost tender.
3. Add taco sauce and remaining ingredients to slow cooker. Cover and cook for 2 hours longer. Stir well and serve.

Pork Sausage Spaghetti

 Serves 6

¾ pound bulk pork sausage

1 onion, chopped

2 cloves garlic, chopped

½ cup grated carrot

1 (14-ounce) can diced
  tomatoes, undrained

1 (6-ounce) can tomato paste

1 cup Beef Stock (page 233)

1 teaspoon dried Italian
  seasoning

1 (12-ounce) package
  spaghetti

¼ cup grated Parmesan
  cheese

Pork sausage makes flavorful spaghetti. The meat is usually used in lasagna, but why not in spaghetti too?

1. In heavy skillet, cook pork with onion, garlic, and carrot until
   pork is browned. Drain off excess fat. Place in 3½-quart
   slow cooker along with tomatoes, tomato paste, Stock, and
   Italian seasoning.
2. Cover and cook on low for 7–8 hours or until sauce is
   blended. Cook spaghetti according to package directions.
   Serve sauce over spaghetti and top with cheese.

Spaghetti in the Slow Cooker

You can cook spaghetti directly in the Crock-Pot if the sauce
is quite liquid. But the spaghetti will get quite soft; it's almost
impossible to cook al dente pasta in the slow cooker. If you like
that type of pasta doneness, go ahead. The pasta will have
more flavor since it's cooked in the sauce rather than just boiling
water.

Pork Adobo

 Serves 6

$ Total Cost: $7.00
Calories: 390.53
Fat: 19.43 grams
Protein: 28.27 grams
Cholesterol: 102.94 mg
Sodium: 385.22 mg

1 (1¼-pound) boneless pork shoulder roast

3 tablespoons apple cider vinegar

3 tablespoons low-sodium soy sauce

½ cup water

3 garlic cloves, minced

1 jalapeño pepper, minced

⅛ teaspoon crushed red pepper flakes

1 cup long grain rice

Serve this variation on a traditional Philippine dish with hot rice, sliced avocado, chopped tomato, and warmed flour tortillas.

1. Trim excess fat from pork and cut into 1-inch cubes. Combine in large bowl with vinegar, soy sauce, water, minced garlic, jalapeños, and pepper flakes and refrigerate overnight.
2. Pour marinated pork and sauce into 3-quart slow cooker. Cover and cook on low for 8–9 hours or until pork is done and very tender. Cook rice as directed on package. Serve pork mixture over rice.

Slow-Cooker BBQ Shredded Pork

Serves 4

💲 Total Cost: $6.91
Calories: 362.90
Fat: 14.97 grams
Protein: 42.08 grams
Cholesterol: 110.50 mg
Sodium: 709.43 mg

1 onion, chopped

2 cloves garlic, minced

1 jalapeño pepper, minced

½ cup taco sauce

¼ cup barbecue sauce

1 tablespoon chili powder

1¼-pound boneless pork loin roast

½ teaspoon salt

⅛ teaspoon cayenne pepper

This delicious tender pork can be served as-is over rice, or use it as a filling for enchiladas or pork wraps with fresh tomatoes.

1. In a 4 to 5-quart Crock-Pot, combine all ingredients. Cover and cook on low for 8–10 hours or until pork is very tender.
2. Remove pork and shred with 2 forks; return to Crock-Pot and cook on high for another 30 minutes. Serve over rice, or with warmed corn or flour tortillas and guacamole.

Make-Ahead Tip

This shredded pork mixture freezes very well. Cool it completely, then pack into hard-sided freezer containers, label well, cover, and freeze up to 3 months. To thaw, let stand in the refrigerator overnight, and then reheat in saucepan over low heat, stirring gently, until hot.

Creamy Mustard Pork Chops

Serves 4

4 boneless pork loin chops

½ teaspoon salt

⅛ teaspoon white pepper

1 tablespoon olive oil

1 onion, sliced

2 tablespoons grainy mustard

¾ cup Chicken Stock (page 234)

1 tablespoon prepared horseradish

2 tablespoons cornstarch

½ cup sour cream

2 tablespoons Dijon mustard

Mustard was made for pork. The spicy, sweet-and-sour taste blends with the sweet and nutty flavor of pork chops. Serve this one with mashed potatoes.

1. Sprinkle pork chops with salt and pepper. In large skillet, heat olive oil over medium heat. Add chops; brown, turning once, for about 4–6 minutes.
2. Place onions in the bottom of a 3-quart slow cooker. Add a layer of pork chops, then spread some of the grainy mustard over. Repeat, using the rest of the pork chops and the mustard.
3. Add Stock to slow cooker. Cover and cook on low for 7–8 hours or until chops are tender and register 155°F.
4. Remove chops from slow cooker and cover to keep warm. In small bowl, combine horseradish, cornstarch, sour cream, and Dijon mustard; mix well. Pour into slow cooker and stir well.
5. Return chops to slow cooker, cover, and cook on high for 30 minutes until sauce is thickened. Serve immediately.

The $7 a Meal Slow Cooker Cookbook

Ham and Cheese Potatoes

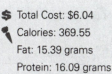

Serves 6

$ Total Cost: $6.04
Calories: 369.55
Fat: 15.39 grams
Protein: 16.09 grams
Cholesterol: 49.61 mg
Sodium: 890.56 mg

½ (32-ounce) package frozen straight cut French fry potatoes

1 onion, chopped

2 cloves garlic, minced

1¼ cups cubed ham

1 cup shredded Swiss cheese

1 (10-ounce) can cream of potato soup

½ cup ricotta cheese

⅛ teaspoon pepper

½ teaspoon dried marjoram

1½ cups frozen baby peas, thawed

¼ cup grated Parmesan cheese

Kids especially will love this recipe. It's hot, creamy, and comforting, made easy by starting with frozen potatoes.

1. In 3½-quart slow cooker, combine potatoes, onions, garlic, ham, and Swiss cheese; mix well. In medium bowl, combine soup, cheese, pepper, and marjoram. Pour over potato mixture.
2. Cover and cook on low for 8–9 hours or until potatoes are tender. Stir in peas and Parmesan cheese. Cover and cook on high for 30–40 minutes or until peas are hot. Serve immediately.

Frozen Potatoes

Frozen potatoes cook very well in the slow cooker. French fries, hash browns, and sliced potatoes—all are delicious. If the recipe cooks for 5–7 hours, thaw and drain the potatoes first. If the recipe cooks for 8 hours or longer, you can use the potatoes straight from the freezer.

Sausage Sweet Potato Supper

 Serves 5

$ Total Cost: $5.98

Calories: 381.38

Fat: 16.93 grams

Protein: 19.43 grams

Cholesterol: 80.42 mg

Sodium: 730.48 mg

1 pound sweet Italian
   sausage links

1 tablespoon butter

1 onion, chopped

2 cloves garlic, minced

2 tablespoons flour

½ teaspoon salt

⅛ teaspoon pepper

2 teaspoons curry powder

¼ cup brown sugar

½ cup Chicken Stock
   (page 234)

½ cup apple cider

2 sweet potatoes, peeled

2 apples, peeled and sliced

2 tablespoons brown sugar

Sweet potatoes, apples, and pork really complement each other. Add curry powder and some onions and garlic, and you have a fabulous one-dish meal.

1. In large skillet, cook sausage until almost done; remove from skillet. Add butter to drippings remaining in skillet. Add onions and garlic; cook and stir until tender, about 6 minutes.
2. Add flour, salt, pepper, and curry powder; cook and stir until bubbly. Add ¼ cup brown sugar, then stir in Chicken Stock and cider. Cook and stir until thickened.
3. Slice sweet potatoes into ⅛-inch thick rounds. Slice the sausage into 1-inch chunks. Layer sweet potatoes, apples, sausage pieces, and onion mixture in 3½-quart slow cooker. Top with 2 tablespoons brown sugar.
4. Cover and cook on low for 9–10 hours or until sweet potatoes are tender. Serve immediately.

Ham with Wild Rice

 Serves 4

 Total Cost: $6.88

Calories: 430.66

Fat: 20.53 grams

Protein: 16.30 grams

Cholesterol: 29.66 mg

Sodium: 730.62 mg

1 onion, chopped

3 cloves garlic, minced

2 (4-ounce) jars sliced mushrooms

1 cup wild rice

2 carrots, sliced

1½ cups cubed cooked ham

1 (10-ounce) can condensed cream of mushroom soup

2½ cups Chicken Stock (page 234)

½ teaspoon dried tarragon leaves

⅛ teaspoon white pepper

¼ cup grated Parmesan cheese

Wild rice cooks perfectly in the slow cooker, unlike white rice. Add some onions, ham, and creamy sauces for an elegant casserole.

1. In 3½ to 4-quart slow cooker, combine onions, garlic, mushrooms, wild rice, carrots, and ham; stir gently.
2. In medium bowl, combine soup, Chicken Stock, tarragon, and pepper; mix well. Pour into slow cooker.
3. Cover and cook on high for 1 hour, then stir food thoroughly. Cover again and cook on low for 6–7 hours or until wild rice and carrots are tender. Stir in cheese and serve.

Condensed Soups

Condensed soups are delicious in slow cooker recipes. They contain stabilizers and emulsifiers which prevent the sauce from separating as it cooks. Look for low sodium varieties to help keep the salt content under control. Match the soup to the recipe; cream of chicken soup adds more flavor to chicken recipes, cream of potato for potato recipes.

CHAPTER 6

CHICKEN—LIGHT MEAT

103 Ranch Casserole

104 Slow-Cooker Simmered Chicken Breasts

105 Chicken Supreme

106 Shredded Chicken for Tacos

107 Chicken with Peppers

108 Chicken con Queso Casserole

109 Fiesta Casserole

110 Updated Chicken Cordon Bleu

111 Chicken Curry

112 Apple Stuffed Chicken Rolls

113 Chicken Tacos

114 Laura's Chicken Risotto

115 Slow-Cooker Chicken and Cheese Soufflé

116 Chicken Dijon

117 Scalloped Chicken

118 Slow-Cooker Chicken à la King

119 Slow-Cooker Chicken Divan

120 Classic Chicken and Dumplings

121 Chicken Lasagna

122 Apple Chicken

123 Spanish Chicken and Rice

Ranch Casserole

 Serves 4

$ Total Cost: $6.95
Calories: 395.34
Fat: 20.32 grams
Protein: 20.73 grams
Cholesterol: 63.62 mg
Sodium: 1391.42 mg

2 tablespoons vegetable oil

4 corn tortillas

2 tablespoons chili powder, divided

1 onion, chopped

4 cloves garlic, minced

1 Slow Cooker Simmered Chicken Breast (page 104)

1 (10-ounce) can condensed nacho cheese soup

1 (8-ounce) can tomato sauce

1 (4-ounce) can chopped green chiles

⅛ teaspoon cayenne pepper

½ cup shredded Cheddar cheese

½ cup shredded pepper jack cheese

Since this casserole cooks for such a long time in the moist environment of the Crock-Pot, the tortillas are fried until crisp before being layered. They will keep their shape and a tiny bit of crunch when the casserole is finished.

1. Heat vegetable oil in large skillet. Cut corn tortillas into eighths and fry, in batches, in oil until crisp and golden. Remove to paper towel to drain; sprinkle fried tortillas with 1 table-spoon chili powder. Set aside.
2. In same skillet, in same oil, cook onion and garlic until crisp-tender. Meanwhile, cube Chicken Breast; reserve skin and bones for Stock (page 234). Add Chicken to onion mixture; remove from heat. In large bowl, combine soup, tomato sauce, green chiles, 1 tablespoon chili powder, and cayenne pepper and mix well.
3. In 3½-quart Crock-Pot, layer half of chicken mixture, fried tortillas, and soup mixture; repeat layers. Cover and cook on low for 8–9 hours or until casserole is bubbling around edges. Sprinkle with cheese, cover, and let stand for 10 minutes before serving.

Slow-Cooker Simmered Chicken Breasts

 Serves 4

Total Cost: $4.40
Calories: 141.90
Fat: 3.07 grams
Protein: 26.68 grams
Cholesterol: 73.10 mg
Sodium: 645.01 mg

4 bone-in, skin-on chicken
   breasts

1 teaspoon salt

⅛ teaspoon white pepper

½ cup water

This chicken is perfect to use in a variety of recipes in this book. You can also use it to make your own chicken salad.

1. Sprinkle chicken with salt and pepper and arrange in 4–6-quart slow cooker. Pour water into slow cooker, cover, and cook on low, rearranging once during cooking, for 7–9 hours or until chicken is fully cooked.
2. Remove chicken to a baking dish and pour any juices remaining in slow cooker over. Cover and chill for 2–3 hours or until chicken is cold. Remove meat from chicken in large pieces and refrigerate up to 2 days, or freeze up to 3 months. Freeze skin and bones for making Chicken Stock (page 234).
3. You can cook chicken thighs or drumsticks using this method too; just increase the cooking time to 8–10 hours.

Chicken in the Slow Cooker

Newer slow cookers cook at hotter temperatures than those manufactured 10 years ago. Because of this change, chicken breasts can overcook. Check boneless, skinless chicken breasts after 5 hours on low. Bone-in breasts should be checked for an internal temperature of 170°F after 7 hours. Dark meat, because it has more fat, isn't in as much danger of overcooking.

Chicken Supreme

 Serves 4

$ Total Cost: $6.90
Calories: 330.21
Fat: 10.58 grams
Protein: 36.01 grams
Cholesterol: 94.47 mg
Sodium: 720.31 mg

2 slices bacon

1 onion, chopped

2 cloves garlic, chopped

⅓ cup apple juice

1 (10-ounce) can condensed mushroom soup

¼ cup evaporated milk

2 carrots, sliced

4 boneless, skinless chicken breasts

1 cup shredded Muenster cheese

This easy dish has a great combination of textures, colors, and flavors. You can also make it with 2 cups of sliced raw turkey breast, or 6 boneless, skinless chicken thighs. For the thighs, cook on low for 8-9 hours.

1. In heavy skillet, cook bacon until crisp. Remove bacon from pan and let drain on paper towels; crumble and refrigerate. Pour off half of the fat from skillet. Cook and stir onions and garlic in remaining drippings for 2–3 minutes, until onions begin to soften. Stir in apple juice, soup, and evaporated milk. Place in a 3½-quart slow cooker, stir in carrots, and top with chicken.

2. Pour apple juice into slow cooker and top with chicken. Cover and cook on low for 6 to 7 hours or until chicken and carrots are tender. Top with Muenster cheese and bacon, cover, and cook on high for 5 to 10 minutes, until cheese is melted.

Shredded Chicken for Tacos

Makes about 3 cups; serves 4

4 boneless, skinless chicken breasts

1 tablespoon chili powder

½ teaspoon cumin

½ teaspoon dried oregano leaves

1 teaspoon salt

⅛ teaspoon pepper

1 onion, finely chopped

½ cup Chicken Stock (page 234)

Cooking chicken breasts in the Crock-Pot makes them extra tender and juicy.

1. In small bowl, combine chili powder, cumin, oregano, salt, and pepper and mix well. Rub this mixture into the chicken breasts and place them in a 3½-quart Crock-Pot along with the chopped onions. Pour Chicken Stock over all. Cover Crock-Pot and cook on low for 5–6 hours, until chicken is completely cooked.
2. Remove chicken from Crock-Pot, shred with forks, and return to Crock-Pot. Mix well and use immediately or refrigerate or freeze for later use.

Ingredient Substitution
Use boneless, skinless chicken thighs in the Crock-Pot instead of breasts if you like a richer flavor. Increase cooking time to 7–9 hours, since the higher fat content in the dark meat means the thighs need longer cooking.

The $7 a Meal Slow Cooker Cookbook

Chicken with Peppers

 Serves 4

$ Total Cost: $6.78

Calories: 308.43

Fat: 15.06 grams

Protein: 24.69 grams

Cholesterol: 88.27 mg

Sodium: 472.78 mg

2 onions, chopped

2 cloves garlic, minced

3 chicken breast halves

½ teaspoon salt

½ teaspoon pepper

½ teaspoon dried thyme leaves

½ cup Chicken Stock (page 234)

2 green bell peppers, sliced

¾ cup sour cream

1 tablespoon cornstarch

2 jalepeño chiles, minced

This colorful dish has a wonderful rich sauce. Serve it with fresh or warmed tortillas and chopped avocados.

1. Place onion and garlic in 3-quart slow cooker. Cut chicken into cubes and sprinkle with salt, pepper, and thyme; add to slow cooker. Pour Chicken Stock over all; cover and cook on low for 5 hours until chicken is almost done.
2. Add peppers and jalapeño to slow cooker and stir. Cover and cook on low for 1–2 hours until chicken is cooked and peppers are tender.
3. Stir sour cream and cornstarch in small bowl. Add to slow cooker; cover and cook on high for 15–20 minutes or until mixture is thickened. Serve with warmed tortillas.

Chicken con Queso Casserole

Serves 5

$ Total Cost: $6.85

Calories: 433.11

Fat: 20.61 grams

Protein: 23.92 grams

Cholesterol: 69.20 mg

Sodium: 834.52 mg

1 tablespoon butter

1 onion, chopped

3 cloves garlic, minced

1 jalapeño pepper, minced

2 Slow-Cooker Simmered Chicken Breasts (page 104)

1 (15-ounce) can pinto beans, rinsed

¾ cup enchilada sauce

⅓ cup tomato sauce

3 cups tortilla chips

1 cup shredded Cheddar cheese

½ cup sour cream

2 tablespoons minced parsley

Sour cream and Cheddar cheese make this hearty casserole very rich and creamy. You could substitute canned taco sauce for the enchilada sauce if you'd like.

1. In heavy skillet, melt butter over medium heat and cook onion, garlic, and jalapeños until crisp-tender. Stir in chicken, drained pinto beans, and enchilada sauce.
2. Grease a 3-quart slow cooker and add tomato sauce. Layer half of chicken mixture, slightly crushed tortilla chips, cheese, and sour cream; repeat layers.
3. Cover and cook on low for 5–6 hours or until vegetables are tender. Sprinkle with parsley and serve.

Recipe Substitutions

Get some thickly sliced cooked turkey from your deli, and cut it into chunks for this easy recipe. Cubed ham would also work well. You could substitute a different type of cheese for the Cheddar. And think about using nacho or Ranch flavored tortilla chips for even more spice.

Fiesta Casserole

 Serves 6

Total Cost: $6.99
Calories: 482.95
Fat: 20.94 grams
Protein: 24.33 grams
Cholesterol: 69.03 mg
Sodium: 693.25 mg

2 cups tortilla chips

1 tablespoon vegetable oil

1 onion, chopped

2 cloves garlic, minced

2 Slow-Cooker Simmered
Chicken Breasts (page
104), chopped

1 (10-ounce) can condensed
nacho cheese soup

1 (14-ounce) can diced
tomatoes, undrained

1 (4-ounce) can chopped
green chiles

1 tablespoon chili powder

⅛ teaspoon cayenne pepper

¾ cup shredded Cheddar
cheese

Since this casserole cooks for such a long time in the
moist environment of the Crock-Pot, crisp tortilla chips
are used instead of plain tortillas.

1. Heat vegetable oil in large skillet and cook onion and garlic
    until crisp-tender. Stir in chicken; remove from heat. In large
    bowl, combine soup, diced tomatoes, green chiles, chili
    powder, and cayenne pepper and mix well.
2. In 3½-quart Crock-Pot, layer half of chicken mixture, tortilla
    chips, and soup mixture; repeat layers. Cover and cook on
    low for 8–9 hours or until casserole is bubbling around
    edges. Sprinkle with cheese, cover, and let stand for 10 min-
    utes before serving.

Updated Chicken Cordon Bleu

 Serves 4

4 boneless, skinless chicken breasts

½ teaspoon salt

⅛ teaspoon white pepper

½ teaspoon dried thyme leaves

4 thin slices boiled ham

1 onion, chopped

2 cloves garlic, minced

3 carrots, sliced

1 (10-ounce) can condensed chicken soup

1 cup shredded Swiss cheese

Instead of being stuffed with ham and cheese, this tender chicken is wrapped in ham and served with a flavorful cheese sauce. Yum.

1. Sprinkle chicken breasts with salt, pepper, and thyme. Wrap a slice of ham around each breast and secure with toothpicks.
2. Place onion, garlic, and carrots in a 4-quart slow cooker. Top with wrapped chicken breasts.
3. In medium bowl, combine remaining ingredients. Pour into slow cooker. Cover and cook on low for 6–8 hours or until chicken is thoroughly cooked. Serve chicken and carrots with sauce.

Boiled Ham

Boiled ham is usually found in the lunch meat section of the supermarket. It is sliced about ⅛-inch thick and is very moist and tender. It adds a great amount of flavor to mild chicken breasts in this delicious recipe. You can substitute thinly sliced deli ham for the boiled ham if you'd like.

The $7 a Meal Slow Cooker Cookbook

Chicken Curry

Serves 4

$ Total Cost: $6.09

Calories: 352.93

Fat: 11.94 grams

Protein: 19.42 grams

Cholesterol: 86.93 mg

Sodium: 269.93 mg

3 boneless, skinless chicken breasts

1 onion, chopped

3 carrots, sliced

1 (8-ounce) can crushed pineapple, undrained

3 cloves garlic, minced

1 cup Chicken Stock (page 234)

1 tablespoon curry powder

1 tablespoon grated gingerroot

½ teaspoon salt

⅛ teaspoon pepper

½ cup Apple Chutney (page 16)

1 tablespoon cornstarch

¼ cup apple juice

Chicken is delicious when cooked with curry and chutney. Serve this one over lots of hot cooked rice.

1. Cut chicken into 1-inch pieces. Place onions, carrots, pineapple, and garlic in a 3½-quart slow cooker. Top with chicken pieces.
2. In medium bowl, combine Stock, curry powder, gingerroot, salt, and pepper; mix well. Pour into slow cooker.
3. Cover and cook on low for 6–8 hours or until vegetables are tender and chicken is thoroughly cooked. In small bowl, combine Chutney, cornstarch, and apple juice; mix well. Stir into slow cooker.
4. Cover and cook on high for 20–30 minutes. Stir thoroughly, then serve over hot cooked rice.

Apple Stuffed Chicken Rolls

Serves 4

$ Total Cost: $6.28

Calories: 309.23

Fat: 8.92 grams

Protein: 20.93 grams

Cholesterol: 80.43 mg

Sodium: 210.24 mg

2 slices oatmeal bread

⅓ cup finely chopped apple

¼ cup raisins

1 tablespoon lemon juice

2 tablespoons butter, melted

1 tablespoon sugar

½ teaspoon salt

4 boneless, skinless chicken breasts

1 onion, chopped

⅓ cup apple juice

½ teaspoon cinnamon

Tender chicken stuffed with an apple-and-raisin mixture will be incredibly popular at your next potluck.

1. Toast bread until golden brown, then cut into cubes. In medium bowl, combine apple, raisins, lemon juice, melted butter, sugar, and salt; mix well. Stir in bread cubes.
2. Arrange chicken breasts on work surface. Pound gently with a meat mallet or rolling pin until ⅓-inch-thick. Divide bread mixture among chicken breasts. Roll up chicken and secure with a toothpick.
3. Place onions in bottom of 4-quart slow cooker. Top with filled chicken rolls. In small bowl, combine apple juice and cinnamon; spoon over chicken.
4. Cover and cook on low for 5 to 7 hours, or until chicken registers 165°F on food thermometer. Remove toothpicks and serve chicken with the cooked onions.

Pounding Chicken

When you're going to stuff chicken breasts, they must be pounded so they are large enough to enclose the filling. Place the chicken breasts, smooth side down, on waxed paper. Cover with more waxed paper. Pound gently, using a rolling pin or meat mallet, starting at center, until chicken is about ⅓-inch thick.

The $7 a Meal Slow Cooker Cookbook

Chicken Tacos

 Serves 4

$ Total Cost: $6.49
Calories: 369.23
Fat: 12.85 grams
Protein: 17.93 grams
Cholesterol: 60.34 mg
Sodium: 482.33 mg

1 onion, chopped

4 cloves garlic, minced

1 jalapeño pepper, minced

2 boneless, skinless chicken breasts

1 tablespoon chili powder

½ teaspoon salt

⅛ teaspoon cayenne pepper

½ cup chunky medium or hot salsa

1 (8-ounce) can tomato sauce

4 taco shells

1 cup grated Cheddar cheese

2 cups shredded lettuce

½ cup sour cream

Tacos are always fun, and when made with chicken they are delightfully different. Use your family's favorite toppings in this easy recipe.

1. In 3½-quart slow cooker, combine onions, garlic, and jalapeño pepper. Sprinkle chicken with chili powder, salt, and cayenne pepper; place on top of onions.
2. Pour salsa and tomato sauce over all. Cover and cook on low for 6–7 hours or until chicken is thoroughly cooked.
3. Using two forks, shred chicken. Stir mixture in slow cooker.
4. Heat taco shells as directed on package. Serve chicken filling with the taco shells and remaining ingredients; let everyone make their own tacos.

Laura's Chicken Risotto

Serves 4

$ Total Cost: $5.98
Calories: 329.94
Fat: 13.23 grams
Protein: 20.42 grams
Cholesterol: 59.03 mg
Sodium: 438.92 mg

1 cup brown rice

1 onion, chopped

3 boneless, skinless chicken breasts, cubed

½ teaspoon salt

⅛ teaspoon pepper

½ teaspoon dried thyme leaves

1½ cups Chicken Stock (page 234)

1 (10-ounce) can cream of chicken soup

1 cup frozen baby peas

2 tablespoons butter

⅓ cup grated Parmesan cheese

Brown rice not only has more fiber and nutrients than white rice, but it cooks well in the slow cooker. Purists may look askance at this recipe, but it's delicious!

1. Combine brown rice and onions in 3½-quart slow cooker. Top with chicken pieces. In large bowl, combine salt, pepper, thyme, Chicken Stock, and canned soup; mix with wire whisk until blended. Pour into slow cooker.
2. Cover and cook on low for 8–10 hours or until rice is tender and chicken is thoroughly cooked, stirring after 4 hours.
3. Stir in peas, butter, and cheese. Cover and cook on high for 20–30 minutes or until peas are hot and butter and cheese are melted. Stir gently and serve.

Risotto

Risotto is traditionally made by cooking short grain or Arborio rice slowly, while stirring constantly. Simmering broth is gradually added to the rice. The rice releases starch as it cooks, which makes the sauce thick and smooth. "Risotto" made in the slow cooker has just about the same texture, with much less work.

Slow-Cooker Chicken and Cheese Soufflé

 Serves 5

Total Cost: $5.80
Calories: 419.90
Fat: 15.33 grams
Protein: 19.83 grams
Cholesterol: 97.94 mg
Sodium: 398.34 mg

4 cups cubed French bread

¾ cup shredded Cheddar cheese

½ cup shredded Swiss cheese

2 Slow-Cooker Simmered Chicken Breasts (page 104), cubed

1 tablespoon olive oil

1 onion, chopped

1 (3-ounce) package cream cheese

1 (13-ounce) can evaporated milk

½ teaspoon dried thyme leaves

½ teaspoon salt

⅛ teaspoon white pepper

3 eggs, beaten

2 tablespoons grated Parmesan cheese

½ teaspoon paprika

A soufflé in the slow cooker! Yes, this recipe is like a cross between a soufflé and a strata. It's hearty and comforting and mildly flavored.

1. In 3½-quart slow cooker, combine bread with Cheddar, Swiss, and cubed cooked chicken; set aside.
2. In medium saucepan, heat olive oil over medium heat. Add onion; cook and stir for 3 minutes. Add to slow cooker and toss gently to combine with bread mixture.
3. Mix cream cheese and evaporated milk in saucepan; cook and stir over low heat until cheese melts. Remove from heat and beat in thyme, salt, and pepper. Then beat in eggs until smooth.
4. Pour into slow cooker and let stand for 15 minutes. Sprinkle with Parmesan cheese and paprika. Cover and cook on low for 3½ to 4½ hours or until soufflé is set. Serve immediately.

Chicken Dijon

Serves 4

$ Total Cost: $6.78
Calories: 349.23
Fat: 13.92 grams
Protein: 23.94 grams
Cholesterol: 85.32 mg
Sodium: 389.53 mg

4 boneless, skinless chicken breasts

½ teaspoon salt

⅛ teaspoon white pepper

½ teaspoon dried tarragon leaves

1 onion, chopped

3 carrots, sliced

1 (10-ounce) container condensed chicken soup

¼ cup Dijon mustard

½ cup apple juice

2 tablespoons cornstarch

¼ cup water

Dijon mustard adds a wonderful kick of spice and piquancy to this simple chicken dish. Serve it with mashed potatoes, noodles, or rice to soak up the flavorful sauce.

1. In 4-quart slow cooker, combine all ingredients except cornstarch and water. Cover and cook on low for 6–7 hours or until chicken registers 165°F with a meat thermometer.

2. In small bowl, combine cornstarch and water; mix well. Add to slow cooker. Cover and cook on high for 20–30 minutes or until sauce is thickened. Serve over hot cooked noodles, rice, or mashed potatoes.

Dijon mustard

Dijon mustard is more expensive than regular yellow mustard, but the unique flavor is worth it. True Dijon mustard is made in a certain way, and is quite strong, with a winey flavor. Buy a small jar and try it. You can find different types of Dijon in the supermarket; country Dijon has herbs, while coarse ground has visible mustard seeds.

Scalloped Chicken

 Serves 4

$ Total Cost: $5.34
Calories: 341.82
Fat: 12.29 grams
Protein: 20.94 grams
Cholesterol: 82.04 mg
Sodium: 459.25 mg

3 tablespoons butter

1 onion, chopped

1 cup chopped apple

1½ cups soft bread crumbs

½ cup raisins

2 tablespoons vegetable oil

2 tablespoons flour

½ teaspoon salt

⅛ teaspoon pepper

1½ cups Chicken Stock (page 234)

½ cup light cream

2 Slow Cooker Simmered Chicken Breasts (page 104), cubed

This hearty casserole is a combination of stuffing, gravy, and chicken, all in one!

1. Spray a 3-quart slow cooker with nonstick cooking spray and set aside. In large skillet, melt 3 tablespoons butter over medium heat. Add onion; cook and stir until tender, about 5 minutes. Add apple; cook and stir for 2 minutes longer.
2. Add bread crumbs to skillet, and toss to coat. Stir in raisins; set aside.
3. In large saucepan, heat oil over medium heat. Add flour, salt, and pepper. Cook and stir until flour begins to brown, about 8–10 minutes. Stir in Stock and cream; cook and stir until sauce bubbles and thickens.
4. Layer half of bread crumb mixture, half of cooked chicken, and half of sauce in prepared slow cooker. Repeat layers. Cover and cook on low for 7–9 hours or until casserole is set and bubbling. Serve immediately.

Slow-Cooker Chicken à la King

 Serves 4

$ Total Cost: $4.89
Calories: 325.93
Fat: 13.92 grams
Protein: 19.38 grams
Cholesterol: 48.92 mg
Sodium: 459.92 mg

2 boneless, skinless chicken breasts, cubed

3 carrots, sliced

1 onion, chopped

2 cloves garlic, minced

1 (3-ounce) package cream cheese, cut into cubes

1 cup milk

1 (10-ounce) can cream of chicken soup

1 teaspoon dried basil leaves

⅛ teaspoon pepper

Chicken à la King is a classic recipe that's comforting and easy to make. And everybody loves it!

1. Place chicken in 3-quart slow cooker. Add carrots, onions, and garlic; mix gently.
2. In food processor or blender, combine cream cheese and milk; process or blend until combined. Pour into medium bowl and add cream of chicken soup, basil, and pepper. Mix well.
3. Pour sauce into slow cooker. Cover and cook on low for 7–9 hours or until chicken and vegetables are tender. Serve over hot cooked noodles, mashed potatoes, biscuits, or baked puff pastry shells.

Chicken à la King

Chicken à la King has been served in the fanciest restaurants and the lowliest diners. It's basically tender chicken with onion and other vegetables served in a cream sauce over crisp toast. It traditionally uses pimentos and peas, but many variations have been created. It's really classic comfort food.

Slow-Cooker Chicken Divan

Serves 4

$ Total Cost: $6.53
Calories: 369.53
Fat: 12.64 grams
Protein: 16.93 grams
Cholesterol: 49.92 mg
Sodium: 539.23 mg

2 cups fresh broccoli florets

2 tablespoons lemon juice

1 onion, chopped

1 (4-ounce) jar sliced mushrooms, drained

2 cups chopped cooked chicken

1 (10-ounce) can cream of broccoli soup

½ cup light cream

¾ cup shredded Swiss cheese

Mushrooms add texture and flavor to this easy recipe. It's a delicious casserole that will please adults and kids alike.

1. Toss broccoli with lemon juice. Place in bottom of 3-quart slow cooker. Top with onions, mushrooms, and chicken.
2. In medium bowl, combine soup with cream and cheese; mix until blended. Pour into slow cooker.
3. Cover and cook on low for 5–6 hours or until thoroughly heated. Stir well, then serve.

Classic Chicken and Dumplings

 Serves 5

$ Total Cost: $6.99
Calories: 469.93
Fat: 20.18 grams
Protein: 18.93 grams
Cholesterol: 54.92 mg
Sodium: 639.23 mg

3 boneless, skinless chicken breasts

½ teaspoon salt

⅛ teaspoon pepper

½ teaspoon paprika

½ teaspoon poultry seasoning

2 stalks celery, sliced

¼ cup chopped celery leaves

3 carrots, sliced

1 onion, chopped

2 cloves garlic, minced

1 (10-ounce) jar condensed cheese soup

1 (10-ounce) can condensed cream of celery soup

1 cup milk

½ (13.8-ounce) tube refrigerated pizza dough

Pizza dough, when cut into small pieces, cooks into fluffy dumplings in this comforting and classic recipe.

1. Cut chicken breasts into cubes. Sprinkle with salt, pepper, paprika, and poultry seasoning; toss to coat. Combine celery, celery leaves, carrots, onions, and garlic in 4-quart slow cooker; mix well. Add chicken and stir.
2. In medium bowl, combine soups and milk; mix well. Pour into slow cooker. Cover and cook on low for 6–7 hours or until chicken and vegetables are tender.
3. On lightly floured surface, roll out the pizza dough to ½-inch thickness and cut into 1-inch pieces. Stir into slow cooker, making sure the dough is evenly distributed. Cover and cook on high for 1 to 1½ hours or until dumplings are cooked through.

Dumplings in the Slow Cooker

Dumplings, whether made from refrigerated dough or from scratch, really do cook well in the Crock-Pot. The secrets are to make sure the liquid is bubbling, make sure the dumplings are fairly small, stir well into the liquid, and don't lift the cover until the minimum cooking time.

The $7 a Meal Slow Cooker Cookbook

Chicken Lasagna

 Serves 5

Total Cost: $7.00
Calories: 485.92
Fat: 20.73 grams
Protein: 21.48 grams
Cholesterol: 73.92 mg
Sodium: 528.93 mg

2 boneless, skinless chicken breasts
½ teaspoon salt
⅛ teaspoon pepper
1 tablespoon butter
1 onion, chopped
2 cloves garlic, minced
1 (18-ounce) jar spaghetti sauce
½ cup water
1 (3-ounce) package cream cheese, softened

1 egg
1 cup ricotta cheese
1 cup frozen cut-leaf spinach, thawed and drained
¼ cup grated Parmesan cheese
5 lasagna noodles
½ cup shredded mozzarella cheese
¼ cup shredded Romano cheese

Lasagna in the slow cooker is a great timesaver and is so easy. You don't have to boil the noodles separately!

1. Cut chicken breasts into 1-inch cubes and toss with salt and pepper. Heat butter in large saucepan over medium heat. Add chicken; cook and stir until chicken is cooked, about 9–11 minutes. Remove chicken from pan with slotted spoon.
2. In drippings remaining in skillet, cook onion and garlic until tender. Stir in spaghetti sauce and water; bring to a simmer.
3. Meanwhile, in medium bowl combine cream cheese, egg, and ricotta cheese; beat until smooth. Stir in drained spinach and Parmesan cheese.
4. Break lasagna noodles in half. Place about 1 cup of the chicken mixture in bottom of 4-quart slow cooker. Top with a layer of lasagna noodles, more chicken mixture, some cream cheese mixture, and mozzarella cheese. Repeat layers, ending with cheese.
5. Sprinkle with Romano cheese, cover, and cook on low for 6–7 hours or until noodles are tender. To serve, scoop down deeply into the slow cooker to get all the layers.

Apple Chicken

Serves 4

💲 Total Cost: $6.74
Calories: 329.12
Fat: 8.49 grams
Protein: 21.48 grams
Cholesterol: 83.04 mg
Sodium: 268.93 mg

4 boneless, skinless chicken breasts

½ teaspoon dried thyme leaves

⅛ teaspoon pepper

½ teaspoon salt

1 onion, sliced

½ cup Chicken Stock (page 234)

¼ cup apple juice

¼ cup brown sugar

2 tablespoons butter, melted

2 Granny Smith apples, sliced

⅓ cup chopped pecans

Chicken, apples, and pecans are classic ingredients in chicken salad. When combined together in a hot casserole, the flavors and textures blend beautifully.

1. Sprinkle chicken with thyme, pepper, and salt. Place onions in bottom of 3-quart slow cooker. Top with chicken.
2. In small bowl, combine remaining ingredients except apples and pecans, and mix well. Pour into slow cooker.
3. Cover and cook on low for 5 hours. Then stir in apples; cover and cook for 1–2 hours longer or until chicken is thoroughly cooked and apples are tender. Sprinkle with pecans and serve over hot cooked rice.

Apples for the Slow Cooker

Tart apples that hold their shape are best for cooking in the slow cooker, especially for main dishes. Granny Smith apples fit this description, and they're among the most inexpensive apples in the supermarket. More expensive apples that will also work include McIntosh, Winesap, and Rome Beauty.

Spanish Chicken and Rice

Serves 4

Total Cost: $6.58
Calories: 385.02
Fat: 14.93 grams
Protein: 18.23 grams
Cholesterol: 45.93 mg
Sodium: 638.29 mg

2 boneless, skinless chicken breasts

½ teaspoon paprika

⅛ teaspoon pepper

½ teaspoon salt

1 tablespoon vegetable oil

1 onion, chopped

2 cloves garlic, minced

¾ cup long grain brown rice

1 green bell pepper, chopped

1 cup barbecue sauce

1 (8-ounce) can tomato sauce

1 cup Chicken Stock (page 234)

2 tablespoons apple cider vinegar

¼ cup chopped fresh parsley

Season this delicious one-dish meal to your liking. If you like it really spicy, add a minced jalapeño pepper or two or substitute cayenne pepper for the regular black pepper.

1. Cut chicken breasts into 1-inch cubes. Sprinkle with paprika, pepper, and salt; mix well. Heat vegetable oil in large skillet over medium heat. Add chicken; cook and stir until chicken starts to brown, about 4–5 minutes.
2. Remove chicken from skillet and place in 3½-quart slow cooker. Add onions and garlic to skillet; cook until onion is tender, stirring to remove pan drippings, about 5 minutes.
3. Add rice to skillet; cook and stir for 3–4 minutes until coated. Add rice mixture to slow cooker.
4. Stir in remaining ingredients except parsley. Cover and cook on low for 6–7 hours or until chicken is thoroughly cooked and rice is tender. Stir in parsley and serve.

CHAPTER 7

CHICKEN—DARK MEAT

125 Spicy Peanut Chicken

126 Slow-Cooker Chicken Verde

127 Slow-Cooker Rotisserie Chicken

128 Italian Slow-Cooker Chicken

129 Texas BBQ Chicken Thighs

130 Chicken Wheat Berry Casserole

131 Slow-Cooker Chicken with Curried Apricot Pilaf

132 Thai Chicken Drumsticks

133 Chicken and Potato Hot Dish

134 Chicken and Bean Cassoulet

135 Chicken and Rice

136 Yogurt Chicken Paprika

137 Easy BBQ Chicken

138 Very Lemon Chicken

139 Chicken Marsala

140 Fiesta Chicken

141 Classic BBQ Chicken

142 Indian Chicken Pilaf

Spicy Peanut Chicken

Serves 4

$ Total Cost: $5.04

Calories: 452.82

Fat: 24.90 grams

Protein: 41.04 grams

Cholesterol: 115.67 mg

Sodium: 705.43 mg

1¼-pounds boneless, skinless chicken thighs

½ cup chunky peanut butter

3 tablespoons low-sodium soy sauce

¼ cup orange juice

1 onion, chopped

1 chopped jalapeño pepper

This simple and well-flavored dish has a marvelous sauce that is creamy and spicy. Serve with prepared couscous.

1. Cut chicken thighs into 2-inch pieces. Place in 3 to 4-quart slow cooker.
2. In medium bowl, combine peanut butter, soy sauce, orange juice, onion, and jalapeños and mix well. Pour into slow cooker and cover. Cook on low for 7 to 8 hours, until done. Stir well and serve over hot cooked rice, pasta, or couscous.

Slow-Cooker Chicken Verde

 Serves 4

1 onion, chopped

3 cloves garlic, chopped

1 (4-ounce) can chopped green chiles

⅓ cup chopped cilantro

1 green bell pepper, chopped

1½ pounds boneless, skin-on chicken thighs

½ teaspoon salt

½ teaspoon garlic pepper

2 tablespoons vegetable oil

Use a Crock-Pot and your chicken will always be tender and perfectly cooked. This delicious dish can be served with different colors of corn tortillas, salsa, and guacamole.

1. In blender container or food processor, combine onions, garlic, green chiles, cilantro, and green pepper. Blend or process until mixture is smooth; set aside.
2. Sprinkle chicken with salt and garlic pepper. Heat oil in heavy skillet and brown chicken, skin side down. As chicken browns, remove it to a 3½ to 4-quart Crock-Pot.
3. When all chicken is browned, add onion sauce to skillet. Cook and stir to remove browned bits from bottom of skillet. Pour over chicken, cover Crock-Pot, and cook on low for 8–9 hours until chicken is tender and thoroughly cooked. Shred chicken, removing skin if desired, and return to sauce.

Chicken Verde

Verde is the Spanish word for "green." Green chiles, bell peppers, and other peppers color and flavor the sauce with freshness. Chicken Verde can be served as-is, over rice pilaf, or used as a filling for enchiladas and burritos. The chicken becomes super tender when cooked in the rich sauce.

Slow-Cooker Rotisserie Chicken

 Serves 4

$ Total Cost: $4.02
Calories: 446.02
Fat: 26.40 grams
Protein: 42.25 grams
Cholesterol: 183.02 mg
Sodium: 804.90 mg

2 pounds chicken thighs and drumsticks

1 teaspoon salt

1 teaspoon paprika

½ teaspoon onion powder

¼ teaspoon garlic powder

½ teaspoon dried rosemary

½ teaspoon dried thyme leaves

1 tablespoon sugar

⅛ teaspoon pepper

⅛ teaspoon cayenne pepper

½ cup Chicken Stock (page 234)

The spice flavors go deep within the chicken in this easy recipe. It really does taste like a rotisserie chicken from the deli.

1. Rinse chicken pieces and dry with paper towel. Loosen skin from flesh and place chicken on large cookie sheet. In small bowl, combine remaining ingredients except Stock and mix well. Sprinkle half this mixture under the chicken skin and rub in well. Sprinkle remaining mixture on the chicken skin and rub in well.

2. Cover chicken and refrigerate for 8–24 hours. When ready to cook, use aluminum foil to make 5 balls about 2-inches in diameter and place these in the bottom of a 4 to 5-quart slow cooker. Place chicken in slow cooker, resting on the aluminum balls. Pour Stock over, then cover and cook on low for 8 to 10 hours, until chicken is very tender and glazed.

Italian Slow-Cooker Chicken

Serves 6

$ Total Cost: $6.91

Calories: 479.20

Fat: 22.34 grams

Protein: 28.97 grams

Cholesterol: 125.03 mg

Sodium: 622.21 mg

2-pounds boneless, skinless chicken thighs

½ cup Italian salad dressing

3 russet potatoes, cut into wedges

3 cloves garlic, chopped

1 onion, chopped

1 (10-ounce) package frozen green beans, thawed

1. Combine chicken with salad dressing in zipper-lock bag. Place in large bowl or casserole and refrigerate for 6–7 hours.
2. When ready to cook, place potatoes, garlic, and onion in the Crock-Pot. Pour chicken and salad dressing over all. Cover and cook on low for 8 hours. Then add green beans to Crock-Pot. Cover and cook on low for 1–2 hours longer or until chicken is thoroughly cooked and vegetables are tender.

Chicken Thighs

Chicken thighs are higher in fat than chicken breasts, so they take longer to cook in the slow cooker. They are also richer tasting, and moister. They are smaller than chicken breasts, so plan on 1½ to 2 per serving. If there's visible fat on them, trim off and discard before cooking.

Texas BBQ Chicken Thighs

 Serves 4

Total Cost: $6.65
Calories: 307.53
Fat: 15.61 grams
Protein: 23.94 grams
Cholesterol: 79.56 mg
Sodium: 628.34 mg

2 tablespoons vegetable oil

1 onion, chopped

2 cloves garlic, minced

1 jalapeño pepper, minced

¼ cup orange juice

1 tablespoon low-sodium soy sauce

2 tablespoons apple cider vinegar

2 tablespoons brown sugar

2 tablespoons Dijon mustard

1 (8-ounce) can tomato sauce

1 tablespoon chili powder

¼ teaspoon pepper

6 boneless, skinless, chicken thighs

Make a double batch of this fabulous barbecue sauce all by itself in your slow cooker and freeze it in ¼-cup portions to use anytime.

1. In a small skillet, heat oil over medium heat. Add onion and garlic; cook and stir until crisp-tender, about 4 minutes. Place in 3–4-quart slow cooker and add jalapeño, orange juice, soy sauce, vinegar, brown sugar, mustard, tomato sauce, chili powder, and pepper.
2. Add chicken to the sauce, pushing chicken into the sauce to completely cover. Cover and cook on low for 8–10 hours or until chicken is thoroughly cooked.

Chicken Wheat Berry Casserole

Serves 6

$ Total Cost: $6.08

Calories: 456.43

Fat: 13.66 grams

Protein: 40.21 grams

Cholesterol: 118.07 mg

Sodium: 637.51 mg

1 cup wheat berries

1½ pounds boneless, skinless chicken thighs

3 carrots, sliced

2 cups frozen corn

1 onion, chopped

3 cloves garlic, minced

2 cups Chicken Stock (page 234)

1 teaspoon cumin

1 teaspoon salt

¼ teaspoon pepper

1 tablespoon cornstarch

¼ cup water

Wheat berries are the whole kernel of wheat and are nutritious and full of fiber. Plus they taste great!

1. Rinse wheat berries and drain well. Cut chicken into 1½-inch pieces and combine with remaining ingredients, except for cornstarch and ¼ cup water, in a 4 to 5-quart slow cooker. Cover and cook on low for 8–9 hours or until wheat berries are tender and chicken is cooked.

2. In small bowl, combine cornstarch and water and blend well. Add to casserole in slow cooker, cover, and cook on high for 20–30 minutes until thickened, then stir again and serve.

Buying Grains in Bulk

One of the best places to buy grains and legumes in bulk is at a food co-op. These stores usually have a high turnover rate and their bulk products are quite fresh. These stores are also great places to find more unusual grains like the wheat berries used in this stew, along with grains like amaranth and quinoa.

The $7 a Meal Slow Cooker Cookbook

Slow-Cooker Chicken with Curried Apricot Pilaf

 Serves 5

 Total Cost: $6.66

Calories: 530.76

Fat: 15.49 grams

Protein: 36.25 grams

Cholesterol: 121.77 mg

Sodium: 400.79 mg

1 tablespoon butter

1 onion, chopped

4 cloves garlic, minced

1 cup long grain brown rice

1 cup apricot nectar

3 carrots, sliced

½ teaspoon salt

⅛ teaspoon white pepper

1 tablespoon curry powder

1 cup Chicken Stock (page 234)

¼ cup finely chopped dried apricots

1¼ pounds boneless, skinless chicken thighs

⅓ cup apricot preserves

The rich flavor of dark meat chicken is accented with the tart and sweet flavor of apricots in this elegant dish.

1. In large skillet, melt butter over medium heat. Add onion and garlic; cook and stir for 5 minutes until crisp-tender. Add brown rice; cook and stir for 2–3 minutes longer until rice is coated with the butter.
2. Pour nectar into skillet; stir until mixture boils. Pour into 4-quart slow cooker. Add carrots, salt, pepper, curry powder, Chicken Stock, and chopped apricots. Top with chicken and spoon apricot preserves over all.
3. Cover and cook on low for 8–9 hours or until rice is tender and chicken is thoroughly cooked.

Thai Chicken Drumsticks

Serves 6

$ Total Cost: $5.39
Calories: 382.95
Fat: 16.93 grams
Protein: 19.42 grams
Cholesterol: 74.90 mg
Sodium: 529.39 mg

2-pounds chicken drumsticks

1 onion, chopped

3 cloves garlic, minced

¼ cup peanut butter

1 (6-ounce) can tomato paste

¼ cup low-sodium soy sauce

⅓ cup Chicken Stock (page 234)

½ cup chunky mild or medium salsa

½ teaspoon ground ginger

¼ teaspoon pepper

¼ teaspoon hot pepper sauce

½ cup chopped peanuts

Peanuts, tomato, and soy make these drumsticks spicy and rich. Some sauce cooked with Chicken Stock and a chili pepper is the perfect accompaniment.

1. Place drumsticks in a 4-quart slow cooker. Add onions and garlic. In medium bowl, stir together remaining ingredients except peanuts. Pour into slow cooker.
2. Cover and cook for 6–8 hours on low, or until internal temperature reaches 170°F. Remove chicken from slow cooker and roll each piece in the chopped peanuts. Arrange on broiler pan. Preheat broiler.
3. Broil chicken 6-inches from heat source, turning frequently, until browned, about 6–8 minutes. Serve immediately with sauce.

Crisp Skin

For crisp skin, you have to brown these drumsticks after they are cooked. But that's easy to do under the broiler, and that step adds wonderful caramelized flavor to the finished dish. Serve with the rest of the sauce. If the sauce needs thickening, uncover and cook on high for 15–20 minutes.

The $7 a Meal Slow Cooker Cookbook

Chicken and Potato Hot Dish

 Serves 5

$ Total Cost: $6.89

Calories: 470.25

Fat: 21.48 grams

Protein: 32.95 grams

Cholesterol: 62.94 mg

Sodium: 320.53 mg

4 boneless, skinless chicken thighs, cubed

1 onion, chopped

3 cloves garlic, minced

1 (4-ounce) jar sliced mushrooms, undrained

1 (16-ounce) package frozen hash brown potatoes, thawed

1 (10.75-ounce) can cream of chicken soup

½ cup Chicken Stock (page 234)

½ cup barbecue sauce

¼ cup grated Parmesan cheese

The easiest way to thaw the potatoes is to let the package stand in the refrigerator overnight. Then drain and mix with the other ingredients.

1. In 3½-quart slow cooker, combine chicken, onions, garlic, mushrooms, and potatoes; mix well.
2. In medium bowl, combine remaining ingredients except cheese; mix well. Pour into slow cooker.
3. Cover and cook on low for 8–9 hours or until chicken is thoroughly cooked. Stir once during cooking time. Add cheese, stir again, and serve.

Chicken and Bean Cassoulet

 Serves 4

1 tablespoon butter

1¼ pounds boneless, skinless chicken thighs, cubed

1 onion, chopped

2 cloves garlic, minced

3 carrots, sliced

1 (15-ounce) can navy beans, drained

1 (15-ounce) can black beans, drained

1 (8-ounce) can tomato sauce

1 cup Chicken Stock (page 234)

½ teaspoon dried marjoram

⅛ teaspoon pepper

1 bay leaf

Beans add rich flavor and nutrition to this simple and classic dish.

1. Heat butter in large saucepan over medium heat. Add chicken; cook and stir until browned, but not cooked through. Remove chicken to plate.
2. Add onions and garlic to saucepan; cook and stir to loosen drippings. Place onions and garlic in 3½-quart slow cooker along with chicken and remaining ingredients. Stir well to combine.
3. Cover and cook on low for 8–9 hours or until chicken is cooked and vegetables are tender. Remove bay leaf and serve.

Cassoulet

Cassoulet is French for "casserole." It's traditionally made with duck breasts and sausage, but this simplified version has just as much flavor, with less fat! It's also much less expensive. Chicken thighs have a similar flavor and richness to duck. Browning the chicken before cooking in the slow cooker also adds more flavor.

Chicken and Rice

 Serves 6

💲 Total Cost: $6.59

Calories: 320.74

Fat: 7.73 grams

Protein: 21.48 grams

Cholesterol: 100.68 mg

Sodium: 264.99 mg

1 tablespoon olive oil

2 pounds chicken parts, skinned

¼ cup flour

½ teaspoon salt

⅛ teaspoon pepper

4 carrots, sliced ½-inch thick

1 cup long grain brown rice

1 onion, chopped

2 cloves garlic, minced

2 cups Chicken Stock (page 234)

1 teaspoon poultry seasoning

⅛ teaspoon white pepper

One-dish meals are a great time saver, not only in preparation but also in cleanup.

1. Heat olive oil in large skillet over medium heat. Sprinkle chicken with flour, salt, and pepper. Brown chicken on both sides in hot oil, turning once, about 10 minutes. Remove chicken from skillet.
2. Add carrots, onion, and garlic; cook and stir for 5 minutes. Place rice in 4-quart slow cooker and top with carrots.
3. Place chicken on top of carrot mixture. Add Stock, poultry seasoning, and pepper. Cover and cook on low for 8–9 hours or until chicken is thoroughly cooked and rice is cooked. Serve immediately.

Yogurt Chicken Paprika

Serves 4

$ Total Cost: $5.52
Calories: 372.99
Fat: 16.09 grams
Protein: 24.48 grams
Cholesterol: 90.95 mg
Sodium: 375.05 mg

6 boneless, skinless chicken thighs

⅛ teaspoon pepper

½ teaspoon salt

¼ cup flour

1 tablespoon olive oil

1 onion, diced

1 cup Chicken Stock (page 234)

1 tablespoon lemon juice

2 tablespoons cornstarch

1 cup plain low-fat yogurt

2 teaspoons paprika

Yogurt and paprika are a classic combination when cooked with chicken. Serve this over hot cooked brown rice.

1. Season chicken with salt and pepper. Roll in the flour to coat. In large skillet, heat oil over medium heat. Add chicken and brown on both sides, about 4 minutes total. Add onion, stock, and lemon juice; bring to a simmer.
2. Place in 3½ to 4-quart slow cooker. Cover and cook on low for 7–9 hours or until tender and thoroughly cooked.
3. Meanwhile, combine cornstarch, yogurt, and paprika in a medium bowl. Add to slow cooker; stir, then cover and cook on high for 30–40 minutes or until sauce is thickened.

Chicken Breasts and Thighs

The white meat and dark meat of chicken cooks at different times, which is why it's difficult to roast a whole chicken to perfection. They are also done at different temperatures. White meat, or the breast, should be cooked to 170°F, while the dark meat, or thighs and wings, should be cooked to 180°F.

Easy BBQ Chicken

Serves 4

$ Total Cost: $6.59
Calories: 346.63
Fat: 15.64 grams
Protein: 25.39 grams
Cholesterol: 119.68 mg
Sodium: 571.85 mg

2 tablespoons buttermilk

¼ cup ketchup

¼ cup chili sauce

3 tablespoons Dijon mustard

2 tablespoons honey

3 cloves garlic, minced

½ teaspoon dried oregano leaves

½ teaspoon dried basil leaves

½ teaspoon salt

¼ teaspoon pepper

2 pounds boneless, skinless chicken thighs

½ teaspoon dried thyme leaves

Buttermilk adds a sweet tanginess to this easy barbecue sauce. Use it to cook pork chops and spareribs too.

1. In large bowl, combine buttermilk, ketchup, chili sauce, mustard, honey, garlic, oregano, basil, thyme, salt, and pepper. Add chicken, turn to coat, cover, and refrigerate for 3 hours.
2. Place in 4-quart slow cooker. Cover and cook on low for 8–9 hours until chicken is tender and thoroughly cooked.

Very Lemon Chicken

Serves 4

$ Total Cost: $6.59
Calories: 302.41
Fat: 9.86 grams
Protein: 28.43 grams
Cholesterol: 92.14 mg
Sodium: 253.28 mg

1½ pounds chicken parts, skinned

2 tablespoons olive oil

⅓ cup lemon juice

2 tablespoons vinegar

1 cup Chicken Stock (page 234)

2 tablespoons slivered lemon zest

½ teaspoon dried oregano leaves

1 onion, chopped

½ teaspoon salt

⅛ teaspoon white pepper

½ teaspoon paprika

2 tablespoons cornstarch

½ cup sour cream

Lemon juice and lemon zest combine to make extremely tender chicken that is very well flavored.

1. Place chicken in 3-quart slow cooker. In small bowl, combine olive oil, lemon juice, vinegar, Stock, lemon zest, oregano, onion, salt, pepper, and paprika; mix well. Pour over the chicken, cover, and cook for 8–9 hours.
2. In small bowl combine cornstarch and sour cream; mix well. Add to slow cooker and stir. Cover and cook on high for 20–30 minutes or until sauce is thickened. Serve immediately.

Lemon Zest

You can remove the zest from a lemon in several different ways. A lemon zester is a sharp tool with small holes that removes the zest in very thin strips. You can also use a sharp paring knife to peel the lemon, removing just the yellow skin and leaving the white pith, which can be bitter.

Chicken Marsala

 Serves 4

$ Total Cost: $5.69

Calories: 348.03
Fat: 5.63 grams
Protein: 21.49 grams
Cholesterol: 69.34 mg
Sodium: 276.89 mg

8 boneless, skinless chicken thighs

3 tablespoons flour

¼ teaspoon salt

⅛ teaspoon pepper

1 tablespoon olive oil

1 minced onion

1 (14-ounce) can diced tomatoes, undrained

½ cup Marsala wine

½ cup Chicken Stock (page 234)

¼ cup chopped flat-leaf parsley

Marsala wine is a sweet, rich wine with a deep amber color. It adds a complex flavor to this easy recipe.

1. Sprinkle chicken with flour, salt, and pepper. Heat olive oil in large skillet over medium heat. Add chicken; cook until lightly browned, about 5 minutes, then remove from heat and place in 4-quart slow cooker.
2. Add onion, tomatoes, wine, and Stock to skillet; bring to a boil. Pour into slow cooker. Cover and cook on low for 8–9 hours or until chicken is thoroughly cooked. Sprinkle with parsley and serve immediately.

Chicken—Dark Meat

Fiesta Chicken

Serves 6

$ Total Cost: $6.79
Calories: 301.95
Fat: 6.96 grams
Protein: 20.41 grams
Cholesterol: 71.93 mg
Sodium: 302.49 mg

1 (8-ounce) can tomato sauce

½ cup orange juice

1 minced onion

½ teaspoon dried oregano leaves

1 teaspoon chili powder

1 clove garlic, minced

¼ teaspoon salt

⅛ teaspoon cayenne pepper

1½-pounds boneless, skinless chicken thighs, cubed

1 tablespoon cornstarch

2 tablespoons water

¼ cup chopped flat-leaf parsley

3 cups hot cooked rice

The combination of flavors and textures in this recipe is really good. If your family likes food spicy, triple the chili powder and double the amount of cayenne pepper.

1. In large skillet, combine tomato sauce, orange juice, onion, oregano, chili powder, garlic, salt, and pepper. Bring to a boil, cover, reduce the heat to low, and simmer for 5 minutes.
2. Pour into 3½-quart slow cooker and add chicken. Cover and cook on low for 7–8 hours or until chicken is thoroughly cooked.
3. In small bowl, combine water, cornstarch, and parsley. Add to slow cooker, stir, cover, and cook on high for 20–30 minutes or until sauce is thickened. Serve over couscous or rice.

Cayenne Pepper

The heat from cayenne peppers, or any hot peppers, comes from capsaicin, a molecule concentrated in the seeds and membranes of the peppers. It is a good source of vitamin A, a powerful antioxidant. Cayenne peppers also contain substance P, which researchers have found to be an anti-inflammatory that fights heart disease.

Classic BBQ Chicken

 Serves 4

$ Total Cost: $5.39
Calories: 431.92
Fat: 15.93 grams
Protein: 25.23 grams
Cholesterol: 75.93 mg
Sodium: 430.25 mg

2-pounds boneless, skinless chicken thighs

½ teaspoon celery salt

¼ teaspoon seasoned salt

¼ teaspoon pepper

2 onions, chopped

4 cloves garlic, minced

1 cup barbecue sauce

1 (6-ounce) can tomato paste

2 tablespoons honey

1 teaspoon dried oregano leaves

Chicken thighs cook perfectly in the slow cooker while staying moist and tender. This flavorful mixture is delicious served with hot cooked rice, cold potato salad, and apple wedges.

1. Sprinkle chicken with celery salt, seasoned salt, and pepper. Place onions in bottom of 4-quart slow cooker and top with chicken and garlic.
2. In medium bowl, combine barbecue sauce, tomato paste, honey, and oregano; mix well. Pour over chicken.
3. Cover and cook on low for 8–9 hours or until chicken is cooked. Using two large forks, shred chicken in the sauce. Serve on split and toasted sandwich rolls or over hot cooked rice.

Indian Chicken Pilaf

 Serves 4

$ Total Cost: $5.86
Calories: 377.46
Fat: 9.81 grams
Protein: 24.95 grams
Cholesterol: 63.94 mg
Sodium: 261.40 mg

2 cups Chicken Stock (page 234)

1 tablespoon curry powder

½ teaspoon ground ginger

½ teaspoon salt

⅛ teaspoon pepper

1 onion, chopped

3 cloves garlic, minced

½ teaspoon cinnamon

1 cup long grain brown rice

1¼-pounds boneless, skinless chicken thighs, cubed

½ cup plain low-fat yogurt

½ cup Apple Chutney (page 16)

A pilaf is a spicy combination of rice and other ingredients. Yogurt is added for a cooling contrast.

1. In 3½-quart slow cooker, combine Stock, curry powder, ginger, salt, pepper, onion, garlic, and cinnamon. Add rice and chicken, cover, and cook on low for 7–8 hours or until the liquid is absorbed and the rice is tender.
2. Stir in yogurt and Chutney and cover and cook on high for 10–20 minutes until hot. Stir again and serve immediately.

Indian Flavors

Indian flavors include curry, ginger, onion, cinnamon, and garlic. These inexpensive ingredients add wonderful flavor to dishes. Chutney is also a classic Indian condiment. You can use any chutney in this easy recipe. Mango chutney is the classic bottled condiment, but it costs more than $4.00 for 8 ounces.

CHAPTER 8

SEAFOOD

144   Sweet and Sour Fish

145   Poor Fisherman's Chowder

146   Uptown Tuna Casserole

147   Slow-Cooker Salmon with Curried Pilaf

148   Shrimp and Potato Tacos

149   Light Snapper Risotto

150   Curried Tuna and Potato Casserole

151   Salmon Meatloaf

152   Red Snapper and Succotash

153   Tex-Mex Fish Burritos

154   Shrimp with Grits

155   Shrimp with Black Beans and Rice

156   Orange Ginger Fish and Sweet Potatoes

157   Salmon with Rice Pilaf

158   Clam Linguine

159   Crab and Spinach Risotto

160   Tuna Dumpling Casserole

161   Clam Chowder

Sweet and Sour Fish

 Serves 4

$ Total Cost: $5.82
Calories: 396.90
Fat: 9.48 grams
Protein: 15.83 grams
Cholesterol: 42.95 mg
Sodium: 289.95 mg

1½ cups long grain brown rice

3 cups water

1 onion, chopped

2 cloves garlic, minced

3 carrots, sliced

1 (8-ounce) can pineapple tidbits

¼ cup ketchup

2 tablespoons sugar

2 tablespoons apple cider vinegar

2 tablespoons cornstarch

2 tablespoons soy sauce

½ teaspoon ground ginger

4 frozen crunchy fish fillets

Everything but the fish cooks in the slow cooker. When you're ready to eat, bake the fish, then place it on the sweet and sour rice mixture.

1. In 3-quart slow cooker, combine all ingredients except cornstarch, soy sauce, and fish. Cover and cook on low for 7–8 hours or until rice is almost tender.
2. Preheat oven to 350°F. In small bowl, combine soy sauce and cornstarch and mix well. Stir into slow cooker. Cover and cook on high for 20–30 minutes or until rice mixture has thickened.
3. Prepare fish as directed on package. When rice mixture is done, place on serving plate. Cut fish fillets in half and place on top of rice mixture. Serve immediately.

Poor Fisherman's Chowder

Serves 4

5 cups water

3 potatoes, peeled and diced

2 carrots, sliced

2 stalks celery, sliced

1 onion, chopped

¼ cup all-purpose flour

1 teaspoon salt

⅛ teaspoon white pepper

1 cup milk

½ pound fish fillets

1 cup small raw shrimp

¾ cup shredded Cheddar cheese

This rich and thick chowder is accented with just enough seafood. If you want to splurge, increase the amount of seafood; crabmeat would be a fabulous addition.

1. In 4-quart slow cooker, combine water, potatoes, carrots, celery, and onion. Cover and cook on low for 6–7 hours or until potatoes are almost tender.
2. In small bowl, combine flour, salt, pepper, and milk and mix well. Stir into slow cooker. Cover and cook on high for 30 minutes.
3. Uncover slow cooker and add fish and shrimp. Cover and cook on high for 25–35 minutes or until shrimp curl and turn pink and fish flakes when tested with fork. Stir the chowder, then add cheese. Turn off heat, cover, and let stand for 10 minutes. Stir again and serve.

Seafood on Sale

Grocery stores often have seafood on sale. When that happens, buy a couple of packages and freeze them. Most seafood freezes very well. If the fish or shrimp isn't in freezer bags, repackage them into freezer-safe bags or containers, label with the purchase date, and freeze. Use within three months.

Uptown Tuna Casserole

Serves 4

Total Cost: $6.59
Calories: 348.92
Fat: 11.34 grams
Protein: 14.28 grams
Cholesterol: 38.23 mg
Sodium: 489.52 mg

2 tablespoons butter

1 onion, finely chopped

1 (10-ounce) can cream of mushroom soup

1 tablespoon curry powder

1 cup milk

1 (12-ounce) can tuna, drained

3 stalks celery, chopped

1 cup shredded Swiss cheese

1 cup red grapes

2 cups gemelli pasta

2 tablespoons grated Parmesan cheese

Red grapes and celery add wonderful flavor and a bit of crunch to this comforting tuna casserole.

1. Preheat oven to 375°F. Spray a 3-quart slow cooker with nonstick cooking spray and set aside.
2. In large saucepan, melt butter over medium heat. Add onion; cook and stir until tender, about 4 minutes. Add soup and curry powder; cook and stir until bubbly, about 3 minutes.
3. Stir in milk, whisking until smooth. Then add tuna. Pour into prepared slow cooker. Cover and cook on low for 5–6 hours or until onion is tender.
4. Add celery, Swiss cheese, and grapes to slow cooker. Cover and cook on low for 30 minutes. Meanwhile, cook pasta as directed on package. Stir into slow cooker along with Parmesan cheese and serve.

Slow-Cooker Salmon with Curried Pilaf

 Serves 4

$ Total Cost: $4.79

Calories: 329.81

Fat: 12.47 grams

Protein: 18.53 grams

Cholesterol: 79.43 mg

Sodium: 459.94 mg

1 tablespoon butter

1 onion, chopped

2 cloves garlic, minced

1½ cups long grain brown rice

3 cups Chicken Stock
(page 234)

2 carrots, sliced

½ teaspoon salt

⅛ teaspoon white pepper

1 tablespoon curry powder

1 (7.1-ounce) pouch salmon,
drained

The rich flavor of salmon is accented with the tart and sweet flavor of curry in this elegant dish.

1. In 3-quart slow cooker, combine all ingredients except salmon. Cover and cook on low for 7–8 hours or until rice is tender.
2. Stir in salmon, cover, and cook on high for 20–30 minutes or until rice is tender and mixture is hot. Uncover and stir, then serve immediately.

Salmon and the Slow Cooker

Most fish doesn't cook very well in the slow cooker because the extended cooking time can easily overcook the flesh. You can adapt recipes by choosing a long-cooking food, like rice or potatoes, then adding the fish at the very end of the cooking time. Make sure that you keep checking the fish; it's done when it flakes easily with a fork.

Shrimp and Potato Tacos

 Serves 4

$ Total Cost: $6.58
Calories: 420.81
Fat: 15.39 grams
Protein: 19.42 grams
Cholesterol: 102.41 mg
Sodium: 358.90 mg

3 potatoes, peeled and cubed

1 onion, chopped

3 cloves garlic, minced

1 tablespoon butter

½ teaspoon salt

1 tablespoon chili powder

⅛ teaspoon cayenne pepper

½ pound frozen cooked tiny shrimp, thawed

4 taco shells

½ cup chopped tomatoes

1 cup shredded pepper jack cheese

Potatoes in tacos? Yes, they add a wonderful texture. This can be made spicier with more chili powder and cayenne pepper.

1. In 4-quart slow cooker, combine potatoes, onions, garlic, butter, salt, chili powder, and cayenne pepper; mix well. Cover and cook on low for 8–9 hours or until potatoes are very tender.
2. Stir in shrimp, increase heat to high, and cook for 20–30 minutes or until shrimp are hot, pink, and curled.
3. Heat taco shells according to package directions. Serve the shrimp mixture with tomatoes and cheese, and let everyone make their own tacos.

Light Snapper Risotto

 Serves 6

$ Total Cost: $6.89
Calories: 320.42
Fat: 9.93 grams
Protein: 15.35 grams
Cholesterol: 53.35 mg
Sodium: 329.97 mg

1 tablespoon olive oil

1 onion, chopped

3 cloves garlic, minced

3 carrots, sliced

1 cup milk

2 cups long grain brown rice

2 cups water

2 cups Chicken Stock
  (page 234)

½ pound thin red snapper
  fillets

1 tablespoon lemon juice

1 tablespoon butter

⅓ cup grated Parmesan
  cheese

2 tablespoons chopped flat-
  leaf parsley

Risotto is a special dish for a party. And it's really easy to make in the slow cooker.

1. In large saucepan, heat olive oil over medium heat. Add onion and garlic; cook and stir for 3 minutes. Add rice; cook and stir for 3 minutes longer.
2. Combine all ingredients except fillets, lemon juice, butter, cheese, and parsley in a 3-quart slow cooker. Cover and cook on low for 6–7 hours, stirring every two hours, until rice is almost tender.
3. Place fish on top of rice mixture; cover and cook for 45–55 minutes until fish flakes when tested with a fork. Stir in lemon juice, butter, and cheese, then cover and let stand for 5 minutes. Uncover, gently stir in parsley, and serve.

Risotto

Risotto is traditionally made with Arborio rice, a short-grain rice with a high starch content. But you can make it with ordinary rice, and using brown rice adds more fiber and B vitamins. Risotto is easy to make in the slow cooker. The occasional stirring helps the rice release more starch, which makes the risotto creamy.

Curried Tuna and Potato Casserole

 Serves 5

$ Total Cost: $4.84

Calories: 359.21

Fat: 12.38 grams

Protein: 14.93 grams

Cholesterol: 32.45 mg

Sodium: 428.64 mg

4 potatoes, peeled

1 tablespoon butter

1 onion, chopped

3 cloves garlic, minced

3 tablespoons flour

1 tablespoon curry powder

½ teaspoon salt

⅛ teaspoon pepper

½ cup heavy cream

½ cup milk

2 stalks celery, chopped

1 (12-ounce) can light tuna, drained

Tuna and potatoes are a nice comforting combination. Add some curry powder and suddenly you have a gourmet dish!

1. Slice potatoes ⅛-inch thick and place in cold water. In large skillet, melt butter over medium heat. Add onion and garlic; cook and stir for 5 minutes. Add flour, curry powder, salt, and pepper; cook until bubbly.
2. Add heavy cream and milk and bring to a simmer. Drain potatoes thoroughly. Layer potatoes, celery, and tuna in 3½-quart slow cooker. Pour cream mixture over all.
3. Cover and cook on low for 7–9 hours, or until potatoes are tender and casserole is bubbling.

Salmon Meatloaf

 Serves 4

$ Total Cost: $4.70
Calories: 341.94
Fat: 13.82 grams
Protein: 14.87 grams
Cholesterol: 45.38 mg
Sodium: 362.21 mg

⅓ cup brown rice

⅔ cup water

1 tablespoon olive oil

¼ cup finely chopped onion

⅓ cup shredded carrot

¼ cup ground almonds

3 tablespoons flour

2 tablespoons sour cream

½ teaspoon salt

⅛ teaspoon pepper

1 egg

1 (14-ounce) can salmon, drained

¼ cup grated Parmesan cheese

2 tablespoons butter

Serve this old-fashioned meatloaf with a gelatin salad and a green salad for a retro meal.

1. In small saucepan, combine rice and water. Bring to a boil, reduce heat, cover, and simmer for 30–40 minutes or until rice is tender and liquid is absorbed.
2. In large saucepan, heat olive oil over medium heat. Add onion and carrot; cook and stir for 4 minutes. Remove from heat and add almonds, flour, sour cream, salt, pepper, and egg. Stir in cooked rice, then add salmon and cheese and mix.
3. Grease 2-quart slow cooker with butter. Form mixture into a loaf that fits into the slow cooker with 1-inch of space all around. Fold two 22-inch long strips of foil into 3" × 22" strips. Place in an "X" position in the bottom of slow cooker, letting ends extend over side.
4. Place loaf in bottom of slow cooker. Cover and cook on low for 6–7 hours or until meatloaf is firm. Remove from slow cooker using foil strips. Let stand for 5 minutes, then slice to serve.

Red Snapper and Succotash

Serves 4

$ Total Cost: $6.73
Calories: 310.92
Fat: 10.27 grams
Protein: 18.94 grams
Cholesterol: 42.58 mg
Sodium: 318.94 mg

1 onion, chopped

1 (10-ounce) package frozen lima beans

2 stalks celery, chopped

2 cups frozen corn kernels

½ teaspoon salt

½ teaspoon ground ginger

⅛ teaspoon pepper

¼ cup apple cider vinegar

¼ cup sugar

2 tablespoons butter

⅓ cup sour cream

½ pound red snapper fillets

Salt and pepper to taste

½ teaspoon paprika

Succotash is a combination of lima beans and corn. Ginger and sour cream add more fabulous flavor. The fish cooks perfectly in the moist heat of the slow cooker.

1. In 3-quart oval slow cooker, combine onions, lima beans, celery, corn, salt, ginger, and pepper; mix gently. In small bowl, combine vinegar and sugar; blend well. Pour into slow cooker.
2. Cover and cook on low for 7–8 hours or until succotash is blended and hot. Stir in butter and sour cream.
3. Sprinkle fillets with salt and pepper to taste, along with paprika. Spoon some of the succotash out of the slow cooker. Layer fish and succotash in slow cooker, making sure no fillets are touching.
4. Cover and cook on low for 1 to 1½ hours or until fish flakes when tested with fork. Stir to break up fish and blend mixture, then serve immediately.

Freezing Fish

Leftover canned fish, like salmon and tuna, freezes very well. If you don't use a whole can, remove the rest from the can and place it in a freezer bag or container, seal, label, and freeze for up to 3 months. To thaw, place in refrigerator overnight. Never store fish in the can, even in the refrigerator or freezer.

The $7 a Meal Slow Cooker Cookbook

Tex-Mex Fish Burritos

 Serves 4

$ Total Cost: $6.48

Calories: 402.94
Fat: 14.29 grams
Protein: 13.57 grams
Cholesterol: 42.89 mg
Sodium: 548.95 mg

1 tablespoon olive oil

1 onion, chopped

1 green bell pepper, chopped

1 (15-ounce) can black beans, drained

1 (4-ounce) can green chiles, drained

24 frozen fish fingers

1 tablespoon chili powder

½ cup Suave Cooked Salsa (page 31)

1 cup shredded Monterey jack cheese

4 (10-inch) flour tortillas

Burritos can be baked or deep fried, or covered with sauce. The method used in this recipe, baking, has the fewest calories, and is delicious for lunch.

1. In small saucepan, heat olive oil over medium heat. Add onion; cook and stir for 3 minutes. Place in 3-quart slow cooker along with bell pepper, beans, and chiles.

2. Cover and cook on low for 6–7 hours or until vegetables are tender.

3. Preheat oven to 400°F. Place fish fingers on cookie sheet. Arrange in single layer. Bake according to package directions.

4. When fish is done, remove from oven. Make wraps by removing bean mixture from slow cooker with slotted spoon and combining with Salsa and cheese. Place on tortillas, put fish on top, then wrap up, folding in ends.

5. Place, seam side down, on cookie sheet. Bake for 15–25 minutes or until tortillas start to brown and cheese is melted. Cut each in half and serve immediately.

Fish Fingers

Fish fingers are usually sold in very large packages, about 3–5 pounds. Store the package in the coldest part of your freezer, and be sure to reseal the package carefully after you remove some food. And be sure to abide carefully by the use by dates on the package. Shop around for the best deal; these products often go on sale.

Shrimp with Grits

Serves 4

$ Total Cost: $6.78
Calories: 439.82
Fat: 15.89 grams
Protein: 12.48 grams
Cholesterol: 84.95 mg
Sodium: 371.92 mg

2½ cups water

1½ cups milk

1 cup quick-cooking grits

½ teaspoon salt

½ teaspoon hot sauce

1 onion, chopped

2 tablespoons butter

1 cup grated sharp Cheddar cheese

3 slices bacon

1 green bell pepper, chopped

2 cloves garlic, minced

1 (8-ounce) can tomato sauce

2 teaspoons chili powder

8 ounces frozen cooked small shrimp, thawed

2 tablespoons cornstarch

3 tablespoons water

Grits, that Southern staple, is a wonderful complement to tender and sweet shrimp served in a spicy tomato sauce. This is a dish to serve when you entertain!

1. In 3-quart slow cooker, combine water, milk, grits, salt, butter, hot sauce, and onions. Cover and cook on low for 8–9 hours or until grits are thick and creamy. Stir in cheese.
2. In large saucepan, cook bacon until crisp. Remove bacon, crumble, and set aside. To drippings in skillet, add garlic and bell pepper and cook until crisp-tender, about 4 minutes.
3. Add tomato sauce and chili powder to saucepan and bring to a simmer. Add shrimp and stir. In small bowl, combine water and cornstarch and mix well. Stir into saucepan and bring to a simmer; simmer until thickened.
4. Spoon grits into a serving dish and top with shrimp mixture. Sprinkle with reserved bacon and serve immediately.

The $7 a Meal Slow Cooker Cookbook

Shrimp with Black Beans and Rice

Serves 4

$ Total Cost: $6.67

Calories: 385.94

Fat: 15.93 grams

Protein: 15.22 grams

Cholesterol: 89.34 mg

Sodium: 402.81 mg

2 cups dried black beans

1 tablespoon olive oil

1 cup brown rice

1 onion, chopped

3 garlic cloves, minced

2 cups Vegetable Broth (page 241)

3 cups water

1 (14-ounce) can diced tomatoes, undrained

½ teaspoon cumin

½ teaspoon salt

⅛ teaspoon cayenne pepper

8 ounces frozen tiny cooked shrimp, thawed

This recipe must be stirred, unlike most slow cooker recipes, so the beans cook evenly.

1. The night before you want to serve this dish, sort beans and rinse well. Cover with cold water and soak overnight. In the morning, drain beans and rinse.
2. Heat olive oil in medium saucepan. Add rice, onion, and garlic; cook and stir for 3–5 minutes or until fragrant. Combine in 3½-quart slow cooker along with beans, onion, garlic, Vegetable Broth, and water. Cover and cook on low for 6 hours, stirring every two hours.
3. Then add tomatoes, cumin, salt, and pepper, stirring well. Cover and cook on low for 2–3 hours longer until rice and beans are tender. Stir in shrimp, cover, and cook for 20 minutes, then serve.

About Tomatoes and Beans

Always cook beans and legumes in a low-acid and low-salt solution. Tomatoes and salt, along with salty ingredients such as bacon or ham, and ingredients high in calcium such as cheese and milk, will slow the softening process. Add these ingredients toward the end of cooking time, especially when you're cooking with a slow cooker.

Orange Ginger Fish and Sweet Potatoes

 Serves 4

3 sweet potatoes, peeled

1 onion, chopped

3 cloves garlic, minced

1 tablespoon minced gingerroot

¼ cup brown sugar

¼ cup orange juice

1 tablespoon butter

½ teaspoon salt

⅛ teaspoon pepper

½ pound fish fillets

½ cup sour cream

2 tablespoons orange marmalade

2 tablespoons orange juice concentrate, thawed

¼ teaspoon ground ginger

Sweet potatoes and onions form the base to cook tender and moist fish fillets in this wonderful recipe. It's a meal in one dish!

1. Cut sweet potatoes into 1-inch cubes and combine in 3½-quart slow cooker with onions, garlic, and gingerroot. In small bowl, combine brown sugar, orange juice, butter, salt, and pepper; mix well. Spoon over potatoes.
2. Cover and cook on low for 7–8 hours or until potatoes are tender when pierced with fork.
3. Place fish fillets on top of potatoes. Cover and cook on low for 1 to 1½ hours, or until fish flakes when tested with fork. Stir mixture to combine.
4. Meanwhile, in small bowl combine sour cream, marmalade, thawed concentrate, and ground ginger; mix well. Serve along with fish and potatoes.

Salmon with Rice Pilaf

 Serves 4

$ Total Cost: $6.89
Calories: 462.93
Fat: 15.29 grams
Protein: 13.78 grams
Cholesterol: 45.37 mg
Sodium: 439.09 mg

1 tablespoon butter

1 onion, chopped

2 cloves garlic, minced

1½ cups long grain brown rice

3 carrots, sliced

2 cups Chicken Stock
(page 234)

½ teaspoon dried dill weed

½ pound salmon fillets

½ teaspoon salt

⅛ teaspoon pepper

¼ cup sour cream

2 tablespoons mustard

½ teaspoon dried dill weed

Rice pilaf cooks to perfection, and then salmon fillets coated with a dill sauce are placed on top to steam until flaky. Yum!

1. In large skillet, melt butter over medium heat. Add onion and garlic; cook and stir until tender, about 5 minutes.
2. Add rice; cook and stir until coated, about 3–4 minutes longer. Transfer to 3-quart slow cooker. Add carrots, Stock, and dill weed.
3. Cover and cook on low for 5–6 hours or until rice is almost tender. Sprinkle salmon with salt and pepper.
4. In small bowl, combine sour cream, mustard, and dill weed. Spread over salmon fillets. Place salmon in slow cooker on top of rice.
5. Cover slow cooker and cook on low for 1 to 1½ hours or until salmon flakes when tested with a fork. Stir to mix fish with the rice pilaf and serve.

Salmon Fillets v. Steaks

Salmon fillets are thinner and cook more quickly than steaks, even in the slow cooker. They are usually cheaper too. Before adding the fillets to the slow cooker, run your fingers over the surface. If you feel any small bones, called pin bones, remove them with a tweezer and discard.

Clam Linguine

Serves 4

$ Total Cost: $6.72

Calories: 473.94

Fat: 15.23 grams

Protein: 16.92 grams

Cholesterol: 56.31 mg

Sodium: 539.90 mg

1 onion, chopped

4 cloves garlic, minced

2 potatoes, peeled and cubed

½ teaspoon salt

⅛ teaspoon pepper

1 (14-ounce) can diced tomatoes with herbs, undrained

1 (6-ounce) can tomato paste

2 cups water

2 (6-ounce) cans clams, undrained

2 tablespoons lemon juice

1 (12-ounce) package linguine pasta

2 tablespoons butter

¼ cup chopped fresh flat-leaf parsley

⅓ cup grated Parmesan cheese

This is an easy method for cooking linguine in clam sauce. You could add more vegetables to the original mixture, to stretch the clams and add nutrition.

1. In 3-quart slow cooker, combine onions, garlic, potatoes, salt, pepper, and water.
2. Cover and cook on low for 7–8 hours or until vegetables are tender. Stir in diced tomatoes, tomato paste, clams with their juice, and lemon juice. Cover and cook on low for 30–40 minutes longer or until clams are hot.
3. About 30 minutes before clam mixture is done, heat a large pot of salted water to boiling. Add linguine; cook according to package directions until almost tender. Drain and toss with butter.
4. Transfer linguine to large serving bowl. Ladle clam mixture into each bowl, and then top with parsley and cheese. Serve immediately.

Crab and Spinach Risotto

 Serves 4

💲 Total Cost: $6.28

Calories: 325.93

Fat: 14.83 grams

Protein: 17.82 grams

Cholesterol: 16.83 mg

Sodium: 453.23 mg

1 tablespoon olive oil

1 tablespoon butter

1 onion, finely chopped

3 cloves garlic, minced

2 cups long grain brown rice

3 cups Chicken Stock
(page 234)

½ teaspoon salt

⅛ teaspoon pepper

1 cup frozen chopped spinach,
thawed

12 ounces flaked surimi

½ cup grated Parmesan
cheese

½ cup grated Muenster
cheese

Here's a shocker: you can make risotto with regular long grain rice. You don't need to buy that expensive Arborio rice.

1. In large saucepan, combine olive oil and 1 tablespoon butter. Cook onion and garlic until crisp-tender, about 4 minutes. Stir in rice; cook and stir for 2 minutes longer.
2. Place rice mixture in 3-quart slow cooker. Add Chicken Stock, salt, and pepper. Cover and cook on low for 6–7 hours or until rice is almost tender.
3. Stir in spinach and surimi. Cover and cook on high for 20–30 minutes or until hot. Add cheese, cover, and turn off heat. Let stand for 10 minutes, then stir and serve.

Surimi

Surimi, also known as artificial crab, is made of real seafood. Pollock is flavored and colored and shaped to resemble crab legs. It does taste remarkably like the real thing, flakes into small pieces too, and is much less expensive than lump crab. Add it at the very end of any recipe so it doesn't overcook.

Tuna Dumpling Casserole

 Serves 6

$ Total Cost: $5.78
Calories: 302.12
Fat: 12.49 grams
Protein: 14.29 grams
Cholesterol: 24.92 mg
Sodium: 632.13 mg

4 carrots, sliced

1 onion, chopped

2 stalks celery, chopped

2 sweet potatoes, peeled and cubed

3 cups Chicken Stock (page 234)

1 (10-ounce) can cream of celery soup

½ teaspoon salt

⅛ teaspoon pepper

1 (12-ounce) can chunk light tuna, drained

2 tablespoons cornstarch

¼ cup apple juice

1 cup biscuit mix

¼ cup grated Parmesan cheese

1 teaspoon dried parsley

⅔ cup light cream

2 tablespoons butter, melted

This meal-in-one is comforting and rich. You could use cooked chicken or ham instead of the tuna if you'd like.

1. In 4-quart slow cooker, combine carrots, onions, celery, sweet potatoes, Stock, soup, salt, and pepper. Cover and cook on low for 7–8 hours or until vegetables are tender.
2. Stir in drained tuna. In small bowl, combine cornstarch with apple juice and mix well; stir into slow cooker. Turn heat to high.
3. In medium bowl combine biscuit mix, cheese, and parsley; mix well. Stir in light cream and melted butter just until blended.
4. Drop biscuit mixture by spoonfuls into slow cooker. Cover and cook on high for 40–50 minutes or until dumplings are cooked through. Serve immediately.

The $7 a Meal Slow Cooker Cookbook

Clam Chowder

Serves 5

$ Total Cost: $6.28
Calories: 402.24
Fat: 15.35 grams
Protein: 24.15 grams
Cholesterol: 74.92 mg
Sodium: 463.12 mg

3 slices bacon

1 tablespoon butter

1 onion, chopped

2 cloves garlic, minced

2 (6-ounce) cans minced clams

2 carrots, sliced

2 stalks celery, chopped

¼ cup chopped celery leaves

3 potatoes, peeled and cubed

½ teaspoon salt

⅛ teaspoon pepper

2 cups Chicken Stock (page 234)

2 cups water

2 tablespoons cornstarch

1 cup heavy cream

This rich and thick chowder is perfect for a gathering after singing Christmas carols. Serve it with tiny oyster crackers and a wilted spinach salad.

1. In large saucepan, cook bacon until crisp. Drain bacon on paper towels, crumble, and refrigerate. Drain all but 2 tablespoons drippings from saucepan and add butter. When butter melts, add onion and garlic; cook and stir until crisp-tender, about 5 minutes.

2. Drain clams, reserving liquid. Place clams in a bowl, cover, and refrigerate. Combine carrots, celery, celery leaves, potatoes, salt, pepper, Stock, water, and reserved clam liquid in 4-quart slow cooker.

3. Cover and cook on low for 7–8 hours or until vegetables are tender. In medium bowl combine cornstarch with cream; stir with wire whisk until smooth. Stir into slow cooker; cover and cook on high for 15 minutes.

4. Stir in reserved bacon and clams. Cover and cook on high for 10–15 minutes or until chowder is thoroughly heated. Serve immediately.

Seafood

CHAPTER 9

VEGETARIAN

163   Slow-Cooker Chili Tortilla Bake
164   Wild Risi Bisi
165   Potato Gratin
166   Brown Rice and Chickpeas
167   Onion and Mushroom Risotto
168   Spanish Lima Beans and Rice
169   Meatless Chili
170   Potato Tacos
171   Potato Pasta
172   Vegetarian Curry
173   Meatless Lasagna
174   Greek Stew over Couscous
175   Cheesy Polenta Casserole
176   Spicy Risotto
177   Ratatouille
178   Vegetarian Spaghetti
179   Caribbean Black Beans and Rice
180   Lemon Garbanzo Wheat Pilaf
181   Garlicky Red Beans
182   Creamy Roasted Corn with Rice

Slow-Cooker Chili Tortilla Bake

 Serves 4

$ Total Cost: $5.68
Calories: 409.16
Fat: 20.45 grams
Protein: 17.70 grams
Cholesterol: 42.31 mg
Sodium: 1082.43 mg

1 tablespoon vegetable oil

1 onion, chopped

2 jalapeño peppers, minced

1 (8-ounce) can tomato sauce

1 cup tomato juice

1 (15-ounce) can black beans, drained

1 tablespoon chili powder

½ teaspoon salt

⅛ teaspoon pepper

6 corn tortillas

1 cup grated Cheddar cheese

½ cup sour cream

Beans and corn combine to make complete protein in this satisfying and savory dish. Make sure you scoop down through the slow cooker to get all the layers.

1. In a medium saucepan, heat oil over medium heat. Add onion and jalapeños; cook and stir until crisp-tender, about 4 minutes. Add tomato sauce, juice, black beans, and seasonings. Simmer for 10 minutes.
2. Place ½ cup of sauce in bottom of 4-quart slow cooker. Top with 1 tortilla and 2 tablespoons cheese. Repeat layers, ending with cheese.
3. Cover slow cooker and cook on low for 6 to 8 hours. Serve with sour cream, if desired.

Wild Risi Bisi

Serves 4

$ Total Cost: $3.69
Calories: 279.32
Fat: 5.93 grams
Protein: 12.93 grams
Cholesterol: 10.32 mg
Sodium: 205.21 mg

1 cup wild rice

1 onion, chopped

3 cloves garlic, minced

2 cups Vegetable Broth
(page 241)

2 cups frozen edamame,
thawed

½ teaspoon salt

⅛ teaspoon pepper

⅓ cup grated Parmesan
cheese

1 tablespoon butter

Risi bisi is an Italian side dish made with plain rice and peas. Using wild rice and soybeans instead ups the nutritional value; adding cheese makes this a delicious light vegetarian main dish.

1. In 3-quart slow cooker, combine wild rice, onion, garlic, and Broth. Cover and cook on low for 7–8 hours or until wild rice is tender.
2. Stir in the edamame, salt, and pepper; cover, and cook on high for 30 minutes. Uncover and add cheese and butter. Turn off heat, cover, and let stand for 10 minutes. Fluff with a fork and serve.

Grains and Legumes

Combining grains and legumes, like wild rice and edamame, provides complete protein, which is the key to a healthy vegetarian diet. By themselves, these ingredients lack key amino acids that your body needs to repair cells. When you combine these foods, your body can make a complete protein.

The $7 a Meal Slow Cooker Cookbook

Potato Gratin

 Serves 6

$ Total Cost: $4.29
Calories: 352.93
Fat: 13.24 grams
Protein: 9.32 grams
Cholesterol: 52.38 mg
Sodium: 325.25 mg

1 tablespoon butter

1 tablespoon olive oil

1 onion, chopped

2 cloves garlic, minced

2 tablespoons flour

½ teaspoon salt

⅛ teaspoon pepper

⅛ teaspoon nutmeg

½ cup milk

½ cup heavy cream

1 (3-ounce) package cream cheese, cubed

½ cup ricotta cheese

5 russet potatoes, peeled, sliced ⅛-inch thick

1¼ cups diced Swiss cheese

¼ cup grated Parmesan cheese

This fabulously rich and creamy vegetarian main dish will be a hit with all ages. You could also serve it as a side dish, but if you do, scoop out small portions.

1. In large saucepan, melt butter with olive oil over medium heat. Add onion and garlic; cook and stir until tender, about 6 minutes.
2. Add flour, salt, pepper, and nutmeg to onion mixture; cook and stir until bubbly. Add milk and cream all at once, stirring with wire whisk; then stir in cream cheese and ricotta cheese. Cook and stir until cheese melts and mixture is smooth.
3. Spray a 3½-quart slow cooker with nonstick cooking spray. Layer ⅓ of potatoes and Swiss cheese in slow cooker. Pour ⅓ of cheese sauce over. Repeat layers, ending with cheese sauce.
4. Sprinkle with Parmesan cheese. Cover and cook on low for 8–9 hours or until potatoes are tender.

Brown Rice and Chickpeas

Serves 6

💲 Total Cost: $3.92

Calories: 242.93

Fat: 8.52 grams

Protein: 5.39 grams

Cholesterol: 21.38 mg

Sodium: 263.45 mg

1 cup brown rice

2 cups Vegetable Broth (page 241), divided

1 onion, chopped

3 carrots, sliced

½ teaspoon salt

⅛ teaspoon pepper

½ teaspoon dried marjoram leaves

1 (15-ounce) can chickpeas, drained

1 (3-ounce) package cream cheese, softened

½ cup sour cream

⅓ cup grated Parmesan cheese

Don't rinse the chickpeas; just drain them. You want some of the liquid they are packed in to help thicken the recipe.

1. In medium saucepan, combine wild rice and 2 cups Vegetable Broth. Bring to a simmer, then pour into 3-quart slow cooker. Add onion, carrots, salt, pepper, and marjoram. Cover and cook on low for 7–8 hours or until rice is tender.

2. Stir in chickpeas, cream cheese, and sour cream. Cover and cook on high for 30–40 minutes or until mixture is hot. Stir in Parmesan cheese and serve.

Brown Rice

Brown rice is just rice that has the husk removed, but the bran layer remains intact. This greatly increases the fiber, iron, and vitamin B content of the rice. Brown rice has a stronger taste than white, but it's nutty and delicious. It cooks well in the slow cooker, while white rice gets mushy.

The $7 a Meal Slow Cooker Cookbook

Onion and Mushroom Risotto

 Serves 6

 Total Cost: $5.74
Calories: 325.23
Fat: 7.43 grams
Protein: 5.94 grams
Cholesterol: 21.22 mg
Sodium: 251.12 mg

2 tablespoons olive oil

1 onion, chopped

2 cups sliced button mushrooms

2 cloves garlic, minced

2 carrots, sliced

½ teaspoon salt

⅛ teaspoon white pepper

1 teaspoon dried tarragon leaves

1 cup long grain brown rice

2 cups Vegetable Broth (page 241)

⅓ cup grated Parmesan cheese

Brown rice provides a healthy alternative to traditional Arborio rice. The vegetables are sautéed beforehand to give added texture and taste to the finished meal.

1. In large saucepan, heat olive oil over medium heat. Add onion and garlic; cook and stir for 3 minutes. Place in 3-quart slow cooker along with remaining ingredients except cheese.
2. Cover and cook on low for 7–8 hours or until rice and vegetables are tender. Stir in cheese, cover, and let stand for 5 minutes, then serve.

Spanish Lima Beans and Rice

 Serves 6

$ Total Cost: $5.36

Calories: 285.23

Fat: 7.43 grams

Protein: 6.94 grams

Cholesterol: 0.0 mg

Sodium: 264.95 mg

1 tablespoon olive oil

1 onion, chopped

3 cloves garlic, minced

½ teaspoon salt

⅛ teaspoon cayenne pepper

1½ cups long grain brown rice

3 cups Vegetable Broth (page 241)

3 tablespoons taco sauce

2 teaspoons chili powder

1 (10-ounce) package frozen lima beans, thawed

1 (14.5-ounce) can diced tomatoes, undrained

1 green bell pepper, chopped

Spanish rice is taken to the next level with the additions of taco sauce and lima beans, which help complete the protein in the rice.

1. In large saucepan, heat olive oil over medium heat. Add onion and garlic; cook and stir for 5 minutes. Sprinkle with salt and pepper, then add rice. Cook and stir for 3–4 minutes until rice is coated.
2. Add to 3-quart slow cooker along with Broth, taco sauce, chili powder, and lima beans. Cover and cook on low for 7–8 hours or until rice is almost tender.
3. Add tomatoes and bell pepper, cover, and cook on low for 1–2 hours longer or until rice is tender. Stir well and serve immediately.

Lima Beans

Lima beans are delicious; they are soft and nutty with a creamy texture. They are sometimes called butter beans. These little nuggets have a significant amount of fiber and are also high in folate, a B vitamin that can help lower the levels of homocysteine. Elevated homocysteine levels can indicate a risk for heart disease.

Meatless Chili

 Serves 4

$ Total Cost: $4.91
Calories: 303.16
Fat: 1.72 grams
Protein: 16.17 grams
Cholesterol: 0.0 mg
Sodium: 1079.32 mg

1 (15-ounce) can black beans, drained

1 (15-ounce) can kidney beans, drained

1 (14-ounce) can diced tomatoes, undrained

1 onion, chopped

4 cloves garlic, minced

1 (6-ounce) can tomato paste

½ teaspoon salt

1 tablespoon chili powder

½ teaspoon dried oregano leaves

3 cups water

2 tablespoons cornstarch

¼ cup water, if necessary

Chili is so good for you; it's full of fiber and vitamins A and C. In addition, the leftovers can be used in so many ways, including Chili Quesadillas (page 215).

1. Combine beans, half of the diced tomatoes, onion, and garlic in 3½-quart slow cooker. Mix the tomato paste into the rest of the can of tomatoes to help dissolve tomato paste. Add salt, chili powder, and oregano to the can of tomatoes and stir well; add mixture and 3 cups water to slow cooker.
2. Cover and cook on low for 7–9 hours or until chili is bubbling. If necessary, you can thicken chili by combining cornstarch with water in a small bowl. Stir this mixture into the chili and cook on high for 30 minutes, until thickened.

Potato Tacos

 Serves 4

$ Total Cost: $5.89
Calories: 363.92
Fat: 12.94 grams
Protein: 10.36 grams
Cholesterol: 21.28 mg
Sodium: 395.23 mg

4 russet potatoes, cubed

1 onion, chopped

3 cloves garlic, minced

2 tablespoons olive oil

½ teaspoon salt

⅛ teaspoon pepper

½ cup water

1 (12-ounce) can evaporated milk

2 tablespoons cornstarch

1 (4-ounce) can chopped green chiles, drained

4 taco shells

1 cup shredded pepper jack cheese

½ cup chopped tomato

Tacos are delicious, inexpensive, and easy on the cook. Let diners assemble their own tacos.

1. In 3-quart slow cooker, combine potatoes, onion, garlic, oil, salt, and pepper and mix well. Pour water over; cover and cook on low for 8–9 hours or until potatoes are tender.

2. In small bowl, combine milk and cornstarch; mix well. Stir into potato mixture along with chiles. Cover and cook on high for 20–30 minutes or until mixture is thickened.

3. Heat taco shells in the oven according to package directions until crisp, about 6–7 minutes. Make tacos with potato mixture, cheese, and tomatoes.

Potato Burritos

You can use this potato filling to make lots of other dishes. Roll it up in tortillas with some more cheese, place in a casserole, top with enchilada sauce, and bake for vegetarian enchiladas. Or roll it up in tortillas, folding in the ends, and deep fry until crisp for potato burritos.

Potato Pasta

 Serves 5

 Total Cost: $4.31
Calories: 375.34
Fat: 6.49 grams
Protein: 5.49 grams
Cholesterol: 11.47 mg
Sodium: 264.95 mg

5 russet potatoes, peeled
and cubed

1 onion, chopped

4 cloves garlic

½ teaspoon salt

⅛ teaspoon pepper

1 teaspoon dried thyme
leaves

½ teaspoon dried marjoram
leaves

1 cup water

1 (12-ounce) package
spaghetti pasta

3 tablespoons olive oil

½ cup grated Parmesan
cheese

3 tablespoons chopped
parsley

Potato and pasta may sound like an odd combination,
but it's rich and filling and delicious.

1. In 4-quart slow cooker, combine all ingredients except olive
   oil, pasta, parsley, and cheese. Cover and cook on low for
   7–9 hours or until potatoes are tender.
2. Cook pasta in large pot of boiling water according to package directions. Drain pasta, reserving ½ cup cooking water,
   and return to pot. Add potato mixture, olive oil, and ¼ cup
   cooking water and toss over medium heat.
3. Add cheese and toss again until a sauce forms, then sprinkle with parsley and serve immediately.

Vegetarian Curry

Serves 4

💲 Total Cost: $6.23
Calories: 375.45
Fat: 10.42 grams
Protein: 9.47 grams
Cholesterol: 0.0 mg
Sodium: 421.56 mg

1 tablespoon olive oil

1 onion, chopped

2 cloves garlic, minced

1 tablespoon minced gingerroot

2 teaspoons curry powder

1 cup wild rice

1 pear, peeled, cored, and chopped

1 apple, peeled and chopped

½ cup dark raisins

¼ cup dried currants

½ teaspoon salt

⅛ teaspoon pepper

1 (15-ounce) can chickpeas, drained

2 cups Vegetable Broth (page 241)

½ cup Apple Chutney (page 16)

Chickpeas and wild rice, a legume and a grain, combine to make a complete protein in this wonderful and delicious one-dish meal.

1. In large skillet, heat olive oil over medium heat. Add onions, garlic, gingerroot, and curry powder; cook and stir for 5 minutes.
2. Place wild rice in bottom of 3-quart slow cooker. Layer pears, apples, raisins, and currants on top.
3. Add salt, pepper, chickpeas, Broth, and Chutney to vegetables in skillet; bring to a simmer. Pour mixture into slow cooker.
4. Cover and cook on low for 8–9 hours or until wild rice is tender. Stir gently to mix.

Curry Powder

Curry powder isn't a single spice, but a combination of several spices. In India, curry powder recipes vary by family! You can make your own; just combine various amounts of turmeric, cumin, ginger, cinnamon, garlic, clove, mustard seed, mace, and fennel. Store it in an airtight container in a cool, dry place.

Meatless Lasagna

 Serves 5

Total Cost: $7.00
Calories: 486.45
Fat: 15.43 grams
Protein: 14.69 grams
Cholesterol: 35.45 mg
Sodium: 429.43 mg

1 tablespoon butter

1 tablespoon olive oil

½ eggplant, peeled and cubed

1 yellow summer squash, peeled and cubed

1 (8-ounce) package sliced fresh mushrooms

1 onion, chopped

2 cloves garlic, minced

1 (6-ounce) can tomato paste

2 cup Vegetable Broth (page 241)

1 teaspoon dried Italian seasoning

½ teaspoon salt

¼ teaspoon pepper

1 cup part-skim ricotta cheese

1 egg

½ (8-ounce) package cream cheese

1 cup shredded mozzarella cheese

¼ cup grated Parmesan cheese, divided

6 lasagna noodles

All the squash and mushrooms add great texture and meaty flavor to this rich and filling dish.

1. In large skillet, heat butter and olive oil on medium heat. Add eggplant; cook and stir until crisp-tender, about 5 minutes. Remove to large bowl with slotted spoon. Add squash and mushrooms to skillet; cook and stir until crisp-tender, about 5 minutes. Remove to same large bowl with slotted spoon.
2. Add onion and garlic to skillet; cook and stir for 5 minutes. Stir in tomato paste, Broth, seasoning, salt, and pepper; bring to a simmer.
3. In another large bowl combine ricotta cheese, egg, and cream cheese; beat until blended. Stir in mozzarella cheese and 2 tablespoons Parmesan cheese.
4. Spray a 4-quart slow cooker with nonstick cooking spray. Add a spoonful of the tomato sauce to the bottom. Top with 2 lasagna noodles, then a layer of the squash mixture. Top with ricotta mixture. Repeat layers, ending with ricotta mixture.
5. Sprinkle top with remaining 2 tablespoons Parmesan cheese. Cover and cook on high for 4–5 hours or until lasagna noodles are tender. Turn off heat, remove cover, and let stand for 15 minutes before serving.

Greek Stew over Couscous

 Serves 4

💲 Total Cost: $6.34

Calories: 365.49

Fat: 14.92 grams

Protein: 12.89 grams

Cholesterol: 10.43 mg

Sodium: 364.99 mg

1 acorn squash, peeled and cubed

1 onion, chopped

2 cloves garlic, minced

2 carrots, sliced

3 cups Vegetable Broth (page 241)

4 cups water

½ teaspoon salt

½ teaspoon dried oregano leaves

⅛ teaspoon pepper

1 (15-ounce) can chickpeas, drained

½ cup golden raisins

1½ cups couscous

⅓ cup crumbled feta cheese

The flavors of Greece mingle in this delicious stew. You can find feta in several flavors: plain; with garlic and herbs; or with tomatoes and herbs.

1. Combine all ingredients except couscous, 1 cup Broth, 2 cups water, and feta in a 3½-quart slow cooker. Cover and cook on low for 9–10 hours or until vegetables are very tender.
2. Place 1 cup Broth and 2 cups water in large saucepan and bring to a boil over high heat. Stir in couscous, cover, and remove from heat. Let stand for 5 minutes, then fluff with fork. Place couscous in large serving bowl.
3. Stir mixture in slow cooker and spoon over couscous. Sprinkle with feta cheese and serve.

Couscous

Couscous is not a grain, as some think; it's pasta. It's actually ground semolina pasta. Since it's ground, and so small, all you have to do is rehydrate it to cook. Be sure to read the package directions to make sure that's how you prepare it. Traditional couscous looks like large beads and is steamed to prepare.

Cheesy Polenta Casserole

Serves 6

Total Cost: $6.12
Calories: 315.64
Fat: 5.29 grams
Protein: 8.49 grams
Cholesterol: 25.94 mg
Sodium: 264.38 mg

1½ cups yellow cornmeal

2½ cups Vegetable Broth (page 241)

1 cup water

1 tablespoon butter

1 teaspoon salt

⅛ teaspoon pepper

1 cup shredded extra-sharp Cheddar cheese

1 (3-ounce) package cream cheese, cubed

1 tablespoon vegetable oil

1 onion, chopped

1 green bell pepper, chopped

1 (8-ounce) can tomato sauce

1 (15-ounce) can chickpeas, drained

½ teaspoon dried oregano

⅛ teaspoon pepper

¼ cup grated Parmesan cheese

You use two slow cookers to make this casserole—one for the topping and one for the polenta—but the time saving is huge!

1. Place cornmeal in a 2-quart slow cooker. In large saucepan, combine Broth, water, butter, salt, and pepper; bring to a boil. Stir into cornmeal.
2. Cover and cook on high for 2 hours, or until liquid is absorbed. Stir polenta thoroughly, add Cheddar and cream cheese and stir gently, and turn off heat.
3. In large skillet, heat vegetable oil over medium heat. Add onion; cook and stir until tender, about 6 minutes. Add bell pepper, tomato sauce, chickpeas, oregano, and pepper; bring to a simmer. Remove from heat.
4. Place polenta in bottom of 3½-quart slow cooker. Top with chickpea mixture, then sprinkle with Parmesan cheese. Cover and cook on low for 5–6 hours or until casserole is thoroughly heated.

Spicy Risotto

Serves 4

Total Cost: $3.99
Calories: 305.25
Fat: 5.39 grams
Protein: 11.19 grams
Cholesterol: 18.95 mg
Sodium: 352.83 mg

1 tablespoon olive oil

1 onion, chopped

2 cloves garlic, minced

1 jalapeño pepper, minced

1½ cups long grain brown rice

½ teaspoon salt

⅛ teaspoon white pepper

½ teaspoon cumin seeds

¼ teaspoon crushed red pepper flakes

3 cups Vegetable Broth (page 241)

½ cup tomato juice

1 tomato, seeded and chopped

⅓ cup heavy cream

¼ cup grated Parmesan cheese

To seed tomato, cut in half and gently squeeze out the seeds and jelly. Then chop coarsely and set aside in a dish until it's time to add them to the recipe.

1. Heat oil in large skillet. Add onions, garlic, and jalapeño pepper; cook and stir for 4–5 minutes. Then stir in rice; cook and stir for 3–4 minutes longer.
2. Place onion mixture in 3-quart slow cooker. Add salt, pepper, cumin seeds, red pepper flakes, Broth, and tomato juice.
3. Cover and cook on high for 2 hours, stirring twice during cooking time. Stir in chopped tomatoes, then continue cooking on high for another 1–2 hours, stirring every half hour, until rice is al dente (slightly firm in the center).
4. Stir in cream and cheese. Uncover and cook for 15–25 minutes longer or until risotto is creamy and hot. Serve immediately.

Ratatouille

 Serves 5

Total Cost: $6.87
Calories: 365.94
Fat: 10.32 grams
Protein: 7.94 grams
Cholesterol: 10.32 mg
Sodium: 352.79 mg

½ teaspoon salt

⅛ teaspoon pepper

½ teaspoon dried oregano leaves

½ teaspoon dried Italian seasoning

1 tablespoon sugar

2 tablespoons olive oil

1 eggplant, sliced ½-inch thick

1 onion, chopped

2 cloves garlic, minced

1 yellow summer squash, sliced

1 tomato, sliced

1 (4-ounce) jar sliced mushrooms, drained

1 green bell pepper, sliced

1 (16-ounce) jar spaghetti sauce

3 tablespoons tomato paste

1 tablespoon balsamic vinegar

¼ cup diced feta cheese

The vegetables will cook down quite a bit in this recipe, so don't be alarmed if the slow cooker is really full right at the beginning.

1. In small bowl combine salt, pepper, oregano, Italian seasoning, and sugar. Mix well and set aside. In large skillet, heat 2 tablespoons olive oil over medium heat. Add eggplant; sauté for 2–3 minutes on each side and then remove eggplant to a separate bowl. Add onions and garlic to skillet; cook and stir for 5 minutes.
2. Spray a 4-quart slow cooker with nonstick cooking spray. Layer all of the vegetables and mushrooms in the slow cooker, sprinkling each layer with some of the salt mixture.
3. In food processor, combine half of the spaghetti sauce with the tomato paste; blend until smooth. Stir in remaining spaghetti sauce along with the vinegar. Pour into slow cooker.
4. Cover and cook on low for 7–9 hours or until vegetables are very tender. Sprinkle with cheese and serve.

Vegetarian Spaghetti

 Serves 5

1 onion, chopped

2 cloves garlic, minced

1 cup shredded carrots

1 (4-ounce) jar mushroom pieces, undrained

1 tablespoon olive oil

1 (6-ounce) can tomato paste

1 (14-ounce) can diced tomatoes, undrained

1 teaspoon dried Italian seasoning

1 bay leaf

½ teaspoon salt

⅛ teaspoon pepper

1 (12-ounce) package spaghetti pasta

¼ cup grated Parmesan cheese

Carrots help keep the sauce from becoming watery, and add nutrition and flavor to this simple dish.

1. Combine all ingredients except pasta and cheese in a 3-quart slow cooker. Cover and cook on low for 8–9 hours, stirring once during cooking time, until sauce is blended and thickened.

2. When sauce is ready, bring a large pot of salted water to a boil. Add pasta; cook according to package directions until al dente. Drain pasta and place on warmed serving dishes. Remove and discard bay leaf. Stir sauce and spoon over pasta. Sprinkle with cheese and serve.

Bay Leaf

Bay leaves grow in bushes that are native to the Mediterranean. They add an earthy, smoky flavor to foods. But the leaves aren't edible. In fact, the spines of the leaves are so thick that they are a health hazard! Never eat a bay leaf, and be very careful to remove and discard it when the food is finished cooking.

Caribbean Black Beans and Rice

 Serves 4

2 tablespoons olive oil

2 onions, chopped

3 cloves garlic, minced

1 green bell pepper

1 cup long grain brown rice

1 (15-ounce) can black beans

1 tomato, chopped

2 cups water

1 tablespoon vinegar

½ teaspoon Tabasco

½ teaspoon salt

¼ teaspoon pepper

3 tablespoons chopped cilantro

Beans and rice are a classic vegetarian combination. Black beans makes this recipe a bit more exotic.

1. In medium skillet, heat olive oil over medium heat. Add onion and garlic; cook and stir for 4 minutes.
2. Place in 3-quart slow cooker along with remaining ingredients except cilantro. Cover and cook on low for 7–8 hours or until rice is tender. Stir well, then sprinkle with cilantro and serve.

Lemon Garbanzo Wheat Pilaf

Serves 4

1 cup cracked wheat

1 (15-ounce) can chickpeas, drained

½ teaspoon salt

⅛ teaspoon pepper

2 cups Vegetable Broth (page 241)

1 onion, chopped

3 cloves garlic, minced

½ teaspoon grated lemon peel

1 green bell pepper, chopped

1 tablespoon olive oil

½ teaspoon ground cumin

¼ cup lemon juice

⅓ cup chopped parsley

Lemon juice and parsley add a bright flavor to this hearty pilaf. Serve with a green salad and some bakery breadsticks.

1. Combine all ingredients except lemon juice and parsley in a 3½-quart slow cooker. Cover and cook on low for 7–8 hours or until wheat is tender.
2. Add lemon juice and parsley to mixture; stir. Uncover and cook on high for 10–15 minutes or until mixture has thickened slightly. Serve immediately.

Bulgur vs. Cracked Wheat

Bulgur is also known as cracked wheat, but the two are not the same. Wheat is a very inexpensive grain that has a rich and nutty taste. The bulgur you buy in the supermarket has usually been parboiled, and can overcook in the slow cooker. Look for real cracked wheat for slow cooker recipes; it's more available in Indian markets.

Garlicky Red Beans

 Serves 6

$ Total Cost: $4.32
Calories: 318.92
Fat: 4.93 grams
Protein: 7.49 grams
Cholesterol: 0.0 mg
Sodium: 359.23 mg

1 pound dried red beans

5 cups water

1 onion, chopped

6 cloves garlic, minced

3 stalks celery, sliced

½ cup ketchup

1 green bell pepper, chopped

1 tablespoon olive oil

1 tablespoon Worcestershire sauce

1 teaspoon Tabasco sauce

1 bay leaf

½ teaspoon dried thyme leaves

½ teaspoon salt

¼ teaspoon pepper

¼ cup chopped parsley

Serve these spicy and well-flavored beans over brown rice for a hearty winter meal.

1. Sort beans and rinse. Place in large bowl, cover with water, cover, and soak overnight.
2. In the morning, drain and rinse the beans. Place in a 4-quart slow cooker and add 5 cups water. Cover and cook on low for 3 hours.
3. Add remaining ingredients except parsley and stir well. Cover and cook on low for 6–7 hours or until beans are tender. Remove bay leaf and discard. Sprinkle with parsley and serve.

Creamy Roasted Corn with Rice

Serves 4

Total Cost: $4.59
Calories: 428.93
Fat: 8.32 grams
Protein: 9.43 grams
Cholesterol: 10.59 mg
Sodium: 403.92 mg

2 cups frozen corn, thawed

1 tablespoon olive oil

1 tablespoon butter

1 onion, chopped

3 cloves garlic, minced

1 cup long grain brown rice

2 cups Vegetable Broth (page 241)

½ teaspoon salt

⅛ teaspoon pepper

⅛ teaspoon nutmeg

1 (3-ounce) package cream cheese, cubed

2 green onions, chopped

Corn and rice make a delicious combination in this easy and flavorful dish. Serve with a molded gelatin salad for a nice lunch.

1. Preheat oven to 400°F. Combine corn with olive oil on a cookie sheet; toss and spread in an even layer. Roast for 15–25 minutes, stirring occasionally, until corn starts to turn brown around the edges. Place in 3-quart slow cooker.
2. Heat butter over medium heat; add onion, garlic, and rice. Cook and stir for 5 minutes, then stir in Broth. Bring to a simmer, then add to slow cooker with corn.
3. Add salt, pepper, and nutmeg, cover, and cook on low for 7–8 hours or until rice is tender. Stir in cream cheese and green onions, cover, and cook on high for 20–30 minutes until cheese is melted. Stir and serve.

Roasting Corn

Corn has a lot of natural sugars, so when it's cooked at high heat, the sugars caramelize and turn brown in the Maillard reaction. This concentrates the flavors and makes the corn slightly chewy. Be careful not to burn the corn; watch it carefully as it roasts and stir occasionally so the edges don't overcook.

CHAPTER 10

SIDE DISHES

184   Sweet Potato Apple Purée

185   Slow-Cooker Red Beans

186   Buttermilk Mashed Potatoes

187   Tex-Mex Rice and Beans

188   Orange Glazed Carrots

189   Drunken Beans

190   Gingered Baked Beans

191   Coriander Carrots

192   Garlicky Green Beans

193   Creamy Cheesy Potatoes

194   Spicy Corn Spoon Bread

195   Sweet and Spicy Carrots

196   Curried Rice

197   Roasted Root Vegetables

198   Buffalo Smashed Potatoes

199   Curried Roasted Squash with Fruit

200   Cashew Rice Pilaf

201   Risi Bisi

202   Crunchy Sweet Potatoes

203   Cheesy Carrots

204   Creamed Corn

205   Garlic and Herb Mashed Potatoes

206   Grandma's Peas and Carrots

207   Tater Tot Casserole

208   Mashed Sweet Potatoes

Sweet Potato Apple Purée

Serves 6

Total Cost: $6.11
Calories: 122.89
Fat: 5.90 grams
Protein: 1.32 grams
Cholesterol: 15.26 mg
Sodium: 374.91 mg

1½-pounds sweet potatoes, peeled and cubed

2 Granny Smith apples, peeled and cubed

1 cup apple juice

3 tablespoons butter

½ teaspoon ground nutmeg

½ teaspoon salt

¼ teaspoon white pepper

Now this is a dish for the holidays! You can keep it warm in the slow cooker for 2 hours after it's done cooking; just stir occasionally.

1. Combine sweet potatoes and apples in 3-quart slow cooker. Pour in apple juice. Cover and cook on low for 8-9 hours or until potatoes and apples are tender.
2. When tender, add butter, nutmeg, salt, and pepper to slow cooker; mash using a potato masher or immersion blender. Can keep in slow cooker for 2 hours on warm, stirring occasionally.

Slow Cooker Red Beans

 Serves 6

1 onion, chopped

3 cloves garlic, minced

2 jalapeño peppers, minced

1 pound dried red beans

6 cups water

2 tablespoons olive oil

1 tomato, seeded and diced

1 tablespoon chili powder

1 teaspoon salt

⅛ teaspoon pepper

½ teaspoon dried oregano

Serve this hearty and rich dish with some cooked Tex-mati rice and some chilled sweet tea or lemonade for a perfect light lunch.

1. In heavy skillet, heat olive oil over medium heat. Add onion, garlic, and jalapenos and cook until crisp-tender, about 4–5 minutes, stirring frequently.
2. Meanwhile, sort over dried beans, then rinse them thoroughly. Place in 4-quart Crock-Pot along with onion mixture and water. Cover and cook on high for 4 hours.
3. Stir beans and add remaining ingredients. Cover and cook on low for 4–6 hours or until beans are very tender.

Vegetarian Main Dish

To make this side dish a main dish, pair it with some cornbread or corn tortillas. Beans provide lots of protein, but not complete protein; they are missing a few key amino acids. Serve it with a grain or some nuts to complete the amino acid spectrum, for an inexpensive vegetarian lunch or dinner.

Buttermilk Mashed Potatoes

 Serves 12

$ Total Cost: $3.49

Calories: 182.26

Fat: 7.93 grams

Protein: 2.87 grams

Cholesterol: 20.97 mg

Sodium: 537.89 mg

3-pounds potatoes, peeled and-quartered

½ cup butter

1 onion, chopped

¾ cup buttermilk

⅛ teaspoon nutmeg

½ teaspoon salt

⅛ teaspoon white pepper

Mashed potatoes don't have to be full of fat. Buttermilk adds a creamy richness to this classic dish.

1. Place potatoes in a 4–5-quart slow cooker and add 1 cup water. Cover and cook on low until tender, about 7–8 hours.
2. When potatoes are done, in small saucepan melt butter over medium heat. Cook onion, stirring occasionally, until tender and slightly caramelized, about 7 minutes.
3. When potatoes are done, drain, return to the slow cooker, add onion mixture, and mash until smooth. Gradually add the buttermilk, stirring constantly. Stir in nutmeg, salt, and pepper. Serve immediately, or cover and hold on low for up to 3 hours, stirring occasionally.

Tex-Mex Rice and Beans

 Serves 6

$ Total Cost: $3.42
Calories: 241.64
Fat: 1.65 grams
Protein: 8.60 grams
Cholesterol: 0.0 mg
Sodium: 520.34 mg

1 (15-ounce) can black beans, rinsed

1¼ cups brown rice

2 cups boiling water

1 cup frozen corn

½ cup chunky salsa

1 jalapeño chile, minced

4 cloves garlic, minced

½ teaspoon salt

⅛ teaspoon white pepper

2 tablespoons lime juice

¼ cup chopped cilantro

Serve this hearty side dish with a simple grilled steak or grilled chicken breasts, with some corn on the cob on the side.

1. In a 3 to 4-quart Crock-Pot, combine beans, rice, water, corn, salsa, chile, garlic, salt, and pepper. Stir well, then cover and cook on low for 2½ to 3 hours, until rice is tender.
2. Stir in lime juice and cilantro, mix well, and serve.

Rice in the Slow Cooker

When cooked in the Crock-Pot, brown rice becomes moist and tender—more tender than when cooked on the stovetop. Do not substitute regular or instant long grain, medium grain, or short grain rice for the brown rice; it will overcook. Even Texmati and Basmati rice do not work well in this appliance.

Orange Glazed Carrots

Serves 6

$ Total Cost: $2.39
Calories: 142.04
Fat: 4.39 grams
Protein: 1.28 grams
Cholesterol: 5.84 mg
Sodium: 248.73 mg

1 tablespoon butter

1 onion, chopped

4 cloves garlic, minced

6 carrots, sliced

½ cup frozen orange juice
concentrate, thawed

2 tablespoons honey

½ teaspoon salt

⅛ teaspoon white pepper

The combination of orange juice, honey, and carrots is truly delicious, and it's also high in vitamins A and C.

1. In medium saucepan, melt butter over medium heat. Add onion and garlic; cook and stir until tender, about 6 minutes. Combine with carrots in 3-quart slow cooker.
2. Add orange juice concentrate, honey, salt, and pepper to saucepan. Bring to a simmer, then pour into slow cooker. Cover and cook on low for 7-8 hours or until carrots are tender and glazed. Serve immediately.

Drunken Beans

 Serves 8

Total Cost: $5.33
Calories: 355.70
Fat: 2.47 grams
Protein: 20.59 grams
Cholesterol: 3.35 mg
Sodium: 840.34 mg

1½ pounds dried pinto beans

3 strips bacon

1 onion, chopped

3 cloves garlic, minced

1 (12-ounce) bottle beer

6 cups water

1 (4-ounce) can diced green chiles

2 cups chunky salsa

1 teaspoon salt

⅛ teaspoon pepper

½ cup chopped cilantro

These beans are made easier by cooking in the Crock-Pot, so you don't have to keep an eye on them. They taste even better the next day; reheat them by pouring into a saucepan and cooking over low heat, stirring frequently, until beans simmer.

1. Sort through beans and rinse thoroughly. Cover with water and let soak overnight.
2. When ready to cook, fry bacon in a heavy skillet until crisp; drain on paper towels, crumble, and refrigerate. Cook onions and garlic in bacon drippings until crisp-tender. Drain beans and add to a 4 to 5-quart Crock-Pot along with onion mixture, beer, and water. Cover and cook on low for 6–7 hours until beans are tender.
3. Stir beans and add chiles, salsa, salt, and pepper. Cover and cook for 1–2 hours longer until beans are very tender. Sprinkle with cilantro and reserved bacon pieces, stir, and serve.

Dried Bean Science

Dried beans and other legumes will not soften if cooked with ingredients that are high in salt or acid. Salsa, which contains lots of tomatoes (which are high in acid), and the salt are added at the end of cooking time in this recipe to ensure success. Make a note of this and adjust other slow cooker recipes as necessary.

Gingered Baked Beans

 Serves 6

$ Total Cost: $4.78
Calories: 210.93
Fat: 8.30 grams
Protein: 4.02 grams
Cholesterol: 7.39 mg
Sodium: 739.05 mg

1 tablespoon butter

1 onion, chopped

½ teaspoon ground ginger

⅓ cup brown sugar

⅓ cup ketchup

2 tablespoons yellow mustard

2 (16-ounce) cans baked beans, undrained

1 (15-ounce) can black beans, drained

Adding ginger to baked beans wakes them up a bit. The onion and ginger become tender and mild during the long cooking time, forming the perfect complement to the beans.

1. In medium skillet, melt butter over medium heat. Add onion; cook and stir until tender, about 6 minutes. Place in 3-quart slow cooker along with ginger, brown sugar, ketchup, and mustard; mix well.
2. Add undrained baked beans and drained black beans; mix well. Cover and cook on low for 7–9 hours.

Coriander Carrots

 Serves 6

$ Total Cost: $2.09
Calories: 78.78
Fat: 4.42 grams
Protein: 0.97 grams
Cholesterol: 5.09 mg
Sodium: 266.95 mg

1 tablespoon olive oil

1 onion, chopped

1 cup water

1 bay leaf

½ teaspoon salt

7 carrots, peeled and thickly sliced

1 tablespoon butter

2 teaspoons ground coriander

2 tablespoons lemon juice

3 tablespoons minced flat-leaf parsley

Coriander and bay leaf add a nice spicy touch to tender carrots. Serve this with grilled chicken or rice dishes.

1. Heat oil in large saucepan over medium heat. Add onion; cook and stir until crisp-tender, about 4 minutes. Add water and bring to a simmer; pour into 4-quart slow cooker.
2. Add remaining ingredients except for parsley and stir. Cover and cook on low for 5–6 hours or until carrots are tender when pierced with a fork. Remove bay leaf and discard; add parsley and serve.

Coriander

Coriander is the seed of the cilantro plant. The fresh leaves of the plant are called cilantro. The coriander seed is dried and ground to produce the spice. It contains a volatile oil that is dense with phytonutrients and contains an antibacterial compound. Its spicy flavor is usually an acquired taste.

Garlicky Green Beans

Serves 5

$ Total Cost: $3.20	1 (16-ounce) package frozen whole green beans
Calories: 58.39	1 onion, chopped
Fat: 2.09 grams	3 cloves garlic, minced
Protein: 1.38 grams	½ teaspoon salt
Cholesterol: 12.39 mg	⅛ teaspoon pepper
Sodium: 205.45 mg	1 cup water
	2 tablespoons butter

When cooked for a long time at low temperatures, garlic becomes tender, mild, and nutty. It adds a wonderful spark of flavor to green beans.

1. Combine all ingredients except butter in 2-quart slow cooker. Cover and cook on high for 2–3 hours or until beans and onions are tender.
2. Drain off water and return ingredients to slow cooker. Add butter, cover, and cook for 30 minutes longer. Stir and serve.

Creamy Cheesy Potatoes

Serves 8

$ Total Cost: $6.98
Calories: 285.23
Fat: 9.24 grams
Protein: 5.48 grams
Cholesterol: 45.29 mg
Sodium: 429.43 mg

1 20-ounce package frozen hash brown potatoes, thawed

1 sweet potato, peeled

1 tablespoon butter

1 onion, chopped

3 cloves garlic, minced

1 10-ounce jar Alfredo sauce

1 (3-ounce) package cream cheese, cubed

¾ cup sour cream

¾ cup shredded Swiss cheese

½ cup milk

1 teaspoon dried basil leaves

⅛ teaspoon pepper

Adding sweet potatoes to a classic, rich dish makes it more nutrient dense; the vitamin A content goes through the roof.

1. Drain the hash brown potatoes and place in a 4-quart slow cooker. Coarsely grate the sweet potatoes and add to the slow cooker; mix gently.

2. In large skillet, heat butter over medium heat. Add onions and garlic; cook and stir until tender, about 6–7 minutes. Add to slow cooker and stir.

3. Add Alfredo sauce, cream cheese, sour cream, Swiss cheese, milk, basil, and pepper to skillet; cook and stir over medium-low heat until cream cheese melts. Pour over potatoes in slow cooker.

4. Cover and cook on low for 8–9 hours or until potatoes are tender and mixture is bubbling. Serve immediately.

Potatoes

Potatoes are a very healthy food, despite being denigrated in the low-carb craze. They contain lots of potassium and fiber, especially if you eat the skin. A chemical in potatoes called kukoamine may help reduce high blood pressure. And they're delicious too; the perfect side dish for everything from baked chicken to ham.

Spicy Corn Spoon Bread

Serves 6

💲 Total Cost: $4.59
Calories: 280.49
Fat: 7.95 grams
Protein: 4.49 grams
Cholesterol: 99.64 mg
Sodium: 380.25 mg

2 (8-ounce) packages corn muffin mix

1 tablespoon chili powder, divided

2 eggs, beaten

⅓ cup milk

⅓ cup sour cream

1 cup frozen corn

1 (4-ounce) can chopped green chiles, drained

¾ cup shredded Colby cheese

⅓ cup mild salsa

Baking bread in the slow cooker makes a moist and tender loaf, more like a spoon bread, which is a cross between a soufflé and bread.

1. In large bowl, combine both packages muffin mix and 2 teaspoons chili powder; mix to combine. In medium bowl, combine eggs, milk, and sour cream; mix well. Add to muffin mix and stir just until combined. Stir in corn.
2. In small bowl, combine drained chiles, cheese, and salsa. Spray a 3½-quart slow cooker with nonstick baking spray containing flour. Spoon half of the muffin mix batter into the slow cooker. Top with the green chile mixture, then add remaining batter. Smooth top and sprinkle with remaining 1 teaspoon chili powder.
3. Cover slow cooker and cook on high for 2–3 hours, or until top springs back when lightly touched. Turn off, uncover, then top with foil, leaving a corner vented, and cool for 20 minutes. Serve by scooping out hot bread with a large spoon.

Sweet and Spicy Carrots

 Serves 8

$ Total Cost: $3.49
Calories: 125.96
Fat: 2.75 grams
Protein: 1.54 grams
Cholesterol: 7.86 mg
Sodium: 279.43 mg

8 carrots, sliced

1 cup orange juice

2 tablespoons butter

¼ cup honey

2 tablespoons brown sugar

⅓ cup apricot preserves

3 tablespoons Dijon mustard

¼ teaspoon salt

⅛ teaspoon white pepper

The combination of sweet apricots and spicy mustard is the perfect complement to tender carrots. Serve this with roast chicken and rice pilaf.

1. In 3-quart slow cooker, combine carrots and orange juice. Cover and cook on low for 7-8 hours or until carrots are tender. Drain, reserving ¼ cup of the liquid.

2. In small saucepan combine remaining ingredients over medium heat; cook and stir until sugar is dissolved. Pour over carrots in slow cooker. Cover and cook on high for 30-40 minutes until carrots are glazed.

Preserves

Read the labels on fruit preserves before you buy them. Some brands can offer a significant amount of vitamin C. You can find low-sugar or sugar-free brands if you're on a low-carb diet. Keep a good supply of them on hand, because they're delicious added to vegetables and a good way to flavor dips and fruit salads.

Curried Rice

 Serves 6

💲 Total Cost: $1.98
🥄 Calories: 219.43
Fat: 2.38 grams
Protein: 2.10 grams
Cholesterol: 5.02 mg
Sodium: 148.43 mg

1 cup Vegetable Broth (page 241)

2 cups water

2 cloves garlic, minced

1½ cups long grain brown rice

2 teaspoons curry powder

1 tablespoon butter

⅛ teaspoon pepper

½ teaspoon salt

½ cup sliced almonds, toasted

Curried Rice is gently seasoned, and the perfect complement to everything from roasted chicken to grilled steak.

1. In small saucepan, bring Broth and garlic to a simmer. Pour into 2-quart slow cooker. Add remaining ingredients except almonds. Stir and cover. Cook on low for 6–7 hours until tender.
2. Turn off slow cooker and add almonds. Let stand for 5 minutes, then fluff to incorporate almonds and mix the rice.

Roasted Root Vegetables

Serves 6

4 russet potatoes

1 rutabaga, peeled

1 parsnip, peeled

2 large carrots, peeled

4 cloves garlic, peeled

1 tablespoon olive oil

½ teaspoon salt

⅛ teaspoon pepper

½ teaspoon dried basil leaves

½ teaspoon dried thyme leaves

Serve this mix of tender and sweet root vegetables as the side dish for a roasted chicken or a glazed spiral-sliced ham.

1. Cut the potatoes, rutabaga, parsnip, and carrots into 1-inch chunks. Leave the garlic cloves whole. Place in 4–5-quart slow cooker. Drizzle with olive oil and sprinkle with salt, pepper, and seasonings.
2. Cover and cook on low for 8–9 hours until the vegetables are tender. Stir gently and serve.

Root Vegetables

Root vegetables are an excellent source of fiber and vitamin A. If you've never tried the more mundane varieties like parsnips and rutabaga, try this recipe. When the vegetables roast for a long time, they become tender and quite sweet with a wonderful caramelized flavor. This could even be the main dish for a vegetarian meal.

Buffalo Smashed Potatoes

Serves 6

$ Total Cost: $5.89
Calories: 329.42
Fat: 12.39 grams
Protein: 5.39 grams
Cholesterol: 24.93 mg
Sodium: 329.94 mg

4 russet potatoes, cubed

2 tablespoons butter

1 onion, chopped

6 cloves garlic, minced

½ cup sour cream

½ cup ricotta cheese

½ teaspoon hot pepper sauce

½ teaspoon salt

⅛ teaspoon white pepper

½ cup crumbled blue cheese

3 tablespoons grated Parmesan cheese

Because you use the potato skins, these potatoes have more fiber than traditional mashed potatoes.

1. In small skillet melt butter; add onion and garlic. Cook and stir until tender, about 5 minutes. Combine in 4-quart slow cooker with potatoes and ½ cup water. Cover and cook on low for 7–8 hours or until potatoes are tender.
2. Drain potatoes and place in large bowl. Mash with potato masher, leaving some large pieces.
3. Preheat oven to 400°F. Add sour cream, ricotta, hot pepper sauce, salt, and pepper to potatoes and mix well. Pile into a 3-quart casserole and top with blue and Parmesan cheeses. Bake for 30–40 minutes or until potatoes are hot and top browns.

Curried Roasted Squash with Fruit

Serves 6

$ Total Cost: $6.49
Calories: 148.32
Fat: 3.28 grams
Protein: 2.81 grams
Cholesterol: 5.02 mg
Sodium: 204.34 mg

1 butternut squash

1 onion, chopped

2 cloves garlic, minced

1 tablespoon olive oil

1 tablespoon curry powder

½ teaspoon salt

⅛ teaspoon pepper

1 apple, chopped

1 tablespoon butter

Roasted squash is naturally sweet. When combined with apples and onions, it makes an elegant and easy side dish.

1. Peel the squash and remove seeds; cut into 1-inch cubes. Combine with onions and garlic in a 4–5-quart slow cooker. Drizzle with olive oil, curry powder, salt, and pepper and toss.
2. Cover and cook on low for 7–8 hours or until squash is almost tender. Add apple, stir, cover, and cook on low for 1 to 1½ hours longer until squash is tender. Stir in butter and serve.

Winter Squash

Winter squash includes the hard-skinned varieties like butternut, acorn, and pumpkin. They are more difficult to work with, but use a sharp knife and be careful. They are very high in vitamin A and fiber. Roasting these vegetables concentrates the flavor and the sugar content.

Cashew Rice Pilaf

Serves 6

Total Cost: $6.29
Calories: 218.90
Fat: 3.28 grams
Protein: 2.01 grams
Cholesterol: 0.0 mg
Sodium: 243.32 mg

1 tablespoon olive oil

1 onion, chopped

2 cloves garlic, minced

½ cup wild rice

1 cup long grain brown rice

2½ cups water

½ teaspoon salt

⅛ teaspoon pepper

½ teaspoon dried thyme leaves

2 carrots, sliced

½ cup chopped toasted cashews

3 tablespoons chopped flat-leaf parsley

Rice pilaf can be served with so many simple main dishes. This one is so hearty it can be a vegetarian main dish.

1. In large saucepan, combine olive oil, onion, and garlic; cook until crisp-tender, about 4 minutes. Add wild and brown rice; cook for 1 minute. Add water, salt, and pepper; bring to a boil.
2. Pour into 3-quart slow cooker and add thyme and carrots. Cover and cook on low for 6–7 hours or until rice is tender. Stir in cashews and parsley and serve immediately.

Risi Bisi

Serves 6

Total Cost: $5.39
Calories: 238.94
Fat: 8.39 grams
Protein: 5.39 grams
Cholesterol: 8.49 mg
Sodium: 238.94 mg

1 tablespoon butter

1 onion, chopped

2 cups long grain brown rice

4 cups water

1 teaspoon dried Italian seasoning

⅛ teaspoon pepper

1½ cups frozen baby peas, thawed

½ cup sour cream

¼ cup grated Parmesan cheese

This side dish combines rice and peas with a little sour cream and cheese that makes it decadent and delicious.

1. In small saucepan, melt butter over medium heat. Add onion; cook and stir for 4 minutes. Add rice; cook and stir for 3 minutes longer. Place into 3-quart slow cooker.
2. Add water, Italian seasoning, and pepper. Cover and cook on low for 5–6 hours or until rice is almost tender.
3. Stir in peas; cover and cook for 30 minutes. Then add sour cream and cheese; cover and cook for 30 minutes longer. Stir and serve immediately.

Risi Bisi

Risi Bisi, or rice with peas, is a classic Italian side dish. It's served in the spring, when fresh peas are available, at Venetian festivals. The combination may sound strange, but it's really delicious. Rice and legumes of any kind are natural partners. This could be a light vegetarian main dish.

Side Dishes

Crunchy Sweet Potatoes

Serves 6

$ Total Cost: $5.89
Calories: 353.94
Fat: 14.49 grams
Protein: 8.43 grams
Cholesterol: 10.43 mg
Sodium: 329.75 mg

4 sweet potatoes, peeled and cubed

¼ cup brown sugar

¼ cup pineapple juice

½ teaspoon cinnamon

2 tablespoons honey

1 teaspoon salt

⅛ teaspoon pepper

2 tablespoons butter

⅓ cup coconut

½ cup granola

Since the granola is added at the end of cooking time, it stays crunchy. This recipe has a wonderful combination of flavors and textures.

1. In 4-quart slow cooker, combine cubed sweet potatoes, brown sugar, pineapple juice, cinnamon, honey, salt, pepper, and butter. Cover and cook on low for 7–9 hours or until potatoes are tender.
2. Using a potato masher, partially mash the potatoes; stir well. In small saucepan over medium heat, toast coconut, stirring frequently, until browned, about 5–7 minutes. Sprinkle over potatoes, then top with granola.
3. Cover and cook on high for 20–30 minutes longer until hot, then serve.

Cheesy Carrots

 Serves 8

$ Total Cost: $4.89
Calories: 289.43
Fat: 15.39 grams
Protein: 10.94 grams
Cholesterol: 78.43 mg
Sodium: 498.23 mg

8 carrots, sliced

1 cup water

2 tablespoons butter

1 (8-ounce) package process American cheese, cubed

1 (3-ounce) package cream cheese, cubed

1 teaspoon dried thyme leaves

⅓ cup milk

Even picky eaters will love this recipe. A creamy, cheesy sauce surrounds tender carrots. It's the perfect side dish for any entrée.

1. In 3-quart slow cooker, combine carrots, water, and butter. Cover and cook on low for 5–6 hours or until carrots are tender.
2. Drain carrots and return to slow cooker. Stir in American cheese, cream cheese, thyme, and milk; mix gently. Cover and cook on low for 2 hours, stirring once during cooking time, until smooth sauce forms. Serve immediately.

American Cheese

American cheese is a highly processed cheese. It's made from real cheese, but has emulsifiers, additives, flavorings, and color added. It's used in many Crock-Pot recipes just because it melts very well and doesn't separate or become rubbery in the low, moist heat. You can substitute shredded Cheddar cheese, but stir it in just at the end of cooking.

Creamed Corn

 Serves 6

1 (16-ounce) package frozen corn

1 (15-ounce) can creamed corn

⅓ cup mascarpone cheese

1 (3-ounce) package cream cheese, cubed

2 tablespoons butter

2 tablespoons honey

⅓ cup milk

⅛ teaspoon pepper

½ teaspoon dried thyme leaves

Corn combined with two kinds of cheese makes one delicious side dish. Try this one alongside a baked ham.

1. In 3-quart slow cooker, combine all ingredients and mix well. Cover and cook on low heat for 3–4 hours until blended.
2. Stir gently to combine. Serve or hold on low heat for 2 hours, stirring occasionally.

Garlic and Herb Mashed Potatoes

Serves 6

Total Cost: $4.39
Calories: 389.42
Fat: 15.39 grams
Protein: 10.43 grams
Cholesterol: 25.39 mg
Sodium: 279.25 mg

6 potatoes, peeled

3 cloves garlic, minced

½ cup water

¼ cup butter, cut into cubes

½ teaspoon dried thyme leaves

1 (3-ounce) package cream cheese, cubed

⅓ cup ricotta cheese

½ cup milk

1 teaspoon salt

⅛ teaspoon pepper

First cook the potatoes to tender perfection in the slow cooker, then mash them with delicious ingredients to make some of the best mashed potatoes anywhere!

1. In a 4-quart slow cooker, combine potatoes with garlic and water. Cover and cook on low for 7–8 hours or until potatoes are tender.
2. Drain potatoes and return to hot slow cooker. Add butter and dried thyme leaves; mash until smooth.
3. Beat in remaining ingredients until potatoes are fluffy. Cover and cook on low for 2 hours longer, stirring once during cooking time. You can hold the potatoes on low for another hour before serving.

Mashed Potatoes

To make the best mashed potatoes, first cook them until quite tender, then return to the hot pot to remove some of the excess moisture. Always add the fat first, because it will coat the starch granules and keep them from clumping together. Then beat in liquids and remaining ingredients. This is the way to make the fluffiest mashed potatoes.

Grandma's Peas and Carrots

Serves 6

$ Total Cost: $3.79
Calories: 128.25
Fat: 3.29 grams
Protein: 2.18 grams
Cholesterol: 10.94 mg
Sodium: 208.35 mg

6 carrots, sliced

1 onion, chopped

2 cloves garlic, minced

½ cup water

2 tablespoons butter

2 tablespoons honey

½ teaspoon salt

⅛ teaspoon white pepper

½ teaspoon dried marjoram leaves

2 cups frozen baby peas

Carrots take a long time to cook in the slow cooker, while peas take just a brief period, mainly to heat through. They both turn out perfectly in this simple recipe.

1. In 3-quart slow cooker, combine all ingredients except peas and mix well. Cover and cook on low heat for 7–8 hours or until carrots are tender.
2. Stir gently and turn heat to high. Add frozen peas and stir again. Cover and cook on high for 15–25 minutes or until peas are hot and tender. Serve immediately.

Tater Tot Casserole

 Serves 6

💲 Total Cost: $5.58

🍗 Calories: 389.25

Fat: 18.93 grams

Protein: 10.42 grams

Cholesterol: 38.91 mg

Sodium: 589.93 mg

1 (16-ounce) bag frozen Tater Tots, thawed

1 (10-ounce) can condensed potato soup

1 (12-ounce) can evaporated milk

¼ cup chopped fresh chives

⅛ teaspoon white pepper

1 cup shredded Cheddar cheese

¼ cup grated Romano cheese

½ teaspoon paprika

This delicious recipe uses Tater Tots to make a rich and creamy side dish. Serve this with fried chicken, some cooked carrots, and a gelatin salad.

1. In 4-quart slow cooker, combine all ingredients except Romano cheese and paprika; mix well. Sprinkle with Romano cheese and paprika.
2. Cover and cook on low for 5–7 hours, stirring twice during cooking time, until mixture is hot and potatoes are tender. Serve immediately.

Tater Tots

Tater Tots is a registered trademark for a type of potato side dish, first made in 1953 by the Ore-Ida company. The grated or shredded potatoes are pressed into ovals, then deep fried. They are crisp and creamy at the same time, and kids love them. They do fall apart a bit in the slow cooker, but still taste delicious.

Mashed Sweet Potatoes

 Serves 6

$ Total Cost: $4.59
Calories: 163.42
Fat: 4.69 grams
Protein: 2.49 grams
Cholesterol: 0.0 mg
Sodium: 238.17 mg

4 large sweet potatoes

1 (6-ounce) can pineapple-
  orange juice, divided

2 tablespoons olive oil

1 tablespoon minced fresh
  ginger root

½ teaspoon salt

⅛ teaspoon pepper

This is the perfect dish for Thanksgiving dinner. Make it about an hour ahead of time and keep the potatoes warm in a slow cooker.

1. Peel the sweet potatoes and cut into 1inch chunks. Place in 4-quart slow cooker; add the pineapple-orange juice. Cover and cook on low for 8-9 hours or until potatoes are tender.
2. Drain and return to hot pot. Add olive oil and ginger root; mash using a potato masher. Add salt and pepper and stir until combined. Serve immediately or hold on warm up to 2 hours.

CHAPTER 11

SANDWICHES

210   Vegetarian Picadillo Sandwiches

211   BBQ Beef Sandwich Filling

212   Chicken Cheese Pitas

213   Meat Filled Pitas

214   Pizza Burgers by the Yard

215   Chili Quesadillas

216   Texas BBQ Beef Sandwiches

217   Creamy Dried Beef Sandwiches

218   Meatball Marinara Sandwiches

219   French Dip Sandwiches

220   Apricot Ham Wraps

221   Sloppy Joes

222   BBQ Sandwiches

223   Beef and Bean Wraps

224   Veggie Submarine Sandwich

225   Enchilada Sandwiches

226   Thai Chicken Wraps

227   Sloppy Janes

228   Greek Pita Turkey Sandwiches

229   Ham and Veggie Wraps

Vegetarian Picadillo Sandwiches

Serves 6

💲 Total Cost: $5.64

Calories: 413.23

Fat: 6.51 grams

Protein: 19.16 grams

Cholesterol: 0.0 mg

Sodium: 548.02 mg

1 tablespoon vegetable oil

1 onion, chopped

1 green bell pepper, chopped

1 (15-ounce) can black-eyed peas, drained

1 (8-ounce) can tomato sauce

1 teaspoon Tabasco sauce

½ teaspoon salt

1 tablespoon cornstarch

2 tablespoons water

½ cup raisins

¼ cup sliced green olives

¼ cup sliced almonds

3 whole wheat pita breads

You can keep this filling in the fridge and let your kids heat up a portion at a time in the microwave oven (about 30 seconds on high) to make their own sandwiches using pita bread.

1. In large skillet, heat olive oil over medium heat. Add onion; cook and stir for 3 minutes. Place in 2-quart slow cooker along with bell pepper, black-eyed peas, tomato sauce, Tabasco, and salt and bring to a simmer.
2. Cover and cook on low for 6–7 hours or until vegetables are tender. Dissolve cornstarch in water and add along with raisins, olives, and almonds to slow cooker. Stir well and cook on high for 15–20 minutes longer. Serve in pita breads.

BBQ Beef Sandwich Filling

Serves 4

$ Total Cost: $6.29
Calories: 302.05
Fat: 7.59 grams
Protein: 42.00 grams
Cholesterol: 102.00 mg
Sodium: 700.09 mg

1 pound beef chuck roast, trimmed
¼ cup Beef Stock (page 233)
¼ cup taco sauce
2 onions, chopped
½ teaspoon salt

⅛ teaspoon pepper
4 cloves garlic, minced
1 jalapeño pepper, minced
2 teaspoons chili powder
⅓ cup ketchup
2 tablespoons lime juice

This hearty sandwich filling is great for a winter party. Double it, cook in a 5-quart Crock-Pot, let the mixture cook all day, and your home will smell wonderful; plus, the filling for the sandwiches is ready whenever you are.

1. Place beef, Stock, taco sauce, onion, salt, pepper, garlic, jalapeño, chili powder, and ketchup in 3-quart Crock-Pot. Cover and cook on low for 7–9 hours or until beef is very tender. Remove beef from Crock-Pot and shred.

2. Return beef to Crock-Pot. Cover and cook on low for 1–2 hours longer. Stir in lime juice, then make sandwiches with shredded beef mixture, warmed flour tortillas or pita bread, and sour cream.

Shredding Beef

It's very easy to shred beef, especially when it's cooked in the moist heat of the Crock-Pot. Remove the beef from the liquid it cooks in and let stand for a few minutes on a large platter. Using 2 forks, pull the meat apart into long strands, returning the shredded meat to the cooking liquid as you work.

Chicken Cheese Pitas

Serves 4

$ Total Cost: $5.76
Calories: 326.58
Fat: 15.83 grams
Protein: 26.00 grams
Cholesterol: 83.91 mg
Sodium: 620.14 mg

1 green bell pepper, chopped

1 onion, chopped

2 cloves garlic, minced

4 boneless, skinless chicken thighs

½ teaspoon salt

⅛ teaspoon pepper

¼ cup Chicken Stock (page 234)

1 cup diced Muenster cheese

¼ cup grated Parmesan cheese

2 tablespoons honey Dijon mustard

3 pita breads, cut in half

6 slices butter lettuce

You can substitute any cheese you'd like in this simple recipe; any vegetable too, for that matter. It's delicious for an easy lunch.

1. Place bell pepper, onion, and garlic in a 3-quart slow cooker. Sprinkle chicken with salt and pepper and add to slow cooker. Pour Stock over all.
2. Cover and cook on low for 7–8 hours or until chicken is thoroughly cooked. Remove chicken from slow cooker, shred, and return to slow cooker.
3. Turn slow cooker off and stir in cheeses. Cover and let stand for 5–8 minutes. Meanwhile, spread mustard inside the cut pita bread halves. Add lettuce, then fill with chicken mixture and serve.

Pita Breads

Pita breads are Greek in origin. The little round breads are hollow inside, so they can be cut in half and filled. They make a nice neat sandwich that's easy to eat. The breads are baked at a very high temperature, which makes the air and water inside turn to steam. They literally "explode" in the oven, but are held together by the gluten in the dough.

The $7 a Meal Slow Cooker Cookbook

Meat Filled Pitas

 Serves 4

$ Total Cost: $6.17
Calories: 395.48
Fat: 18.23 grams
Protein: 27.10 grams
Cholesterol: 80.40 mg
Sodium: 849.23 mg

¾ pound ground beef

1 cup mushrooms, chopped

1 onion, chopped

2 cloves garlic, minced

1 (8-ounce) can tomato sauce

½ teaspoon dried oregano

½ teaspoon salt

⅛ teaspoon cayenne pepper

⅓ cup grated Parmesan cheese

2 pita breads

4 leaves Romaine lettuce, shredded

1 cup grated mozzarella cheese

You can make the filling ahead of time, then chill it in the fridge. Let your family take out about ⅓ cup at a time, heat in the microwave, then fill the pita breads and eat!

1. Cook ground beef in medium skillet until browned, stirring to break up meat. Combine in 2-quart slow cooker with mushrooms, onion, garlic, tomato sauce, oregano, salt, and pepper.
2. Cover and cook on low for 6–7 hours or until mixture is hot and blended. Stir in Parmesan cheese.
3. Make sandwiches with lettuce, pita breads, meat filling, and mozzarella cheese.

Pizza Burgers by the Yard

 Serves 6

1 onion, chopped

3 cloves garlic, minced

1 (4-ounce) can sliced mushrooms

½ (12-ounce) package meat-less crumbles, thawed

½ (6-ounce) can tomato paste

½ teaspoon dried basil leaves

½ teaspoon dried oregano leaves

¼ teaspoon cayenne pepper

½ loaf Italian bread

2 tablespoons butter, softened

1 cup shredded part-skim mozzarella cheese

¼ cup grated Parmesan cheese

This is the sandwich to make when you're serving a crowd! You can double the mixture and cook it in a 6-quart Crock-Pot to serve 12. Top it with anything that strikes your fancy.

1. In 3-quart slow cooker, combine onion, garlic, mushrooms, crumbles, tomato paste, basil, oregano, and pepper. Cover and cook on low for 5–7 hours or until mixture is hot and vegetables are tender.
2. Preheat oven to broil. Cut loaf in half lengthwise and place cut side up on cookie sheet. Spread butter over each piece of bread. Broil for 1–2 minutes or until bread is almost crisp.
3. Spread crumbles mixture on each half of loaf. Broil about 6-inches from heat source for 7–9 minutes or until hot. Remove from oven and sprinkle with cheeses. Return to oven and broil for 3–5 minutes longer until cheese melts and begins to bubble. Cut into slices to serve.

Chili Quesadillas

 Serves 6

$ Total Cost: $6.11
Calories: 408.21
Fat: 22.26 grams
Protein: 14.92 grams
Cholesterol: 50.58 mg
Sodium: 875.23 mg

8 (8-inch) flour tortillas

½ cup sour cream

1 (4-ounce) can green chiles, drained

1 cup shredded Cheddar cheese

½ cup shredded Swiss cheese

2 tablespoons butter

2 cups Homemade Chili (page 289)

This hearty dish could serve 8–10 as an appetizer (cut into eighths). If you'd like, top it with sour cream and more cheese.

1. In small bowl, combine sour cream with green chiles and mix well. Place tortillas on work surface. Spread mixture onto all tortillas. Top with cheeses, then put tortillas together to make four quesadillas.
2. Melt butter on large skillet over medium heat until sizzling. Add quesadillas and cook, turning once, until tortillas are toasted and cheese is melted. While quesadillas are cooking, heat Chili in microwave until hot.
3. Cut quesadillas into-quarters and place on serving dish; spoon hot Chili over all. Serve immediately.

Quesadillas

You can make quesadillas out of practically anything. They are an excellent way to use up leftovers. Try Veggie Quesadillas, made of leftover cooked vegetables, some taco sauce, and shredded cheese. Or Turkey Quesadillas are a delicious way to use up leftovers after Thanksgiving, and give the meat a new taste.

Texas BBQ Beef Sandwiches

Serves 4

1 pound chuck roast, cubed

½ cup cola

1 onion, chopped

3 cloves garlic, minced

1 jalapeño pepper, minced

½ cup taco sauce

2 tablespoons mustard

4 Kaiser rolls

Cola adds a sweet and caramel flavor to a chuck roast, which mimics a barbecued flavor. This recipe can easily be doubled to serve a crowd.

1. In 3-quart slow cooker, combine all ingredients except mustard and rolls. Cover and cook on low for 7–9 hours or until beef is very tender.
2. Using two forks, shred beef and stir mixture. Using a slotted spoon, remove beef and vegetables from the liquid in the slow cooker. Combine with mustard in medium bowl.
3. Make sandwiches with the meat mixture and rolls. Serve immediately.

Creamy Dried Beef Sandwiches

Serves 4

💲 Total Cost: $7.00
Calories: 450.46
Fat: 28.43 grams
Protein: 15.28 grams
Cholesterol: 88.29 mg
Sodium: 793.42 mg

3 green onions, chopped

5 ounces dried beef

½ (8-ounce) package cream cheese

⅓ cup milk

2 tablespoons mustard

1 tomato, sliced

8 slices cracked wheat bread

2 tablespoons butter

Dried beef becomes mellow and tender when cooked with a mustard flavored cream cheese mixture. This makes a wonderful sandwich filling.

1. Cut the dried beef into ¼-inch cubes. Rinse briefly and drain. Combine in 2-quart slow cooker with onions, cream cheese, milk, and mustard. Cover and cook on low for 2 hours, stirring twice during cooking time.
2. Spread bread with butter and toast, if desired. Make sandwiches with the hot filling, the bread, and tomato. Serve immediately.

Dried Beef

There are many different types of dried beef. Bunderfleisch, from Switzerland, is like a thinly sliced beef jerky. Bresaola, from Italy, is similar to prosciutto but is more highly flavored. And plain old dried beef in America, usually sold in jars, was the source for Chipped Beef on Toast, an old diner recipe from the 1950s.

Meatball Marinara Sandwiches

Serves 4

$ Total Cost: $6.88

Calories: 495.30

Fat: 22.81 grams

Protein: 26.01 grams

Cholesterol: 120.44 mg

Sodium: 1042.43 mg

¾ pound lean ground beef

¼ cup dry bread crumbs

3 tablespoons milk

1 egg

½ teaspoon dried Italian seasoning

½ teaspoon salt

⅛ teaspoon pepper

1 (14-ounce) jar tomato pasta sauce

4 hoagie buns

½ cup shredded Monterey jack cheese

Tender meatballs cooked in pasta sauce are the perfect filling on toasted hoagie buns topped with melted cheese.

1. In large bowl combine beef, bread crumbs, milk, egg, Italian seasoning, salt, and pepper and mix gently but thoroughly. Form into 16 meatballs. Heat large skillet over medium heat and brown meatballs, shaking pan to turn, about 2–3 minutes.
2. Drain well and add to 3-quart slow cooker. Top with pasta sauce. Cover and cook on low for 7–8 hours or until meatballs are thoroughly cooked.
3. Split and toast the hoagie buns. Top with meatballs, some of the sauce, and shredded cheese. Serve immediately.

French Dip Sandwiches

 Serves 4

$ Total Cost: $7.00
Calories: 513.13
Fat: 22.42 rams
Protein: 39.01 grams
Cholesterol: 103.23 mg
Sodium: 734.66 mg

1 pound bottom round beef roast

1 teaspoon seasoned salt

⅛ teaspoon pepper

2 tablespoons oil

2 cups Beef Stock (page 233)

1 bay leaf

3 cloves garlic, minced

1 teaspoon dried thyme

4 crusty French sandwich buns

2 tablespoons butter

These sandwiches are stuffed with very tender beef cooked in the slow cooker.

1. Trim excess fat off beef and rub with salt and pepper. Heat oil in large skillet and brown beef on all sides, about 8 to 10 minutes. Place beef in 3-quart slow cooker with remaining ingredients except buns and butter.
2. Cover and cook on low for 8 to 9 hours, until beef is very tender. Remove beef from broth and strain broth. Slice beef thinly against the grain.
3. Toast sandwich buns and spread with butter. Pile beef in buns and make sandwiches. Serve strained broth on the side for dipping.

French Dip

These sandwiches didn't originate in France. They got their name from the French rolls the beef is served in. The sandwiches themselves are rather plain; it's the savory and highly flavored broth they are served with that adds much of the appeal. Each diner gets a small cup of the broth to dip the sandwich in as they eat.

Sandwiches

Apricot Ham Wraps

 Serves 4

Total Cost: $6.59
Calories: 304.91
Fat: 6.39 grams
Protein: 10.29 grams
Cholesterol: 39.29 mg
Sodium: 429.05 mg

½ pound fully cooked ham, cubed

½ cup apricot preserves

1 onion, chopped

3 cloves garlic, minced

⅓ cup chopped dried apricots

2 tablespoons prepared mustard

1 green bell pepper, chopped

½ cup sour cream

2 tablespoons cornstarch

This delicious recipe has so many flavors and it's pretty too. Serve with tortillas, or with romaine lettuce for wraps.

1. In 5-quart slow cooker, combine ham, preserves, onions, garlic, apricots, and mustard; mix well. Cover and cook on low for 8 hours.
2. Add bell peppers to slow cooker. Cover and cook on low for 1 hour. In small bowl, combine sour cream and cornstarch. Stir into ham mixture. Cover and cook on low for 30 minutes.
3. Gently stir mixture. Serve in homemade buns, tortillas, or lettuce wraps. Can be served warm or cold.

Sloppy Joes

 Serves 4

 Total Cost: $5.63
Calories: 428.91
Fat: 16.28 grams
Protein: 19.21 grams
Cholesterol: 46.02 mg
Sodium: 493.01 mg

¾ pound 80% lean ground beef

1 onion, chopped

3 cloves garlic, minced

2 carrots, chopped

1 (6-ounce) can tomato paste

½ cup tomato juice

1 tablespoon chili powder

1 tablespoon Worcestershire sauce

4 hoagie buns, split and toasted

This sandwich filling is rich and flavorful, just right for a cold winter day. You can serve this filling in plain hamburger buns too.

1. In large skillet, cook ground beef until browned, stirring to break up meat. Drain thoroughly, but do not wipe out skillet. In a 3-quart slow cooker, combine cooked beef with onions, garlic, and carrots; mix well.
2. In skillet that you used for the beef, combine tomato paste, juice, chili powder, and Worcestershire sauce. Bring to a simmer over medium heat, stirring until a sauce forms. Pour into slow cooker.
3. Cover and cook on low for 5–6 hours. Toast buns and serve with the beef filling.

Sloppy Joe Filling

There are many uses for Sloppy Joe filling. Spread it between tortillas with some cheese and grill to make Sloppy Quesadillas. It can also be enclosed in crescent roll dough and baked, for neater sandwiches. And it also makes an excellent hot dip with tortilla chips.

BBQ Sandwiches

 Serves 4

 Total Cost: $6.83
Calories: 431.89
Fat: 14.21 grams
Protein: 43.29 grams
Cholesterol: 69.28 mg
Sodium: 402.55 mg

½ pound boneless beef chuck roast

¼ pound boneless pork loin roast

1 onion, chopped

3 stalks celery with leaves, chopped

½ cup barbecue sauce

½ cup ketchup

¼ cup brown sugar

2 tablespoons apple cider vinegar

4 onion buns, split and toasted

Combining beef and pork makes a rich and savory sandwich filling. You can also use tortillas to make wrap sandwiches.

1. Cut beef and pork into 2-inch cubes. Place onions and celery in bottom of 3-quart slow cooker and top with meat.
2. In medium bowl combine remaining ingredients except onion buns; stir well. Pour into slow cooker. Cover and cook on low for 8–9 hours or until meat is very tender. Stir well, using a fork if necessary, to help break up meat.
3. To serve, spoon some barbecue on the onion buns, making sandwiches.

Beef and Bean Wraps

 Serves 5

$ Total Cost: $6.58
🔥 Calories: 479.04
Fat: 20.42 grams
Protein: 16.32 grams
Cholesterol: 42.78 mg
Sodium: 481.50 mg

¾ pound 80% lean ground beef

1 onion, chopped

2 cloves garlic, minced

1 (15-ounce) can refried beans

1 (10-ounce) can enchilada sauce

1 tablespoon chili powder

½ teaspoon salt

⅛ teaspoon pepper

5 (7-inch) corn tortillas

½ cup shredded Cheddar cheese

½ cup sour cream

2 cups shredded lettuce

These are basically burritos, made in the slow cooker. The refried beans add a rich flavor and smooth texture to this hearty filling.

1. In large skillet, cook ground beef with onions and garlic over medium heat, stirring to break up beef, until beef is thoroughly cooked.
2. Drain beef mixture and combine with refried beans, enchilada sauce, chili powder, salt, and pepper in 3-quart slow cooker; mix well.
3. Cover and cook on low for 8–9 hours until mixture is hot and blended. If necessary, thicken with a mixture of 2 tablespoons cornstarch and ¼ cup water; cover and cook on high for 20–30 minutes.
4. Serve mixture with tortillas, cheese, sour cream, and lettuce, and let people make their own wraps.

Refried Beans

Refried beans add great flavor and texture to sandwiches and many other recipes. They are a very inexpensive and delicious source of protein, fiber, and B vitamins. You can find them in several varieties and flavors. Look for vegetarian refried beans to avoid lard. Flavored beans are usually made with onions, garlic, and chiles.

Veggie Submarine Sandwich

Serves 5

$ Total Cost: $6.33
Calories: 304.12
Fat: 7.01 grams
Protein: 8.34 grams
Cholesterol: 29.17 mg
Sodium: 258.30 mg

1 onion, chopped

1 zucchini, sliced

1 yellow summer squash, sliced

½ pound fresh green beans, trimmed

2 cloves garlic, minced

½ teaspoon salt

⅛ teaspoon white pepper

½ cup water

3 tablespoons mustard

3 tablespoons honey

⅓ cup mayonnaise

5 hoagie buns, split

1 cup shredded Cheddar cheese

Vegetables cook to tender perfection in the slow cooker to save you time and energy. Then make a buffet and let everybody create their own masterpiece!

1. Combine all vegetables in 3-quart slow cooker. Sprinkle with salt and pepper; toss. Pour water into slow cooker. Cover and cook on low for 4–6 hours or until vegetables are tender.
2. Drain vegetables and place in large bowl. In medium bowl, combine mustard, honey, and mayonnaise; mix well.
3. Lay out the split buns, cheese, mayonnaise mixture, and vegetables. Let people make their own sandwiches.

Enchilada Sandwiches

 Serves 5

1 onion, chopped

2 cloves garlic, minced

1 jalapeño pepper, minced

1 cup enchilada sauce

1 (15-ounce) can black beans, drained

½ cup Suave Cooked Salsa (page 31)

2 teaspoons chili powder

½ teaspoon salt

⅛ teaspoon pepper

½ (8-ounce) package cream cheese, cubed

5–6 (8-inch) flour tortillas

1 cup shredded CoJack cheese

1½ cups shredded lettuce

You can use this filling to make enchiladas, too. Just roll up flour or corn tortillas with the filling and some cheese, place in a greased baking dish, top with more cheese, and bake until hot.

1. In 3-quart slow cooker, combine the onions, garlic, jalapeño peppers, enchilada sauce, black beans, Salsa, chili powder, salt, and pepper. Mix well.
2. Cover and cook on low for 8–9 hours or until mixture is thoroughly cooked. Stir cream cheese into slow cooker.
3. Uncover and cook on high for 20–30 minutes or until mixture is thickened. Serve with tortillas and remaining ingredients to make wrap sandwiches.

Beans

There are many types of beans, or legumes, which are all nutritious and delicious. Black beans, kidney beans, Great Northern beans, and black-eyed peas can all be found in dried and canned forms. The canned type is more expensive, but is much easier to use. Drain the beans and rinse them before using for best results.

Thai Chicken Wraps

 Serves 4

$ Total Cost: $5.28

Calories: 356.92

Fat: 16.39 grams

Protein: 21.17 grams

Cholesterol: 57.39 mg

Sodium: 519.12 mg

¾ pound ground chicken

1 onion, chopped

2 cloves garlic, minced

1 tablespoon minced fresh gingerroot

2 tablespoons low-sodium soy sauce

¾ cup Chicken Stock (page 234)

⅓ cup peanut butter

1 tablespoon sugar

⅛ teaspoon pepper

2 tablespoons cornstarch

3 tablespoons lemon juice

1 cup shredded carrots

46 large lettuce leaves

These flavorful wrap sandwiches are a good healthy choice for lunch on the porch.

1. In large skillet, cook chicken until almost done, stirring to break up meat. Drain chicken and place in 3-quart slow cooker.
2. Add onions, garlic, gingerroot, Chicken Stock, soy sauce, peanut butter, sugar, and pepper; stir.
3. Cover and cook on low for 4–5 hours or until chicken is thoroughly cooked and mixture is hot and blended. In small bowl, combine cornstarch and lemon juice and mix well. Stir into slow cooker.
4. Cover and cook on high for 20–25 minutes or until mixture thickens. To serve, set out filling, shredded carrots, and lettuce leaves to use for wraps.

Sloppy Janes

 Serves 4

💲 Total Cost: $6.29
🍴 Calories: 349.18
Fat: 12.84 grams
Protein: 20.74 grams
Cholesterol: 78.39 mg
Sodium: 419.28 mg

¾ pound ground turkey

1 onion, chopped

2 cloves garlic, minced

2 stalks celery

2 carrots, chopped

1 (6-ounce) can tomato paste

½ cup tomato juice

1 teaspoon dried basil leaves

½ teaspoon salt

⅛ teaspoon pepper

4 slices American cheese

4 hamburger buns, split

What do you call a Sloppy Joe filling made from turkey? Sloppy Janes, of course! These delicious sandwiches are lower in fat.

1. In large skillet, cook turkey until browned, stirring to break up meat. Drain thoroughly, but do not wipe out skillet. In a 3-quart slow cooker, combine cooked turkey with onions, garlic, celery, and carrots; mix well.

2. In skillet that you used for the turkey, combine tomato paste, juice, basil, salt, and pepper. Bring to a simmer over medium heat, stirring until a sauce forms. Pour into slow cooker.

3. Cover and cook on low for 6–7 hours. Place one slice American cheese on each split hamburger bun, and make sandwiches with the turkey filling.

Sloppy Janes

Like Sloppy Joes (page 221), this is a versatile recipe that can be flavored in many ways. For Greek Sloppy Janes, add some oregano instead of basil, a tablespoon of lemon juice, use feta cheese, add some olives, and serve on onion buns. For Tex-Mex Sloppy Janes, use taco sauce instead of tomato juice, add a jalapeño pepper, and use pepper jack cheese.

Greek Pita Turkey Sandwiches

Serves 4

$ Total Cost: $6.12
Calories: 429.93
Fat: 15.92 grams
Protein: 22.16 grams
Cholesterol: 54.79 mg
Sodium: 392.55 mg

¾ pound spicy bulk turkey sausage

1 onion, chopped

2 cloves garlic, minced

2 tablespoons flour

1 cup Chicken Stock (page 234)

½ teaspoon salt

⅛ teaspoon pepper

½ teaspoon lemon peel

½ teaspoon dried oregano leaves

½ cup plain yogurt

¼ cup grated Parmesan cheese

1 cucumber, peeled, seeded, and chopped

2 tablespoons lemon juice

¼ cup crumbled feta cheese

4 whole wheat pita breads

Greek flavors include lemon, feta, yogurt, oregano, and olives. This easy sandwich is simple to make and fun, too.

1. In large skillet, brown sausage with onions and garlic over medium heat, stirring to break up meat. When done, sprinkle with flour; cook and stir for 1 minute.
2. Add Stock; cook and stir to loosen pan drippings. Bring to a boil. Add salt, pepper, lemon peel, and oregano.
3. Pour into 2-quart slow cooker. Cover and cook on low for 6–7 hours or until turkey is thoroughly cooked.
4. Meanwhile, combine remaining ingredients except pita breads in large bowl; cover and refrigerate.
5. When turkey is done, use a slotted spoon to remove the mixture from the slow cooker. Make sandwiches with the pita breads and the yogurt filling; serve immediately.

The $7 a Meal Slow Cooker Cookbook

Ham and Veggie Wraps

 Serves 5

💲 Total Cost: $6.33
Calories: 308.18
Fat: 10.42 grams
Protein: 9.32 grams
Cholesterol: 56.27 mg
Sodium: 493.54 mg

1 onion, chopped

2 carrots, sliced

3 potatoes, peeled and cubed

1 teaspoon dried basil leaves

1 cup Chicken Stock (page 234)

1 green bell pepper, chopped

1½ cups cubed cooked ham

½ cup mayonnaise

¾ cup shredded Cheddar cheese

5 flour tortillas

You can add just about any vegetable to this simple and hearty wrap sandwich. Think about using different colors and flavors of tortillas to add interest to the spread.

1. Place onions, carrots, potatoes, basil, and Stock in 3-quart slow cooker. Cover and cook on low for 6 hours or until vegetables are almost tender.
2. Add bell peppers and ham to slow cooker. Cover and cook on low for 2–3 hours longer or until ham is hot and bell peppers are crisp-tender.
3. Drain mixture and place in large bowl. Add mayonnaise and cheese, and mix well. Make wraps with flour tortillas; serve immediately.

Variations

Use any veggies you'd like in this simple recipe. Remember that more tender vegetables cook in a shorter amount of time, so add them during the last 2 hours of cooking time. Root vegetables take the longest time to cook of any ingredient, so make sure they are in the bottom of the slow cooker.

CHAPTER 12

SOUPS

231 Chicken and Rice Stewp

232 Bacon and Black-Eyed Pea Soup

233 Beef Stock

234 Chicken Stock

235 Vegetable Dumpling Soup

236 Black Bean Soup

237 Puffy Dumplings

238 Slow-Cooker Pozole

239 Old-Fashioned Chicken Soup

240 Spinach Beet Borscht

241 Vegetable Broth

242 Updated Onion Soup

243 Split Pea Soup

244 Autumn Soup

245 Minestrone

246 Vichyssoise

247 Golden Potato Soup

248 Lima Bean Soup

249 Broccoli Cheese Soup

250 Creamy Ginger-Pumpkin Soup

251 Chicken Corn Soup

252 Curried Chicken Noodle Soup

253 Beer Cheese Soup

254 Tex-Mex Soup

255 French Onion Soup

256 Slow-Cooker Stroganoff Soup

Chicken and Rice Stewp

 Serves 4

 Total Cost: $6.60
Calories: 440.69
Fat: 13.76 grams
Protein: 39.85 grams
Cholesterol: 119.27 mg
Sodium: 893.12 mg

1 pound boneless, skinless
   chicken thighs
2 tablespoons flour
1 teaspoon paprika
½ teaspoon salt
⅛ teaspoon pepper
3 carrots, sliced
1 onion, chopped

2 cloves garlic, minced
2 cups Chicken Stock
   (page 234)
3 cups water
1 (14-ounce) can diced
   tomatoes, undrained
½ cup long grain rice
2 cups frozen green beans

A "stewp" is like a stew and a soup combined; it's thicker than a soup but not as thick as a stew.

1. Cut chicken thighs into 1-inch pieces and sprinkle with flour, paprika, salt, and pepper. Toss well to coat evenly.
2. Place carrots, onion, and garlic in 3-quart slow cooker and top with coated chicken. Add Chicken Stock, water, and undrained tomatoes and mix well.
3. Cover slow cooker and cook on low for 8 hours. Turn slow cooker to high, add rice and green beans, and cook for 60 to 80 minutes longer until chicken is done and rice and vegetables are tender.

Bacon and Black-Eyed Pea Soup

Serves 6

4 slices bacon

1 onion, chopped

4 cloves garlic, minced

1 tablespoon chili powder

3 cups Chicken Stock (page 234)

3 cups water

1 (14-ounce) can diced tomatoes with chiles

2 (15-ounce) cans black-eyed peas, drained

3 carrots, sliced

1 cup grated Muenster cheese

This rich soup simmers all day in your Crock-Pot. Serve it with corn bread made from a mix for a fabulous lunch or dinner.

1. In heavy skillet, cook bacon over medium heat until crisp; remove bacon, drain on paper towels, crumble, and set aside in refrigerator.
2. In drippings remaining in skillet, cook onion and garlic, until vegetables are crisp-tender, about 4–5 minutes. Place in a 4 to 5-quart Crock-Pot. Add remaining ingredients except bacon and cheese to Crock-Pot, cover, and cook on low for 8–9 hours until vegetables are tender.
3. Add reserved bacon to soup, stir, and cook on high for 20–30 minutes. Top with cheese and serve.

Food Lore

Black-eyed peas are considered a good luck food in the South. Every Southerner eats this legume in one form or another on New Year's Eve and New Year's Day to guarantee good luck for the rest of the year. Serve this soup at your New Year's party and join the tradition. You could use dried beans instead of canned in this recipe to save $1.00.

Beef Stock

 Yields 12 cups

3-pounds leftover beef bones and trimmings

10 cups water

2 onions, chopped

2 carrots, chopped

3 cloves garlic, minced

1 tomato, chopped

¼ cup chopped celery leaves

2 teaspoons salt

½ teaspoon pepper

1 bay leaf

1 teaspoon dried thyme leaves

Once again your slow cooker comes to the rescue to make a rich and flavorful Beef Stock.

1. Preheat oven to 400°F. Place beef bones, onions, and carrots on baking sheet. Roast for 40–50 minutes or until bones begin to brown.
2. Combine bones, onions, and carrots, and trimmings with all ingredients in a 5–6-quart slow cooker. Cover and cook on low for 8–10 hours. When stock tastes rich, strain and refrigerate overnight. The next day, remove the fat from the surface of the stock and discard. Freeze stock up to 3 months.

Chicken Stock

Yields 12 cups

$ Total Cost: $2.98
Calories: 98.69
Fat: 6.94 grams
Protein: 6.78 grams
Cholesterol: 31.75 mg
Sodium: 42.64 mg

2 pounds leftover chicken backs, bones, necks

2 onions, chopped

2 carrots, chopped

3 cloves garlic, minced

1 tablespoon olive oil

10 cups water

3 celery stalks, chopped

¼ cup chopped celery leaves

2 teaspoons salt

½ teaspoon pepper

Use your slow cooker to make Chicken Stock for a big batch with almost no work at all. Freeze in 1-cup portions or in ice cube trays.

1. Preheat oven to 400°F. Place chicken, onions, and carrots on baking sheet and drizzle with olive oil. Roast for 30–40 minutes or until chicken begins to brown.
2. Combine roasted chicken, onions, and carrots with all ingredients in a 5–6-quart slow cooker. Cover and cook on low for 8–10 hours. When stock tastes rich and chickeny, strain and refrigerate overnight. The next day, remove the fat from the surface of the stock and discard. Freeze stock up to 3 months.

Cheapest Chicken Stock

If you buy bone-in chickens, chicken breasts, chicken thighs, or drumsticks for a recipe, save the bones and store them in the freezer until you have a couple of pounds. Season the stock however you'd like. And yes, you can use the bones after they have been cooked; in that case, don't roast them first, just simmer.

Vegetable Dumpling Soup

 Serves 6

$ Total Cost: $6.30
↘ Calories: 426.03
Fat: 23.53 grams
Protein: 10.12 grams
Cholesterol: 115.89 mg
Sodium: 555.64 mg

2 tablespoons olive oil

1 onion, chopped

4 cloves garlic, minced

3 carrots, sliced

3 cups Vegetable Broth (page 241)

5 cups water

2 cups frozen corn

1 cup frozen green beans

1 yellow summer squash, sliced

1 teaspoon dried Italian seasoning

1 Recipe Puffy Dumplings (page 237)

⅓ cup grated Parmesan cheese

Dumplings add great texture to this rich vegetable soup. All you need to add is a fruit salad, and dinner is complete.

1. In 5-quart slow cooker, combine all ingredients except Dumplings and cheese. Cover and cook on low for 7–8 hours or until vegetables are tender.
2. Prepare dough for Dumplings. Turn slow cooker to high. Drop dumplings by teaspoonfuls into simmering soup. Cover and simmer for 20–25 minutes or until dumplings are puffed and cooked through. Sprinkle with cheese and serve.

Black Bean Soup

Serves 6

$ Total Cost: $3.74
Calories: 334.23
Fat: 3.87 grams
Protein: 20.07 grams
Cholesterol: 3.60 mg
Sodium: 249.57 mg

1 pound dried black beans

1 onion, chopped

3 cloves garlic, minced

2 stalks celery, minced

1 jalapeño pepper, minced

1 tablespoon chili powder

½ teaspoon salt

¼ teaspoon cayenne pepper

4 cups water

4 cups Chicken Stock (page 234)

2 tablespoons masa harina

⅓ cup water

Black beans, also called turtle beans, make the most wonderful soup. Their meaty flavor and creamy texture enhance the vegetables in this easy recipe.

1. Sort and rinse black beans and cover with cold water. Let stand overnight. In the morning, drain beans, discard soaking water, and combine in a 4 to 5-quart Crock-Pot with remaining ingredients except masa harina and ⅓ cup water. Cover and cook on low for 8–10 hours until beans are soft.

2. Turn Crock-Pot to high. In small bowl, mix masa harina with water and blend well. Stir into soup, mixing well. Cook on high for 30 minutes, stirring once during cooking, until soup is thickened. Serve with sour cream and guacamole.

Ham Bones

You can add a ham bone to any bean soup recipe. You can usually buy ham bones right in your supermarket's meat aisle. You may have to ask the butcher for the bones. A ham bone adds a rich flavor to soups, especially when long simmered as in Crock-Pot recipes. If you can't find one, substitute 1 cup of chopped cooked ham.

The $7 a Meal Slow Cooker Cookbook

Puffy Dumplings

 Serves 8

$ Total Cost: $1.54
Calories: 183.47
Fat: 13.06 grams
Protein: 3.82 grams
Cholesterol: 84.17 mg
Sodium: 251.66 mg

½ cup water

½ cup milk

½ cup butter

1 cup flour

¼ teaspoon salt

2 eggs

You can add these little dumplings, based on cream puff dough, to any broth or soup recipe. Be sure to simmer the dumplings covered for best results.

1. In medium saucepan, combine water, milk, and butter and bring to a full boil over high heat. Add flour and salt all at once. Cook and stir until mixture forms a ball and cleans sides of pan. Remove from heat and add eggs, one at a time, beating well after each addition.
2. Have soup at a simmer on high heat in the slow cooker. Drop Dumpling dough into the pot, working quickly, using a teaspoon for each dumpling. Cover pot and simmer for 20–25 minutes without lifting lid. Uncover pot and check if dumplings are cooked through. If not, cover and simmer another 2–4 minutes.

Slow-Cooker Pozole

 Serves 4

$ Total Cost: $6.04	¾ pound boneless pork loin roast
Calories: 302.12	

Total Cost: $6.04
Calories: 302.12
Fat: 12.00 grams
Protein: 19.13 grams
Cholesterol: 53.58 mg
Sodium: 892.42 mg

¾ pound boneless pork loin roast

1 onion, chopped

2 cloves garlic, minced

1 (15-ounce) can hominy, drained

4 cups water

1 (4-ounce) can diced green chiles, undrained

1 tablespoon chili powder

1 teaspoon cumin

1 teaspoon salt

½ teaspoon dried oregano

Chiles, pork, and hominy combine in your slow cooker to make a rich hearty soup perfect for a cold day. Serve it with a crisp green salad and some hot corn bread.

1. Cut pork into 1-inch cubes and place in a 3½-quart Crock-Pot with all remaining ingredients; stir well. Cover and cook on low for 6–8 hours until pork is very tender.
2. Serve soup in warmed bowls and garnish with sour cream, tortilla chips, and chopped avocado.

Slow Cooker Hints
Make sure that your Crock-Pot is filled ½ to ⅔ full for best results. Don't lift the lid to stir the food or check on progress, especially when cooking on low, because you lose 20 minutes of cooking time each time it's lifted. Place vegetables on the bottom and chop or slice food so it's all the same size.

Old-Fashioned Chicken Soup

Serves 6

Total Cost: $6.57
Calories: 324.54
Fat: 13.90 grams
Protein: 25.48 grams
Cholesterol: 84.96 mg
Sodium: 677.69 mg

2 tablespoons vegetable oil

8 bone-in chicken thighs

2 tablespoons flour

1 teaspoon salt, divided

¼ teaspoon pepper, divided

1 onion, chopped

4 cloves garlic, minced

3 stalks celery, chopped

4 carrots, peeled and sliced

1 bay leaf

1 teaspoon dried thyme leaves

3 cups Chicken Stock (page 234)

5 cups water

2 cups egg noodles

You can use Puffy Dumplings (page 237) instead of the egg noodles; be sure to add the cost numbers for Puffy Dumplings if you choose to use them instead.

1. In large stockpot, heat oil over medium heat. Sprinkle chicken with flour, ½ teaspoon salt, and ⅛ teaspoon pepper, and place, skin side down, in the hot oil. Cook until browned, about 4–6 minutes, then remove and set aside. To drippings remaining in skillet, add onion and garlic; cook and stir, scraping up pan drippings, until crisp tender, about 4 minutes.
2. Place onion mixture in 4-quart slow cooker. Add chicken and all remaining ingredients except egg noodles. Cover and cook on low for 8–9 hours or until chicken and vegetables are tender.
3. Remove chicken from slow cooker; remove and discard skin and bones. Tear chicken into bite-sized pieces and return to soup.
4. Turn heat to high. Either drop egg noodles into the soup, or drop Puffy Dumpling batter into soup by teaspoonfuls; cover and simmer the noodles for 10–15 minutes; the Dumplings for 20–25 minutes, or until egg noodles or Dumplings are cooked through. Remove bay leaf and serve soup immediately.

Spinach Beet Borscht

Serves 5

$ Total Cost: $6.65
Calories: 269.43
Fat: 9.66 grams
Protein: 11.28 grams
Cholesterol: 21.58 mg
Sodium: 832.43 mg

4 slices bacon

1 onion, chopped

3 cloves garlic, minced

2 (15-ounce) cans sliced beets

1 (6-ounce) can tomato paste

3 cups Chicken Stock (page 234)

½ teaspoon dill seed

½ teaspoon salt

⅛ teaspoon pepper

1 tablespoon apple cider vinegar

2 cups spinach leaves, chopped

½ cup sour cream

¼ cup chopped parsley

A hot bacon and beet soup is poured over spinach leaves to wilt the leaves and make them tender. A sour cream garnish finishes the soup to perfection.

1. In medium saucepan, cook bacon until crisp; remove bacon to paper towel to drain; crumble and refrigerate. In drippings remaining in saucepan, cook onion and garlic until tender, about 5 minutes.
2. Combine onion mixture with beets, tomato paste, Chicken Stock, dill seed, salt, and pepper in 3-quart slow cooker. Cover and cook on low for 6-7 hours until vegetables are soft.
3. Using an immersion blender or potato masher, mash some of the beets, leaving some whole. Stir in apple cider vinegar.
4. Divide spinach leaves among six soup bowls and pour hot soup over spinach. Garnish with sour cream, reserved bacon, and parsley.

Purchased Broths and Stocks

Purchased broths and stocks, although inexpensive, are far more expensive than home-made broth. They are also much higher in sodium. Boxed stocks are the most expensive, but taste the closest to homemade. Take some time to make homemade stock. It's easy in the slow cooker, and you can freeze it for later use.

Vegetable Broth

Yields 8 cups

$ Total Cost: $2.44
Calories: 39.52
Fat: 1.86 grams
Protein: 0.74 grams
Cholesterol: 0.0 mg
Sodium: 323.22 mg

2 tablespoons olive oil

2 onions, chopped

3 carrots, chopped

2 tomatoes, sliced

3 stalks celery, sliced

4 cloves garlic

1 teaspoon salt

¼ teaspoon white pepper

7 cups water

These really are the best vegetables to use when making your own broth. You could also add bell peppers and a turnip, but don't use potatoes; they make the broth cloudy.

1. In large heavy skillet, heat olive oil over medium high heat. Add onions and carrots; cook and stir until vegetables begin to brown. Remove to 4 to 5-quart slow cooker. Add 1 cup water to drippings remaining in skillet; bring to a boil; boil for 1 minute, stirring to loosen drippings in bottom of pan.
2. Pour mixture into slow cooker; add remaining ingredients. Cover and cook on low for 8–10 hours.
3. Strain broth, discarding vegetables. Let the broth cool for 30 minutes, then strain into freezer containers and seal. Freeze up to 3 months. To thaw, let stand in refrigerator overnight.

Updated Onion Soup

 Serves 6

Total Cost: $6.26
Calories: 354.69
Fat: 15.06 grams
Protein: 12.37 grams
Cholesterol: 33.57 mg
Sodium: 372.43 mg

1 tablespoon vegetable oil

3 tablespoons butter, divided

4 large onions, chopped

3 cloves garlic, minced

½ cup dry white wine

1 tablespoon dried thyme
   leaves

½ teaspoon pepper

3 cups Chicken Stock
   (page 234)

2 cups Beef Stock (page 233)

1 cup water

6 slices French bread, toasted

⅓ cup grated Parmesan
   cheese

1 cup grated Gruyere cheese

Using Chicken Stock and Beef Stock lightens up traditional Onion Soup. This soup is a whole meal—don't serve it as a starter because it's too filling.

1. In 2-quart Crock-Pot, heat oil and 1 tablespoon butter with high heat. Add onions and garlic. Cook, stirring every hour, until onions begin to turn brown, about 4–5 hours.
2. Add the wine, thyme, and pepper and stir well. Transfer to a 4-quart Crock-Pot, then add both kinds of Stock and water, cover, and cook on high for 2–3 hours until soup is blended.
3. Preheat the broiler. Spread the French bread with remaining 2 tablespoons butter. In a small bowl, combine the cheeses. Sprinkle cheeses over the bread.
4. Ladle the soup into ovenproof bowls. Top each serving with a slice of the bread. Place on a heavy duty cookie sheet and slide under the broiler. Broil for 2 to 3 minutes or until cheese bubbles and starts to brown. Serve immediately.

Sliced or Chopped?

You can slice or chop onions when making onion soup. Chopped onions make the soup easier to eat because they fit neatly onto a soup spoon, while the thin slices can slip off the spoon. The flavor will be the same with either type of prepared onion, so it's your choice.

Split Pea Soup

 Serves 6

$ Total Cost: $3.49
Calories: 389.14
Fat: 5.58 grams
Protein: 19.10 grams
Cholesterol: 0.0 mg
Sodium: 663.02 mg

2 tablespoons vegetable oil

1 onion, chopped

3 carrots, sliced

3 celery stalks, sliced

2 cloves garlic, minced

½ teaspoon dried thyme leaves

¼ teaspoon pepper

1 teaspoon Worcestershire sauce

½ teaspoon Tabasco sauce

1 bay leaf

2 cups dried green split peas, rinsed

8 cups water

1 pound potatoes, peeled and diced

1 teaspoon salt

Split peas don't need to be soaked before cooking like whole peas do.

1. In 4–5-quart slow cooker, combine all ingredients. Cover and cook on low for 8–9 hours or until peas and potatoes are tender.
2. Using a potato masher, partially mash some of the peas and potatoes. Cover Crock-Pot and cook on high for 10–15 minutes or until soup is thickened and blended. Serve immediately.

Autumn Soup

Serves 4

 Total Cost: $6.97

Calories: 322.40

Fat: 6.13 grams

Protein: 14.89 grams

Cholesterol: 64.97 mg

Sodium: 324.12 mg

4 cups Chicken Stock (page 234)

1 onion, chopped

3 cloves garlic, minced

2 slices firm white bread, cut into cubes

2 Granny Smith apples, peeled, cored, and chopped

½ butternut squash, seeded, peeled, and cubed

1 tablespoon fresh rosemary leaves, minced

½ teaspoon dried marjoram leaves

½ teaspoon pepper

1 egg

1 cup buttermilk

The squash gives this one-pot meal a beautiful golden color. It's also delicious served cold; you may need to thin it with some additional buttermilk.

1. In a 4–5-quart slow cooker, combine Stock, onion, garlic, bread, apples, and the squash. Cover and cook on low for 6–7 hours or until squash is tender.

2. Using an immersion blender, purée the soup. Add rosemary, marjoram, and pepper. In a small bowl, combine egg and buttermilk and beat well. Stir some of the hot soup into the egg mixture, beating with a wire whisk. Add all of the warmed egg mixture to the soup.

3. Cover and cook on high for 10–15 minutes, stirring twice, until steam rises, but do not let the soup simmer. Serve immediately.

Preparing Squash

Winter squashes can take some skill to prepare. Using a sharp chef's knife, cut the squash in half. Once it is cut in half, turn the squash cut side down and cut each half in half. Scoop out the seeds with a large spoon, then use a swivel-bladed peeler to remove the skin. Cut the squash into cubes and proceed with the recipe.

Minestrone

 Serves 4

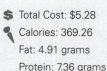 Total Cost: $5.28
Calories: 369.26
Fat: 4.91 grams
Protein: 7.36 grams
Cholesterol: 4.0 mg
Sodium: 392.53 mg

1 onion, chopped

3 cloves garlic, minced

1 (14-ounce) can diced tomatoes, undrained

2 cups Vegetable Broth (page 241)

3 cups water

½ teaspoon salt

½ teaspoon dried thyme leaves

1 (15-ounce) can garbanzo beans, drained

1 zucchini, sliced

2 cups chopped cabbage

1 cup small shell pasta

¼ cup grated Parmesan cheese

Minestrone is a classic Italian soup made from vegetables, beans, and pasta. There are many variations around; this simple one is satisfying and inexpensive.

1. Combine all ingredients except zucchini, cabbage, pasta, and cheese in 4-quart slow cooker. Cover and cook on low for 7 hours.
2. Add zucchini and cabbage and stir well; cover and cook on low for 1–2 hours longer until vegetables are tender.
3. Turn slow cooker to high and stir in pasta. Cover and cook on high for 20–30 minutes longer or until pasta is tender. Sprinkle with cheese and serve immediately.

Vichyssoise

 Serves 6

$ Total Cost: $3.90

🍗 Calories: 320.53

Fat: 8.65 grams

Protein: 8.92 grams

Cholesterol: 27.14 mg

Sodium: 612.53 mg

2 tablespoons butter

1 onion, finely sliced

3 potatoes, peeled and diced

2 cups Chicken Stock (page 234)

2 cups water

2 tablespoons cornstarch

2 cups whole milk

½ teaspoon salt

⅛ teaspoon white pepper

½ cup heavy cream

2 tablespoons minced fresh parsley

This classic soup, which sounds so expensive, is just potato and leek soup, blended until smooth and served hot or cold. Because leeks are expensive, onions are a good substitute.

1. In skillet, melt butter over medium heat. Add onions; cook and stir until translucent. Transfer to a 4-quart slow cooker and add potatoes, Stock, and water; cover and cook on low for 6–7 hours until potatoes are tender.

2. Purée the soup either by using an immersion blender, a standard blender, or forcing the soup through a sieve. Return to slow cooker.

3. In small bowl combine cornstarch with 1 cup whole milk and mix well. Add to slow cooker along with remaining milk, salt, pepper, and cream, then cover and cook on high for 20–30 minutes until soup is slightly thickened. Soup can be served hot with a sprinkling of parsley, or chilled and served cold with some diced fresh chives.

Blending Hot Liquids

Hot liquids expand in the blender, so whether you're blending a soup or a sauce, don't fill the blender all the way to the top. Filling it half way and blending in batches is the safest way. Remember to cover the lid with a folded kitchen towel; hold onto the towel to keep the lid down.

Golden Potato Soup

 Serves 6

$ Total Cost: $5.64
Calories: 325.03
Fat: 11.71 grams
Protein: 10.44 grams
Cholesterol: 35.33 mg
Sodium: 683.42 mg

1 sweet potato, peeled and cubed

5 russet potatoes, peeled and cubed

1 onion, chopped

1 carrot, chopped

3 cups Chicken Stock (page 234)

4 cups water

1 teaspoon salt

3 tablespoons butter

1 (12-ounce) can evaporated milk

Carrots and sweet potatoes add lots of Vitamin A and lend a golden tint to this easy and inexpensive soup.

1. Combine all ingredients except the butter and milk in a 4–5-quart slow cooker. Cover and cook on low for 8–9 hours until potatoes are tender.
2. Using an immersion blender or potato masher, mash the soup until smooth. Stir in butter and milk; turn heat to high. Cover and cook for 30–40 minutes or until soup is hot and blended.

Lima Bean Soup

 Serves 6

 Total Cost: $6.48

Calories: 379.32

Fat: 7.40 grams

Protein: 21.15 grams

Cholesterol: 26.13 mg

Sodium: 893.26 mg

12-ounce package lima beans	1 teaspoon salt
1 onion, chopped	¼ teaspoon pepper
2 carrots, sliced	1 teaspoon dried oregano leaves
3 cloves garlic, minced	
3 potatoes, peeled and cubed	3 cups Beef Stock (page 233)
8 ounces kielbasa, sliced	3 cups water
	1 bay leaf

Lima beans are delicious, pillowy, and nutty-tasting, with a soft texture. They're a nice choice for this flavorful soup.

1. Sort lima beans and rinse, then cover with cold water and soak overnight. In the morning, drain beans and rinse again.
2. Combine all ingredients in 5-quart slow cooker. Cover and cook on low for 8–9 hours or until beans and potatoes are tender. Remove bay leaf and using a potato masher, mash some of the beans and potatoes.

Dried Beans

Dried beans are one of the cheapest foods in the supermarket, and they are so good for you. Beans are full of fiber and B vitamins, and are fat and sodium-free. Dried beans take a bit more work, but are well worth it. You can soak the beans overnight, or cover with water and boil for 2 minutes, then let stand for 1 hour; use as directed.

Broccoli Cheese Soup

Serves 6

$ Total Cost: $5.77
🌶 Calories: 349.52
Fat: 20.12 grams
Protein: 15.91 grams
Cholesterol: 59.73 mg
Sodium: 497.23 mg

1 tablespoons butter

1 tablespoon olive oil

1 onion, chopped

2 cloves garlic, minced

⅛ teaspoon pepper

½ teaspoon dried basil leaves

1 (10-ounce) package frozen cut broccoli

3 cups Chicken Stock (page 234)

1 (10-ounce) can condensed Cheddar cheese soup

2 cups milk

1 (3-ounce) package cream cheese, cubed

1 cup diced process American cheese

The combination of cream cheese and American cheese makes a mild and creamy soup that everyone will love. The condensed soup adds extra flavor and texture.

1. Turn 4-quart slow cooker to high. Add butter and olive oil and heat until melted. Add onions and garlic. Cook, uncovered, for 30 minutes.
2. Stir onions and garlic, then add pepper, basil, broccoli, stock, and soup. Stir well, then cover and cook on low for 5–6 hours or until broccoli is very tender.
3. Turn off slow cooker. Using an immersion blender or potato masher, purée the broccoli in the soup. Stir in remaining ingredients.
4. Cover and cook on low for 1–2 hours or until cheese melts and soup is hot. Stir to combine, then serve immediately.

Creamy Ginger-Pumpkin Soup

Serves 4

1 (15-ounce) can solid-pack pumpkin

1 onion, chopped

2 cloves garlic, minced

1 teaspoon ground ginger

4 cups Chicken Stock (page 234)

1 cup water

1 teaspoon salt

¼ teaspoon white pepper

½ teaspoon dried marjoram leaves

½ cup heavy cream

¼ cup sour cream

2 tablespoons cornstarch

Pumpkin soup is creamy, velvety, hearty, and delicious. It tastes like an expensive treat, but doesn't cost much.

1. In 3-quart slow cooker, combine pumpkin with onions, garlic, and ginger; mash to combine. Gradually stir in Stock, stirring with wire whisk until blended.
2. Add water, salt, pepper, and marjoram. Stir to combine. Cover and cook on low for 5–6 hours or until soup is hot and blended.
3. In medium bowl combine heavy cream, sour cream, and cornstarch; mix well. Stir into soup, cover, and cook on high for 30 minutes or until soup is hot.

Canned Pumpkin

Use only solid-pack canned pumpkin in soup recipes, unless it calls for pumpkin pie filling. Pumpkin pie filling has extra ingredients, including sugar, seasonings, and emulsifiers, which will make the soup too sweet and thin. Read labels carefully, and make sure that the ingredient list specifies just pumpkin and salt.

Chicken Corn Soup

 Serves 6

$ Total Cost: $6.88
Calories: 306.32
Fat: 13.85 grams
Protein: 19.56 grams
Cholesterol: 56.52 mg
Sodium: 592.64 mg

2 tablespoons butter

1 tablespoon vegetable oil

1 onion, chopped

3 cloves garlic, minced

2 boneless, skinless chicken
breasts, cubed

1 (10.75-ounce) can cream
of chicken soup

2 cups Chicken Stock
(page 234)

3 cups water

½ teaspoon dried basil leaves

⅛ teaspoon pepper

1 cup frozen corn

1 (15-ounce) can cream-style
corn

1 cup shredded Swiss cheese

This delicious soup is slightly creamy and perfect with
the Swiss cheese melting into each spoonful.

1. In large skillet, melt butter and oil over medium heat. Add
   onion and garlic; cook and stir until crisp-tender, about 5
   minutes. Place in 4-quart slow cooker.
2. Add remaining ingredients except cheese to slow cooker.
   Keep cheese refrigerated until ready to serve. Stir to blend.
   Cover and cook on low for 7–8 hours or until chicken is
   thoroughly cooked and soup is blended. Stir in cheese until
   melted, and serve.

Curried Chicken Noodle Soup

Serves 4

$ Total Cost: $5.08
Calories: 339.18
Fat: 13.90 grams
Protein: 23.24 grams
Cholesterol: 72.64 mg
Sodium: 620.35 mg

2 tablespoons butter

1 tablespoon olive oil

2 boneless, skinless chicken breasts

½ teaspoon salt

⅛ teaspoon pepper

2 tablespoons curry powder

1 onion, chopped

3 carrots, sliced

4 cups Chicken Stock (page 234)

2 cups water

2 cups egg noodles

Curry powder adds great flavor and a touch of the exotic Near East to this classic soup.

1. In large skillet, heat butter and olive oil over medium heat. Sprinkle chicken with salt, pepper, and 1 tablespoon curry powder. Add to skillet; cook, turning once, for 4–5 minutes or until chicken begins to brown.

2. Remove chicken from skillet. Add onions to skillet; cook and stir until crisp-tender, about 5 minutes; remove from heat.

3. Place carrots in 4-quart slow cooker. Add onions and chicken to slow cooker along with 1 tablespoon curry powder. Pour stock and water over all.

4. Cover and cook on low for 5–6 hours or until chicken and vegetables are tender. Remove chicken from slow cooker and shred. Return chicken to slow cooker; add noodles and stir.

5. Turn heat to high and cook for 15–20 minutes or until noodles are tender. Serve in warmed bowls, topped with minced green onion if desired.

Pasta in the Slow Cooker

It's difficult to cook pasta in the Crock-Pot, mainly because it overcooks so easily. Cooking pasta in soups, which have more liquid, works better than cooking pasta in a sauce. Be sure that you measure carefully and check the pasta consistency at the earliest time specified by the recipe.

The $7 a Meal Slow Cooker Cookbook

Beer Cheese Soup

 Serves 6

1 onion, chopped

2 carrots, chopped

3 cloves garlic, minced

1 teaspoon dried thyme leaves

½ teaspoon salt

⅛ teaspoon pepper

1 (16-ounce) bottle beer

3 cups Chicken Stock (page 234)

2 cups milk

2 cups shredded sharp Cheddar cheese

2 tablespoons cornstarch

¼ cup grated Parmesan cheese

3 cups popped popcorn

The alcohol doesn't fully cook out of this soup, so serve it only to adults.

1. In 3–4-quart slow cooker, combine onion, carrots, garlic, thyme, salt, pepper, beer, and Chicken Stock. Cover and cook on low for 8–9 hours.
2. Add milk to slow cooker; cook on low for 1 hour. In medium bowl, mix Cheddar cheese with cornstarch and toss to coat. Add to slow cooker, cover, and cook on high for 20–25 minutes or until cheese is melted and soup is thickened. Stir in Parmesan cheese, then serve with popcorn.

Tex-Mex Soup

 Serves 4

$ Total Cost: $5.37
🍦 Calories: 260.34
Fat: 8.38 grams
Protein: 20.93 grams
Cholesterol: 44.96 mg
Sodium: 728.13 mg

1 tablespoon vegetable oil

1 onion, chopped

½ pound boneless pork chops

1 (14-ounce) can diced
  tomatoes, undrained

½ teaspoon dried oregano
  leaves

½ teaspoon salt

⅛ teaspoon crushed red
  pepper flakes

1½ cups water

1 cup enchilada sauce

1 cup Chicken Stock (page 234)

This rich soup uses canned enchilada sauce for a kick.
You could also use taco sauce if you'd like.

1. Heat vegetable oil in a saucepan over medium heat and
   cook onion until crisp-tender. Meanwhile, cut pork chops
   into 1-inch pieces, discarding excess fat. Add to pan; cook
   and stir until pork is browned, about 4 minutes.
2. Add along with remaining ingredients to 3-quart slow
   cooker. Cover and cook on low for 7–8 hours or until pork is
   thoroughly cooked and mixture is slightly thickened. Garnish
   with fresh cilantro, tortilla chips, and sour cream.

French Onion Soup

 Serves 6

$ Total Cost: $6.13
Calories: 330.34
Fat: 12.08 grams
Protein: 12.79 grams
Cholesterol: 24.05 mg
Sodium: 462.92 mg

1 tablespoon olive oil

5 onions, chopped

4 cloves garlic, minced

1 teaspoon sugar

½ cup dry red wine

4 carrots, sliced

5 cups Beef Stock (page 233)

½ teaspoon salt

⅛ teaspoon pepper

½ teaspoon dried marjoram leaves

1 (3-ounce) package low-fat cream cheese, softened

1 cup shredded Swiss cheese

6 slices French bread

Making this classic soup in the slow cooker helps reduce the fat. All you have to do at the end is ladle it into bowls and top with cheese toasts.

1. In 4 to 5-quart slow cooker, combine olive oil, onions, garlic, and sugar. Cover and cook on high for 1–2 hours, stirring occasionally, until the onions are deep golden brown. Halfway through cooking time, add the red wine. Do not let this burn.

2. Add carrots, Stock, salt, pepper, and marjoram. Cover and cook on low for 4–5 hours. Meanwhile, in small bowl, combine cream cheese and Swiss.

3. Preheat broiler. Spread cheese mixture on bread slices and broil until cheese begins to brown. Spoon soup into hot bowls and top with bread.

Slow Cooking Onions

Because the onions won't fill the slow cooker at least halfway, you'll need to stir them occasionally to prevent burning. For this reason, in the first step you can't just set the slow cooker and walk away. The method used in this recipe causes the onions to become very sweet and caramelized, and they add great flavor to this classic soup.

Slow-Cooker Stroganoff Soup

Serves 6

$ Total Cost: $6.77

Calories: 352.34

Fat: 9.38 grams

Protein: 24.97 grams

Cholesterol: 54.25 mg

Sodium: 478.19 mg

¾ pound sirloin tip, cubed

1 onion, chopped

4 cloves garlic, minced

3 carrots, sliced

½ teaspoon salt

½ teaspoon dried thyme leaves

⅛ teaspoon pepper

3 cups Beef Stock (page 233)

2 cups water

½ cup sour cream

2 tablespoons flour

2 cups egg noodles

Stroganoff made into soup makes a festive addition to any meal. Serve in warmed soup bowls.

1. In 4-quart slow cooker, combine beef, onions, garlic, carrots, salt, thyme, pepper, Beef Stock, and water. Cover and cook on low for 7–8 hours or until beef and vegetables are tender.
2. In small bowl combine sour cream with flour. Add 1 cup of the hot liquid from slow cooker; mix with wire whisk. Add sour cream mixture to slow cooker. Cover and cook on high for 20–25 minutes or until soup thickens. Stir in egg noodles; cook for 6–7 minutes longer until noodles are tender.

CHAPTER 13

SALADS

258   Layered Chicken and Bean Salad

259   Chicken Slaw Salad

260   Ham and Potato Salad

261   Beef Taco Salad

262   German Potato Salad

263   Classic Chicken Salad

264   Tex-Mex Steak and Potato Salad

265   Chicken and Wild Rice Salad

266   Potato Seafood Salad

267   Black-Eyed Pea and Rice Salad

268   Curried Barley and Potato Salad

269   Potato Salad

270   Wild Rice Salad

271   Grandma's Best Chicken Salad

272   Southwest Potato Salad

273   Ham and Wild Rice Salad

274   Chicken Taco Salad

Layered Chicken and Bean Salad

 Serves 6

$ Total Cost: $6.35
Calories: 425.34
Fat: 19.42 grams
Protein: 20.83 grams
Cholesterol: 83.49 mg
Sodium: 430.25 mg

2 cups Slow Cooker Red Beans (page 185), cooled

2 Slow Cooker Simmered Chicken Breasts (page 104), cubed

3 cups spinach leaves

2 cups torn lettuce

1½ cups frozen corn, thawed

1 cup salsa

½ cup sour cream

1 cup grated Muenster cheese

Layered salads are easy to make and inexpensive, but they look festive and fancy.

1. Prepare Beans and Chicken; chill if hot.
2. Combine spinach leaves and lettuce in serving bowl. Top with beans, then corn. Spoon salsa on top. Add chicken, then sour cream and cheese.
3. Cover and chill for 3–4 hours. To serve, toss salad together and serve immediately.

Chicken Slaw Salad

Serves 4

$ Total Cost: $4.89

Calories: 328.49

Fat: 11.23 grams

Protein: 26.93 grams

Cholesterol: 80.43 mg

Sodium: 263.49 mg

4 cups chopped purple cabbage

2 cups chopped green cabbage

1 green bell pepper, chopped

½ cup mayonnaise

¼ cup buttermilk

½ teaspoon dried dill weed

3 Slow Cooker Simmered Chicken Breasts (page 104), cubed

1 cup frozen peas, thawed

This easy salad can be varied in many ways. Add different chopped vegetables, add chopped ham or turkey, or add cubed cheese; whatever you have on hand.

1. Combine all ingredients in large bowl. Cover and chill for 3–4 hours before serving.

Cabbage

Cabbage is one of the cheapest foods in the supermarket, and it's so good for you. It's a member of the cruciferous family, with tons of antioxidants and cancer-fighting properties. It is in season year-round, and has a fresh taste and wonderful crisp crunch. Add it to everything from salads to Crock-Pot stews.

Ham and Potato Salad

 Serves 5

3 potatoes, peeled and cubed

1 sweet potato, peeled and cubed

1 onion, chopped

2 cloves garlic, minced

½ cup Chicken Stock (page 234)

1 cup cubed ham

½ cup mayonnaise

½ cup plain yogurt

¼ cup milk

¼ cup yellow mustard

½ teaspoon salt

⅛ teaspoon pepper

1 teaspoon dried basil leaves

1 green bell pepper, chopped

4 stalks celery, chopped

Cooking ham and potatoes together in the slow cooker makes a wonderful base for a ham salad. Add dressing and it's waiting for you in the fridge!

1. In 3½-quart slow cooker, combine potatoes, sweet potatoes, onions, garlic, stock, and cubed ham. Cover and cook on low for 8–9 hours or until potatoes are tender when pierced with fork. Drain if necessary.
2. In large bowl, combine mayonnaise, yogurt, milk, mustard, salt, pepper, and dried basil; mix well. Remove hot potato mixture from slow cooker with large slotted spoon or sieve. Stir into dressing in bowl, then add remaining ingredients and stir gently to coat.
3. Cover and refrigerate for 3–4 hours or until salad is cold. Stir gently before serving.

Beef Taco Salad

Serves 5

$ Total Cost: $6.85
Calories: 444.84
Fat: 22.94 grams
Protein: 24.11 grams
Cholesterol: 75.71 mg
Sodium: 802.43 mg

¾ pound ground beef

1 onion, chopped

2 cloves garlic, minced

1 jalapeño chile, minced

1 tablespoon chili powder

¾ cup taco sauce

¾ cup cubed processed American cheese food

3 cups shredded lettuce

1 green bell pepper, chopped

1½ cups corn chips

¾ cup shredded Cheddar cheese

Processed cheese food, a classic Tex-Mex ingredient, is made with emulsifiers so it melts perfectly, every time. There's really no substitute.

1. In heavy skillet, cook ground beef, onion, garlic, and jalapeño until beef is browned, stirring to break up meat. Drain if necessary, place in 2-quart slow cooker. Add chili powder and taco sauce.
2. Cover and cook on low for 6–7 hours or until vegetables are tender. Uncover and stir in cheese food. Cover and cook on low for 30 minutes longer.
3. Place lettuce, bell pepper, and corn chips on serving plate. Top with beef mixture, then sprinkle with Cheddar cheese. Serve immediately.

Make-Ahead Tips

Ground beef, processed cheese food, taco sauce, and corn chips are the "authentic" Tex-Mex ingredients in this yummy salad. You can make the beef mixture ahead of time, but don't add the cheese. Refrigerate until you're ready to eat, then reheat beef mixture, add cheese, and proceed with the recipe.

German Potato Salad

Serves 6

$ Total Cost: $5.08

Calories: 371.06

Fat: 14.32 grams

Protein: 10.82 grams

Cholesterol: 36.55 mg

Sodium: 630.45 mg

3 slices bacon

1 onion, chopped

2 cloves garlic, minced

6 potatoes, peeled and chopped

½ pound Polish sausage, sliced

¾ cup water

½ teaspoon salt

⅛ teaspoon pepper

½ cup apple cider vinegar

⅓ cup brown sugar

3 tablespoons cornstarch

⅓ cup sour cream

Hot salads like this one are good for a cold winter night. The small amounts of bacon and sausage are really just used for flavor.

1. In medium skillet, cook bacon until crisp. Drain on paper towels, crumble, and set aside. Drain fat from skillet. Cook onion and garlic in drippings remaining in skillet for 3–4 minutes.
2. Combine bacon, onion, garlic, potatoes, sausage, water, salt, and pepper in 4-quart slow cooker. Cover and cook on low for 7–8 hours or until potatoes are tender.
3. In small bowl combine vinegar, brown sugar, and cornstarch; stir well. Stir into slow cooker; cover and cook on high for 20–30 minutes. Then stir in sour cream; cook on high for 10–15 minutes until hot. Serve immediately.

Classic Chicken Salad

 Serves 4

$ Total Cost: $6.93
Calories: 300.52
Fat: 9.88 grams
Protein: 37.03 grams
Cholesterol: 110.52 mg
Sodium: 606.43 mg

5 boneless, skinless chicken breasts

½ teaspoon salt

⅛ teaspoon pepper

½ teaspoon dried thyme leaves

½ cup Chicken Stock (page 234)

1 onion, chopped

2 cloves garlic, minced

½ cup mayonnaise

⅓ cup sour cream

2 tablespoons milk

½ cup chopped celery

2 tablespoons chopped parsley

A classic chicken salad consists mostly of perfectly cooked chicken, along with a creamy dressing and some onion.

1. Combine chicken, salt, pepper, thyme, Chicken Stock, onion, and garlic in 4-quart slow cooker. Cover and cook on low for 6–7 hours or until chicken is thoroughly cooked.
2. In large bowl, combine remaining ingredients and mix until smooth. Remove chicken from slow cooker and cut into 1-inch cubes. Add to dressing as you work. Remove onions from slow cooker with slotted spoon and add to chicken mixture.
3. Fold everything together, cover, and chill for 3–4 hours before serving.

Chicken Breasts

Boneless, skinless chicken breasts have a tendency to overcook in the newer slow cookers. Most will cook to 165°F in about 6 hours. If you have a new slow cooker, check the chicken after 5 hours just to be sure. Bone-in, skin-on chicken breasts cook in 7–8 hours.

Salads

Tex-Mex Steak and Potato Salad

Serves 4

$ Total Cost: $6.38
Calories: 386.94
Fat: 16.93 grams
Protein: 26.39 grams
Cholesterol: 71.49 mg
Sodium: 450.21 mg

¾ pound sirloin tip

2 teaspoons chili powder

½ teaspoon salt

⅛ teaspoon pepper

3 potatoes, peeled and cubed

1 onion, chopped

2 cloves garlic, minced

1 jalapeño pepper, minced

1 (16-ounce) jar mild salsa

½ cup mayonnaise

⅓ cup plain yogurt

1 green bell pepper, chopped

½ cup cubed pepper jack cheese

¼ cup chopped fresh cilantro

Cooking sirloin tip and potatoes together until tender is a wonderful way to make a lot of salad with ease. This is a good choice for a summer picnic.

1. Cut sirloin into 1-inch pieces. Sprinkle with chili powder, salt, and pepper. Place potatoes, onions, garlic, and jalapeño in bottom of 3-quart slow cooker. Top with beef. Pour half of the salsa over all. Cover and cook on low for 8–9 hours or until beef and potatoes are tender.
2. In large bowl, combine remaining salsa, mayonnaise, yogurt, bell pepper, and cheese; mix well. Remove hot beef mixture from slow cooker with large slotted spoon or sieve and add to mixture in bowl. Stir gently to coat. Discard liquid left in slow cooker.
3. Cover and refrigerate for 4–5 hours until cold. Stir gently before serving, and top with cilantro.

Chicken and Wild Rice Salad

Serves 5

💲 Total Cost: $6.49

🥄 Calories: 429.94

Fat: 20.54 grams

Protein: 21.79 grams

Cholesterol: 89.43 mg

Sodium: 439.55 mg

1 cup wild rice

1 onion, chopped

3 boneless, skinless chicken breasts, cubed

2 cups Chicken Stock (page 234)

½ teaspoon salt

¼ teaspoon pepper

1 teaspoon dried thyme leaves

½ cup apple juice

¾ cup mayonnaise

½ cup yogurt

¼ cup apple juice

1 cup seedless red grapes

2 stalks celery, chopped

Yes, you can make a salad in the slow cooker! This easy recipe cooks the chicken and wild rice together, so all you have to do is add a dressing and a few more ingredients and then chill the salad.

1. In 3½-quart slow cooker, combine wild rice and onion. Place chicken on top. Sprinkle with salt, pepper, and thyme, then pour Stock and ¼ apple juice over all.

2. Cover and cook on low for 6–7 hours or until wild rice is tender and chicken is cooked.

3. In large bowl, combine mayonnaise, yogurt, and apple juice. Remove chicken mixture from slow cooker using large slotted spoon or sieve and stir into mayonnaise mixture along with remaining ingredients.

4. Cover and chill for 3–4 hours until cold. Stir gently before serving.

Wild Rice

Wild rice is not a rice, but a grass seed. It grows wild in the northern states, especially Wisconsin and Minnesota. Look for the longest grains you can find, because they cook perfectly in the Crock-Pot. If you use broken grains, they will become mushy during the long cooking time.

Potato Seafood Salad

Serves 5

$ Total Cost: $7.00
Calories: 335.22
Fat: 11.38 grams
Protein: 15.93 grams
Cholesterol: 108.45 mg
Sodium: 502.64 mg

4 russet potatoes

1 onion, chopped

2 cloves garlic, minced

½ teaspoon salt

⅛ teaspoon white pepper

2 cups water

¼ pound red snapper fish fillets

¼ pound frozen small cooked shrimp, thawed

1½ cups frozen peas

½ cup mayonnaise

½ cup plain yogurt

¼ cup seafood cocktail sauce

¼ cup whole milk

You could add even more seafood to this recipe if you'd like, stirring in drained canned crab or salmon with the potato mixture.

1. Peel potatoes and cut into cubes. Combine in 3-quart slow cooker with onions and garlic. Sprinkle with salt and pepper, then pour water over all.
2. Cover and cook on low for 8–9 hours or until potatoes are tender.
3. Turn heat to high. Place red snapper fillets on potato mixture. Cover and cook on high for 30 minutes or until fish flakes easily with fork.
4. In large bowl, combine remaining ingredients and mix well. Remove fish and potato mixture from slow cooker with large slotted spoon or sieve and add to mixture in bowl. Stir gently to coat. Cover and chill for 4–5 hours until cold. Stir gently before serving.

Black-Eyed Pea and Rice Salad

Serves 5

1½ cups dried black-eyed peas

½ cup wild rice

1 onion, chopped

1 jalapeño pepper, minced

2 carrots, sliced

4 cups water

½ cup mayonnaise

¼ cup buttermilk

3 tablespoons Dijon mustard

2 tablespoons apple cider vinegar

½ teaspoon salt

½ teaspoon dried thyme leaves

⅛ teaspoon pepper

1 yellow summer squash, sliced

The peas and rice combine to provide complete protein in this excellent and colorful main dish salad.

1. Sort and rinse peas. Place in large saucepan and cover with water. Bring to a boil; boil hard for two minutes. Remove saucepan from heat, cover, and let stand for 2 hours.
2. Drain peas and place in 3-quart slow cooker with wild rice, onions, jalapeño pepper, carrots, and water. Cover and cook on low for 8–9 hours or until peas and rice are tender. Drain well.
3. In large bowl, combine mayonnaise, buttermilk, mustard, vinegar, salt, thyme, and pepper; mix well. Stir in squash and rice mixture.
4. Cover and chill for 4–5 hours. Stir gently before serving.

Black-Eyed Peas

Black eyed peas are a traditional southern legume usually eaten with ham. If eaten on New Year's Eve, they promise good luck for the whole year. If you can't find them, you can substitute dried black beans, kidney beans, or Great Northern Beans. Whichever type you use, sort them over carefully and rinse well before cooking.

Curried Barley and Potato Salad

Serves 5

$ Total Cost: $5.98
Calories: 402.93
Fat: 15.23 grams
Protein: 13.29 grams
Cholesterol: 30.22 mg
Sodium: 439.25 mg

1 cup pearl barley

3 russet potatoes

1 onion, chopped

2 cloves garlic, minced

½ teaspoon salt

⅛ teaspoon white pepper

3 cups water

½ cup mayonnaise

⅓ cup plain yogurt

¼ cup mustard

2 tablespoons milk

1 teaspoon dried tarragon leaves

1 red bell pepper, chopped

1 cup frozen corn, thawed

Barley adds a great chewy texture and nutty flavor to potato salad. You can find vegan mayonnaise, yogurt, and milk if you're serving strict vegans.

1. Place barley in the bottom of 3-quart slow cooker. Peel potatoes and cut into cubes. Place on top of barley along with onions and garlic. Sprinkle with salt and pepper, then pour the water over all.
2. Make sure barley is covered with liquid. Cover and cook on low for 8–9 hours or until potatoes and barley are tender.
3. In large bowl, combine mayonnaise, yogurt, mustard, mustard, milk, and tarragon; mix well with wire whisk. Stir in remaining ingredients and mix well.
4. Remove hot potato mixture from slow cooker with large slotted spoon or sieve. Add to bowl and stir gently to coat. Cover and chill for 4–5 hours until cold. Stir gently before serving.

Potato Salad

 Serves 6

$ Total Cost: $4.39
Calories: 245.93
Fat: 12.47 grams
Protein: 8.38 grams
Cholesterol: 26.93 mg
Sodium: 529.21 mg

4 russet potatoes

1 onion, chopped

2 cloves garlic, minced

½ teaspoon salt

⅛ teaspoon pepper

1 cup water

½ cup mayonnaise

¼ cup whipped salad dressing

2 tablespoons Dijon mustard

¼ cup milk

4 chopped green onions

⅓ cup thinly sliced radishes

Cook your potatoes so easily in the slow cooker. They turn out tender and moist, with practically no effort on your part, perfect for potato salad.

1. Peel potatoes and cut into cubes. Combine in 3-quart slow cooker with onions and garlic. Sprinkle with salt and pepper, then pour water over.
2. Cover and cook on low for 8–9 hours or until potatoes are tender. Drain potato mixture.
3. In large bowl, combine remaining ingredients and mix well. Add hot potato mixture and stir gently to coat. Cover and chill for 4–5 hours until cold. Stir gently before serving.

Potatoes for Salad

Many people like to use red potatoes for potato salad, but russet potatoes actually absorb the flavors of the dressing better. They will absorb the flavors of salt, pepper, onion, and garlic when cooking in the slow cooker, then when added to the dressing while hot, will absorb even more.

Wild Rice Salad

 Serves 5

💲 Total Cost: $6.22

Calories: 306.23

Fat: 11.29 grams

Protein: 8.29 grams

Cholesterol: 21.28 mg

Sodium: 469.52 mg

1 cup wild rice

½ cup brown rice

1 onion, chopped

2 cups water

1 cup apple juice

½ teaspoon salt

⅛ teaspoon pepper

½ teaspoon dried thyme leaves

½ cup mayonnaise

½ cup sour cream

2 tablespoons tarragon vinegar

1 tablespoon sugar

1 red bell pepper, chopped

½ pint grape tomatoes

Wild rice and brown rice cook well in the slow cooker. This salad can be made into a main dish salad with the addition of 3–4 cups chopped cooked chicken.

1. In 2-quart slow cooker, combine wild rice, brown rice, onions, water, and apple juice. Add salt, pepper, and thyme; stir.
2. Cover and cook on high for 3–4 hours or until liquid is absorbed and the rice is tender.
3. In large bowl, combine mayonnaise, sour cream, tarragon vinegar, and sugar; mix well. Add bell peppers and tomatoes.
4. Drain rice mixture if any liquid remains, and stir into mayonnaise mixture. Cover and chill for 3–4 hours. Stir gently before serving.

The $7 a Meal Slow Cooker Cookbook

Grandma's Best Chicken Salad

 Serves 4

$ Total Cost: $5.67
Calories: 483.02
Fat: 22.18 grams
Protein: 20.16 grams
Cholesterol: 84.55 mg
Sodium: 102.33 mg

2 Slow Cooker Simmered Chicken Breasts (page 104), cubed

1 cup seedless red grapes, cut in half

3 stalks celery, chopped

½ cup golden raisins

¼ cup dark raisins

½ cup mayonnaise

¼ cup vanilla yogurt

¼ teaspoon salt

⅛ teaspoon white pepper

½ teaspoon paprika

¼ cup heavy whipping cream

You could serve this salad on split and toasted English muffins, in pita breads, or with lettuce to make low-carb wraps.

1. In large bowl, combine cubed Chicken Breasts, grapes, celery, golden and dark raisins; toss gently.
2. In medium bowl, combine mayonnaise, yogurt, salt, pepper, and paprika. In small bowl, beat cream until stiff peaks form. Fold into mayonnaise mixture.
3. Fold mayonnaise mixture into chicken mixture. Cover and chill for 1–2 hours.

Raisins

Dark and golden raisins are made from two different varieties of grapes. The lighter raisins are treated with sulfur dioxide and heated to maintain their light color. Dark raisins are usually dried just with heat, or in the sun. All raisins are naturally sweet. You can substitute one for the other in any recipe.

Southwest Potato Salad

Serves 6

$ Total Cost: $5.12
Calories: 339.23
Fat: 14.26 grams
Protein: 12.57 grams
Cholesterol: 32.68 mg
Sodium: 572.32 mg

4 russet potatoes

1 onion, chopped

3 cloves garlic, minced

1 jalapeño pepper, minced

1 tablespoon chili powder

½ teaspoon salt

⅛ teaspoon pepper

1 cup water

½ cup mayonnaise

½ cup plain yogurt

⅛ teaspoon cayenne pepper

¼ cup salsa

1½ cups frozen corn, thawed

1 cup cherry tomatoes

Cook the potatoes for this spicy salad in the slow cooker. If you don't like spicy food, leave out the jalapeño peppers.

1. Peel potatoes and cut into cubes. Combine in 3-quart slow cooker with onions, garlic, and jalapeños. Sprinkle with chili powder, salt, and pepper; then pour water into slow cooker.
2. Cover and cook on low for 8–9 hours or until potatoes are tender. Drain potato mixture.
3. In large bowl, combine mayonnaise, yogurt, pepper, and salsa. Add hot potato mixture, corn, and tomatoes and stir gently to coat. Cover and chill for 5–6 hours until cold. Stir gently before serving.

Ham and Wild Rice Salad

➤ Serves 5

💲 Total Cost: $6.32
🔥 Calories: 401.34
Fat: 20.21 grams
Protein: 21.69 grams
Cholesterol: 45.29 mg
Sodium: 749.02 mg

½ cup wild rice

1 onion, chopped

1 cup cubed ham

1 cup Chicken Stock (page 234)

½ cup water

½ teaspoon salt

¼ teaspoon pepper

1 teaspoon dried thyme leaves

¾ cup zesty Italian salad dressing

1 cup cherry tomatoes

3 stalks celery, chopped

This easy recipe cooks the ham and wild rice together, so all you have to do is add a dressing and a few more ingredients and then chill the salad.

1. In 2-quart slow cooker, combine wild rice and onion. Place ham on top. Sprinkle with salt, pepper, and thyme, then pour Stock and water over all.
2. Cover and cook on low for 6–7 hours or until wild rice is tender.
3. Remove ham mixture from slow cooker using large slotted spoon or sieve and place in large bowl. Add salad dressing and remaining ingredients. Cover and chill for 3–4 hours until cold. Stir gently before serving.

Premade Salad Dressings

There are many different types and varieties of salad dressings on the market. Zesty Italian salad dressing does have more flavor than regular Italian. The dressings that are sold in the produce aisle need to be kept refrigerated, and they cost more than the bottled dressings in the condiment aisle.

Chicken Taco Salad

 Serves 4

$ Total Cost: $5.36
Calories: 438.95
Fat: 19.43 grams
Protein: 16.84 grams
Cholesterol: 78.94 mg
Sodium: 469.32 mg

3 cups Lentil and Chicken
   Chili (page 299)

4 cups mixed lettuce

2 cups tortilla chips

1 cup cherry tomatoes

1 cup frozen corn, thawed
   and drained

1 cup grated Cheddar cheese

¼ cup chopped cilantro

Any chili is delicious layered on a salad using this technique. You could add bell peppers, black beans, and more cheese if you'd like.

1. Prepare Chili. If using leftovers, reheat in microwave for 1–2 minutes, stirring twice, until steaming.
2. Layer lettuce, chips, tomatoes, and corn on serving plates. Top with chili and cheese. Sprinkle with cilantro and serve immediately.

CHAPTER 14

STEWS, CHILIS, AND CHOWDERS

276   Classic Beef Stew

277   Southwest Chicken Stew

278   Ribollita

279   Black Bean Stew

280   Beef Chili with Beans

281   Everything Stew

282   Wild Rice Cauliflower Chowder

283   Vegetable-Barley Stew

284   Three-Bean Chili

285   Lentil Stew

286   Sausage and Potato Stew

287   Potato Corn Chowder

288   Turkey Wild Rice Chowder

289   Homemade Chili

290   Classic Beef Barley Stew

291   Jalepeño Chili

292   Salmon Chowder

293   Simple Burger Stew

294   Bean and Sausage Chowder

295   Thick Potato Chowder

296   A Bowl of Red

297   Triple Corn Chowder

298   White Chicken Chili

299   Lentil and Chicken Chili

300   Buffalo Chicken Chowder

301   Ham Chowder

Classic Beef Stew

 Serves 4

$ Total Cost: $6.58
Calories: 397.81
Fat: 8.13 grams
Protein: 37.13 grams
Cholesterol: 84.15 mg
Sodium: 709.92 mg

¾ pound round steak, cubed

3 carrots, sliced

1 onion, chopped

3 cloves garlic, minced

1 teaspoon dried thyme

⅛ teaspoon pepper

3 russet potatoes, peeled and cubed

2 cups Beef Stock (page 233)

3 cups water

2 tablespoons cornstarch

2 tablespoons Worcestershire sauce

1½ cups frozen baby peas

A classic stew has a rich beefy flavor and lots of tender vegetables. The slow cooker is perfect for this easy recipe.

1. Combine meat, carrots, onions, garlic, thyme, pepper, potatoes, Beef Stock, and water in 3 to 4-quart Crock-Pot. Cover and cook on low for 8–10 hours, until beef and vegetables are tender.
2. Half an hour before serving, combine Worcestershire sauce and cornstarch in small bowl and mix well; add with peas to Crock-Pot. Cover and cook on high for 20 to 30 more minutes, until peas are hot and stew is thickened.

Southwest Chicken Stew

Serves 6

$ Total Cost: $6.97
Calories: 329.87
Fat: 10.02 grams
Protein: 29.57 grams
Cholesterol: 79.51 mg
Sodium: 876.03 mg

1 pound boned, skinned chicken thighs

1 tablespoon chili powder

½ teaspoon salt

⅛ teaspoon pepper

1 onion, chopped

4 cloves garlic, minced

1 jalapeño pepper, minced

1½ cups frozen corn

½ (29-ounce) can puréed tomatoes

1 (15-ounce) can pinto beans, drained

2 cups Chicken Stock (page 234)

2 cups water

Chicken thighs make a richer stew because they contain more fat than breasts. This excellent stew is mild; to make it spicier, add another jalapeño.

1. Cut chicken thighs into 1-inch pieces and toss with chili powder, salt, and pepper to coat. Combine in 4-quart slow cooker with onion, garlic, jalapeño pepper, and corn, and top with undrained tomatoes, drained beans, Stock, and water.
2. Cover and cook on low for 8 to 9 hours, until chicken is tender and thoroughly cooked.

Beans in the Slow Cooker

Surprisingly, canned beans do not overcook when cooked in the Crock-Pot for 8–9 hours. To save more money, you can use dried beans. Sort and rinse the beans, then soak overnight. Drain when you're ready to cook, then add the beans to the slow cooker along with twice the volume of water. Cook as the recipe directs.

Ribollita

Serves 6

💲 Total Cost: $6.59

Calories: 556.87

Fat: 12.63 grams

Protein: 26.16 grams

Cholesterol: 18.20 mg

Sodium: 880.32 mg

¾ pound dried Great Northern beans

3 cups water

2 cups Beef Stock (page 233)

1 tablespoon olive oil

1 tablespoon butter

1 onion, chopped

4 cloves garlic, chopped

2 potatoes, peeled and cubed

½ teaspoon salt

¼ teaspoon pepper

2 cups chopped red cabbage

3 carrots, peeled and sliced

2 stalks celery, chopped

6 whole wheat dinner rolls

2 tablespoons butter

1 (14.5-ounce) can pureed tomatoes

¼ cup grated Parmesan cheese

Ribollita means "re-boiled" in Italian. It's a vegetable and bean soup thickened with leftover bread. Made in the slow cooker, it's a c-inch.

1. Sort beans and rinse. Place in large pot and cover with water; bring to a boil. Boil for 2 minutes, then remove from heat, cover, and let stand for 2 hours. Drain well and pour beans into 5–6-quart slow cooker; add water and Stock.

2. In heavy saucepan, heat olive oil and 1 tablespoon butter over medium heat. Add onions and garlic; cook and stir for 3–4 minutes until vegetables start to soften. Add to slow cooker with potatoes, salt, and pepper; stir well.

3. Add cabbage, carrots, and celery to slow cooker. Cover and cook on low for 7–8 hours until vegetables and beans are almost tender.

4. Meanwhile, slice rolls in half and spread cut sides with butter. Place under broiler or in toaster oven; broil or toast until crisp and golden brown. Cut rolls into 1-inch pieces and stir into soup along with tomatoes. Cover and cook on low for 1–2 hours until bread has softened. Stir the soup well and serve with Parmesan cheese.

Black Bean Stew

 Serves 4

1 tablespoon olive oil

1 onion, chopped

2 cloves garlic, minced

1 (15-ounce) can black beans, drained

1½ cups frozen corn

1 (10.75-ounce) can condensed tomato soup

2 cups Vegetable Broth (page 241)

2 cups water

¼ teaspoon pepper

1 tablespoon chili powder

½ cup brown rice

Combining legumes, such as these black beans, with grains (the corn and rice) makes a complete protein out of this healthy and simple stew.

1. In small saucepan, heat olive oil over medium heat. Add onion and garlic; cook and stir until tender, about 6 minutes. Combine with all remaining ingredients in 3–4-quart slow cooker.

2. Cover and cook on low for 7–9 hours or until rice is tender. Serve immediately.

About Canned Foods

Canned foods are totally prepared and ready to eat. They can be higher in sodium than the raw variety of the food. Look for lower sodium types (read labels!). You can also rinse the food before use to reduce the sodium content. Beans and vegetables such as corn and peas especially benefit from rinsing.

Beef Chili with Beans

Serves 4

¾ pound round steak

1 tablespoon chili powder

½ teaspoon salt

1 onion, chopped

4 cloves garlic, chopped

1 jalapeño pepper, chopped

⅛ teaspoon cayenne pepper

1 cup tomato juice

1 cup Beef Stock (page 233)

1 (15-ounce) can black beans, drained

1 (8-ounce) can tomato sauce

1 (16-ounce) jar salsa

1 cup water

This hearty chili is perfect for a cold winter evening. Serve it with an easy corn bread, with some brownies for dessert.

1. Cut steak into 1-inch cubes and toss with chili powder and salt. Place onion, garlic, and jalapeño pepper in 4-quart slow cooker.
2. Top with beef, cayenne pepper, tomato juice, Stock, black beans, tomato sauce, salsa and water.
3. Cover slow cooker and cook on low for 8 to 9 hours, until beef is tender. Remove about ⅓ of the beans from the slow cooker, mash, and return to pot. Cook for an additional 20–30 minutes, until mixture is thickened.

Everything Stew

Serves 4

$ Total Cost: $2.12
Calories: 347.76
Fat: 11.74 grams
Protein: 19.92 grams
Cholesterol: 49.54 mg
Sodium: 540.24 mg

2 cups tomato juice

3 cups water

1 cup cooked ground beef
or chicken

2 cups cooked vegetables

½ teaspoon hot sauce

3 tablespoons potato flakes

1 cup small pasta

1 cup shredded Cheddar
cheese

After the stew is complete, taste it for seasoning and see if you need to add more salt or pepper.

1. In 3-quart slow cooker, combine tomato juice, water, and meat. Cover and cook on low for 4–5 hours until hot.
2. Add remaining ingredients except cheese and turn slow cooker to high. Cover and cook on low for 15–20 minutes or until stew is thickened and pasta is tender. Stir in cheese, and serve immediately.

Storing Leftovers

If you want to make a soup or stew from leftovers, keep a hard-sided freezer container in your freezer specifically designated for those ingredients. Add cooked meats and bits of cooked vegetables, making sure to keep track of when you started collecting the food. Use it within three months of the original preparations.

Wild Rice Cauliflower Chowder

Serves 6

Total Cost: $6.62
Calories: 309.23
Fat: 14.65 grams
Protein: 11.98 grams
Cholesterol: 37.25 mg
Sodium: 503.11 mg

1 tablespoon olive oil

1 tablespoon butter

1 onion, chopped

4 cloves garlic, minced

½ teaspoon salt

⅛ teaspoon white pepper

½ teaspoon dried tarragon
  leaves

½ cup wild rice, rinsed

3 carrots, sliced

2 cups Chicken Stock
  (page 234)

3 cups water

1½ cups frozen corn

2 cups frozen cauliflower
  florets

½ cup light cream

3 tablespoons cornstarch

1 cup shredded Swiss cheese

This creamy soup is delicious served with some toasted garlic bread or hot corn bread. It's warming and hearty.

1. In large saucepan, heat olive oil and butter over medium heat. Add onion and garlic and cook and stir until crisp tender, about 4 minutes.
2. Place wild rice in 4-quart slow cooker and sprinkle with salt, pepper, and tarragon. Top with onion mixture, carrots, Stock, and water. Cover and cook on low for 8–9 hours or until wild rice is tender.
3. Add corn and cauliflower to slow cooker and cook on low for 2 hours longer. In small bowl, combine cream and cornstarch and blend well. Stir into slow cooker and cook on high for 5–10 minutes longer or until soup is thickened. Stir in cheese and serve.

Vegetable-Barley Stew

 Serves 8

💲 Total Cost: $6.89

📍 Calories: 378.52
Fat: 10.47 grams
Protein: 26.96 grams
Cholesterol: 56.10 mg
Sodium: 855.27 mg

¾ pound beef round steak

2 tablespoons flour

1 teaspoon salt

1 teaspoon paprika

2 tablespoons olive oil

2 onions, chopped

3 cups Beef Stock (page 233), divided

4 carrots, thickly sliced

3 potatoes, cubed

1 (8-ounce) package sliced mushrooms

4 cups water

1 teaspoon dried marjoram leaves

1 bay leaf

¼ teaspoon pepper

¾ cup hulled barley

This amount of meat adds rich flavor without increasing the cholesterol or saturated-fat content of the stew.

1. Trim beef and cut into 1-inch pieces. Sprinkle with flour, salt, and paprika and toss to coat. In large skillet, heat olive oil over medium heat. Add beef; brown beef, stirring occasionally, for about 5–6 minutes. Remove to 5 to 6-quart slow cooker.

2. Add onions to skillet along with ½ cup Beef Stock. Bring to a boil, then simmer, scraping the bottom of the skillet, for 3–4 minutes. Add to slow cooker along with all remaining ingredients.

3. Cover and cook on low for 8–9 hours, or until barley and vegetables are tender. Stir, remove bay leaf, and serve immediately.

Barley

Barley contains a substance called beta-glucan that has been shown to be effective in reducing cholesterol levels in clinical studies. You can buy barley in several forms. Hulled barley is the most nutritious, while pearl barley is more polished and cooks more quickly. Barley flakes and grits are also available for quick-cooking recipes.

Three-Bean Chili

 Serves 6

1 cup dried black beans

1 cup dried kidney beans

1 cup dried pinto beans

2 jalapeño peppers, minced

2 onions, chopped

4 cloves garlic, minced

4 cups water

4 cups Beef Stock (page 233), divided

1 (14-ounce) can diced tomatoes, undrained

1 (8-ounce) can tomato paste

⅛ teaspoon pepper

Chili without meat but with beans is rich and satisfying. If you love hot food, use habanero peppers instead of the jalapeños.

1. Pick over beans and rinse well; drain and place in large bowl. Cover with water and let stand overnight. In the morning, drain and rinse the beans and place them into a 4 to 5-quart slow cooker.
2. Add peppers, onions, and garlic to slow cooker. Add water and 3 cups stock to the slow cooker. Stir well. Cover and cook on low for 8 hours, or until beans are tender.
3. Add canned tomatoes to slow cooker. In small bowl, combine remaining 1 cup stock with the tomato paste; stir with whisk to dissolve the tomato paste. Add to slow cooker along with pepper. Cover and cook on low for 1–2 hours longer or until chili is thick.

Lentil Stew

 Serves 6

$ Total Cost: $3.72
Calories: 309.15
Fat: 3.63 grams
Protein: 19.34 grams
Cholesterol: 7.73 mg
Sodium: 736.53 mg

1 onion, chopped

3 cloves garlic, minced

3 carrots, sliced

½ teaspoon dried thyme leaves

4 cups Vegetable Broth (page 241)

2 cups water

1½ cups brown lentils

½ teaspoon salt

¼ teaspoon pepper

1 (14-ounce) can diced tomatoes, undrained

¼ cup chopped flat-leaf parsley

¼ cup grated Parmesan cheese

Lentils are small and tender and have a wonderful meaty, nutty taste. Serve this stew with some cheese bread.

1. In 4-quart Crock-Pot, combine onion, garlic, carrots, thyme, Broth, water, lentils, salt, and pepper. Cover and cook on low for 7–8 hours or until lentils are tender.
2. Add tomatoes and stir. Cover and cook on high heat for 20–30 minutes or until stew is hot and blended. Top with parsley and cheese and serve.

Lentils

Lentils are the "fast food" of the legume world. They don't need to be presoaked or pre-cooked. In fact, they will cook in only about an hour on the stovetop. They are great for slow cookers because all you have to do is add them to the appliance, add water and other ingredients, and turn it on.

Sausage and Potato Stew

Serves 8

$ Total Cost: $7.00

Calories: 305.77
Fat: 14.26 grams
Protein: 13.62 grams
Cholesterol: 39.05 mg
Sodium: 644.96 mg

2 slices bacon

½ pound Polish sausage

1 onion, chopped

3 cloves garlic, minced

3 potatoes, peeled and cubed

4 cups Chicken Stock
  (page 234)

2 cups water

2 cups frozen corn

1 (13-ounce) can evaporated
  milk

2 tablespoons cornstarch

¼ cup chopped chives

Bacon and Polish sausage add rich flavor to this creamy and thick stew. Serve it with crisp breadsticks from the bakery.

1. In large skillet, cook bacon until crisp. Drain on paper towels, crumble, and refrigerate. Cut sausage into 1-inch slices and cook for 2–3 minutes in bacon drippings. Remove and place in 4-quart slow cooker.
2. Add onion and garlic to skillet; cook and stir for 4 minutes. Pour all ingredients from skillet into slow cooker. Add potatoes, stock, water, and frozen corn.
3. Cover and cook on low for 8 hours. In small bowl, combine cornstarch and evaporated milk; mix well. Add to slow cooker along with reserved bacon.
4. Cover and cook on high for 30–40 minutes, or until stew is thickened. Sprinkle with chives and serve.

Potato Corn Chowder

 Serves 4

$ Total Cost: $5.03
Calories: 370.42
Fat: 9.28 grams
Protein: 15.06 grams
Cholesterol: 30.35 mg
Sodium: 817.23 mg

3 russet potatoes, peeled

1 onion, chopped

3 cloves garlic, minced

2 cups Chicken Stock (page 234)

½ teaspoon salt

⅛ teaspoon white pepper

½ teaspoon dried tarragon leaves

2 cups water

2 cups frozen corn

1 green bell pepper, chopped

2 tablespoons cornstarch

1 (13-ounce) can evaporated milk

This simple recipe is full of rich ingredients that are good for you. You can also use white corn in this recipe, but yellow corn is prettier.

1. Chop the potatoes and combine in 4-quart Crock-Pot with onion, garlic, Stock, salt, pepper, tarragon, and water. Cover and cook on low for 6–7 hours or until vegetables are tender.
2. Using a potato masher, mash half of the vegetables; stir in corn and green bell pepper and turn heat to high.
3. In a small bowl, combine cornstarch with milk and mix well. Stir into Crock-Pot, cover, and cook on high for 30–40 minutes or until soup is thickened and vegetables are tender. Stir well and serve immediately.

Chowders

Chowders are usually thick soups with a milk base and potatoes and flour added for thickening. They can be made vegetarian or with any meat, including chicken, ham, beef, and seafood. Most chowders are mild in flavor, relying on the ingredients to provide seasoning. You can make your chowder as thick or thin as you like.

Turkey Wild Rice Chowder

Serves 6

2 tablespoons butter

1 onion, chopped

3 cloves garlic, minced

1 (½-pound) turkey tenderloin, cubed

3 tablespoons flour

½ teaspoon salt

¼ teaspoon pepper

1 teaspoon dried thyme leaves

4 cups water

½ cup wild rice, rinsed

4 carrots, sliced

1 (8-ounce) package sliced mushrooms

1 cup frozen corn

2 cups Chicken Stock (page 234)

½ cup heavy whipping cream

You can buy fresh mushrooms already sliced at the grocery store. When you're doing a lot of cooking, that's a great timesaver.

1. In large skillet, melt butter over medium heat, then add onions and garlic; cook and stir for 4 minutes. Remove onions and garlic with slotted spoon to 4–5-quart slow cooker.
2. On shallow plate, combine flour, salt, pepper, and thyme. Toss cubed turkey in this mixture. Brown turkey in remaining drippings in skillet, stirring frequently, about 4–5 minutes total. As turkey browns, add it to slow cooker. Add water to skillet and bring to a boil, stirring to loosen drippings.
3. Place wild rice, carrots, and mushrooms in slow cooker. Add mixture from skillet along with frozen corn and Stock. Stir to combine.
4. Cover and cook on low for 8–9 hours or until turkey is thoroughly cooked and rice and vegetables are tender. Stir in cream; cover and cook for 20 minutes longer until hot. Serve topped with croutons, if desired.

Homemade Chili

Serves 4

$ Total Cost: $6.43
Calories: 404.19
Fat: 14.36 grams
Protein: 29.52 grams
Cholesterol: 70.55 mg
Sodium: 1049.34 mg

¾ pound 80% lean
   ground beef
1 onion, chopped
3 cloves garlic, minced
1 (15-ounce) can kidney
   beans, drained
1 (14-ounce) can diced
   tomatoes, undrained

1 (6-ounce) can tomato paste
1 tablespoon chili powder
1 teaspoon cumin
1½ cups water
½ teaspoon salt
2 tablespoons cornstarch
2½ cups water

This chili cooks all day in the slow cooker, so you can do other things. It's thick, hearty, and filling; all the things chili should be!

1. In large skillet, cook ground beef, onion, and garlic until beef is browned and vegetables are tender, stirring occasionally. Drain well. Combine with all remaining ingredients except cornstarch and ¼ cup water in 3½-quart slow cooker.
2. Cover and cook on low for 8–10 hours. In small bowl, combine cornstarch with ¼ cup water and mix well. Stir into chili, then turn heat to high and cook for 15–20 minutes or until chili is thickened. Serve immediately.

Canned Beans

Very often canned beans go on sale; when they do, stock up! Mark the purchase date on each can with an indelible marker or grease pencil and store the cans in your pantry. Be sure to rotate the cans and use the oldest first. Discard any cans that are dented, bulging, or leaking.

Classic Beef Barley Stew

 Serves 6

$ Total Cost: $7.00
Calories: 340.12
Fat: 11.67 grams
Protein: 31.59 grams
Cholesterol: 79.89 mg
Sodium: 506.71 mg

1 pound beef stew meat, cubed

3 tablespoons flour

1 teaspoon paprika

½ teaspoon salt

⅛ teaspoon pepper

1 tablespoon olive oil

1 tablespoon butter

1 onion, chopped

3 cloves garlic, minced

3 carrots, peeled and sliced

¾ cup medium pearl barley

3 cups Beef Stock (page 233)

3 cups water

1 bay leaf

Barley is a wonderful grain; it's chewy and nutty tasting. In this hearty stew, with beef and vegetables, it's filling and warming.

1. Trim excess fat from stew meat. On large plate, combine flour, paprika, salt, and pepper; mix well. Toss beef in this mixture to coat.
2. Heat olive oil and butter in large skillet. Add beef cubes; brown, stirring, on all sides, about 5–6 minutes.
3. Remove beef from skillet and place in 4-quart slow cooker. Add onions and garlic to skillet; cook and stir until crisp-tender, about 5 minutes, stirring to loosen pan drippings.
4. Add onions and garlic to slow cooker. Add all remaining ingredients. Cover and cook on low for 7–9 hours or until barley and vegetables are tender. Remove bay leaf and serve.

Jalepeño Chili

 Serves 4

 Total Cost: $7.00
Calories: 389.90
Fat: 15.04 grams
Protein: 22.96 grams
Cholesterol: 59.64 mg
Sodium: 1203.21 mg

¾ pound ground beef

1 onion, chopped

2 teaspoons chili powder

¼ teaspoon salt

⅛ teaspoon pepper

1 (4-ounce) can chopped jalapeños, undrained

1 (8-ounce) can tomato sauce

1 (14-ounce) can diced tomatoes with garlic, undrained

1 (15-ounce) can kidney beans, drained

2 tablespoons cornstarch

½ cup water

Serve this easy chili with sour cream, shredded Cheddar or pepper jack cheese, and chopped tomato for a nice contrast.

1. In large saucepan, cook ground beef and onion over medium heat, stirring frequently to break up meat, about 6 minutes. When beef is browned, drain and place in 3½-quart slow cooker.
2. Add all remaining ingredients, except cornstarch and water, and stir. Cover and cook on low for 7–8 hours or until chili is blended. Combine cornstarch and water in a small bowl; stir into chili. Cover and cook on high for 15–20 minutes until thickened.

Five-Way Chili

In Cincinnati, "five-way" chili means chili served with spaghetti, Cheddar cheese, beans, and chopped raw onions. If you vary the additions, you'll be serving "two-way" (with spaghetti), "three-way" (spaghetti and cheese), and "four-way" (three-way plus raw onions). One-way, of course, is plain chili.

Salmon Chowder

 Serves 4

$ Total Cost: $6.64
Calories: 364.89
Fat: 15.07 grams
Protein: 20.04 grams
Cholesterol: 59.22 mg
Sodium: 676.49 mg

2 slices bacon

1 onion, chopped

2 cloves garlic, minced

2 potatoes, peeled and cubed

2 cups frozen corn

4 cups Chicken Stock (page 234)

1 teaspoon dried thyme leaves

½ teaspoon dried dill weed

½ teaspoon salt

⅛ teaspoon pepper

¾ cup heavy cream

⅓ cup potato flakes

1 (7.1-ounce) pouch salmon, drained

Salmon packaged in a pouch already has the skin and bones removed, saving you a lot of work. This creamy chowder is a great way to showcase this fish.

1. In large skillet, cook bacon until crisp. Drain bacon on paper towel, crumble, and refrigerate. Add onions and garlic to skillet; cook and stir for 5 minutes to loosen pan drippings.
2. Place potatoes and corn in 4-quart slow cooker. Add onion mixture to slow cooker along with stock, thyme, dill weed, salt, and pepper. Cover and cook on low for 7–9 hours or until potatoes are tender.
3. Stir in cream, potato flakes, salmon, and reserved bacon. Cover and cook on high for 20–30 minutes or until chowder is thick and hot. Serve immediately.

Simple Burger Stew

Serves 6

$ Total Cost: $6.97
Calories: 364.80
Fat: 18.42 grams
Protein: 17.88 grams
Cholesterol: 41.05 mg
Sodium: 732.53 mg

1 pound ground beef

1 tablespoon olive oil

2 onions, chopped

4 carrots, sliced

3 cloves garlic, minced

1 (10.75-ounce) can cream of mushroom soup

2 cups water

3 russet potatoes, sliced

1 cup frozen peas

½ teaspoon dried tarragon leaves

½ teaspoon salt

⅛ teaspoon pepper

This easy and wholesome stew cooks in the slow cooker so you can go about your day without worrying about it. Serve it with a gelatin salad and some breadsticks.

1. Brown ground beef in large skillet. Remove meat from skillet with slotted spoon and place in 5-quart slow cooker. Drain all but 1 tablespoon of drippings from skillet. Add olive oil, then cook onion and carrots in drippings for 3–4 minutes until glazed. Add to beef in slow cooker.
2. Add garlic, soup, water, potatoes, tarragon, salt, and pepper to slow cooker. Cover and cook on low for 6–7 hours until potatoes are tender.
3. Add peas to slow cooker; cover and cook on high for 15–20 minutes until hot. Serve immediately.

Soup Science

Soup is one of the most forgiving recipes in all of food science. You can add almost anything to it, and leave everything out but the liquid. It's a great way to use leftover vegetables and meats. Just remember, if the ingredients are already cooked, add them at the very end; you just want to reheat them, not overcook them.

Bean and Sausage Chowder

Serves 6

 Total Cost: $6.28

Calories: 459.12

Fat: 5.96 grams

Protein: 29.05 grams

Cholesterol: 17.01 mg

Sodium: 927.43 mg

1 pound Great Northern beans

¾ pound sweet Italian sausage

1 onion, chopped

4 cloves garlic, minced

3 potatoes, peeled and chopped

6 cups water

1 (14-ounce) can diced tomatoes, undrained

1 (8-ounce) can tomato sauce

½ teaspoon salt

⅛ teaspoon pepper

This hearty soup is perfect for cold winter evenings. It stretches a small amount of sausage to serve six people! To splurge, add some cooked link sausage.

1. Sort beans and rinse thoroughly. Drain and place in large pot; cover with water. Bring to a boil and boil for 2 minutes. Then cover pot, remove from heat, and let stand for 1 hour.
2. Cook sausage in large skillet until browned; drain off all but 1 tablespoon drippings. Cook onion and garlic in drippings over medium heat until crisp tender, about 4 minutes.
3. Drain beans and rinse well. Cut sausage into 1-inch pieces. Combine in 4–5-quart slow cooker with 6 cups water, onion, garlic, and potatoes. Cover and cook on low for 8 hours.
4. Then stir in tomatoes, tomato sauce, salt, and pepper; cover and cook on low for 1–2 hours longer, until beans and potatoes are tender. If you'd like, you can mash some of the beans and potatoes, leaving others whole, for a thicker chowder.

Thick Potato Chowder

 Serves 6

6 large russet potatoes

2 onions, chopped

3 cups Chicken Stock (page 234) or water

3 cups water

1 teaspoon salt

⅛ teaspoon pepper

1 (13-ounce) can evaporated milk

¼ cup potato flakes

1 cup grated Swiss cheese

½ teaspoon dried thyme leaves

If you have potatoes on hand, you have a meal! This thick chowder will feed a crowd and won't cost you an arm and a leg.

1. Peel potatoes and cut into cubes. Place in 4–5-quart slow cooker along with onions, Stock, water, salt, and pepper. Cover and cook on low for 6–8 hours until potatoes are tender.
2. Using a potato masher, mash some of the potatoes directly in the slow cooker. Stir in evaporated milk, potato flakes, cheese, and thyme. Cover and cook for 20–30 minutes longer until soup is thick and cheese has melted. Serve immediately.

Potato Nutrition

Potatoes have gotten a bad reputation because of the low-carb craze. But these tubers have nourished populations for generations. They are high in fiber, low in fat, and are a good source of Vitamins C and B. In addition, potatoes are very inexpensive and filling, and can be used in many ways.

A Bowl of Red

 Serves 4

💲 Total Cost: $6.90

Calories: 377.75

Fat: 14.40 grams

Protein: 37.35 grams

Cholesterol: 40.35 mg

Sodium: 710.32 mg

1 pound beef round steak	3 cups Beef Stock (page 233)
¼ cup flour	2 jalapeño chiles, minced
1 teaspoon paprika	2 teaspoons chile paste
2 tablespoons vegetable oil	1 tablespoon chili powder
2 onions, chopped	½ teaspoon dried oregano
4 cloves garlic, minced	½ teaspoon salt
2 dried ancho chiles	¼ teaspoon pepper
1 cup water	

This is the classic Texas-Mexican chili, which has sustained many a traveler with its hearty ingredients and fiery taste. No beans or tomatoes are allowed in this chili: just beef, chiles, and onions.

1. Cut beef into 1-inch pieces and toss with flour and paprika. Heat oil in large skillet over medium heat. Sauté coated beef in batches until brown, about 4–5 minutes per batch. Remove each batch when cooked and place in 4-quart slow cooker. Cook onions and garlic in drippings until crisp-tender, about 4–5 minutes.
2. Meanwhile, soak ancho chiles in ½ cup hot water for about 20 minutes. Drain and purée chiles and ¼ cup water in blender or food processor.
3. Add to slow cooker along with remaining ingredients. Cover and cook on low for 8–9 hours, stirring occasionally, until beef is tender and chili is thickened.

Triple Corn Chowder

Serves 4

$ Total Cost: $6.85

Calories: 380.21

Fat: 19.52 grams

Protein: 9.07 grams

Cholesterol: 59.92 mg

Sodium: 812.53 mg

1 onion, chopped

2 tablespoons butter

2 cups frozen corn

1 (15-ounce) can creamed corn

2 cups Chicken Stock (page 234)

2 tablespoons corn flour

1 cup heavy cream

½ red bell pepper, chopped

1 (4-ounce) can diced chiles

½ teaspoon cumin

Chowders are thicker than soups and usually have cheese or another dairy product in the recipe. Serve this hearty chowder with some breadsticks and a fruit salad.

1. In small saucepan, cook onion in butter until crisp-tender, about 4 minutes. Place in 3-quart slow cooker along with frozen corn, creamed corn, and half of the Chicken Stock. Cover and cook on low for 7-8 hours.

2. In small saucepan, combine remaining Chicken Stock with corn flour; bring to a boil, stirring constantly.

3. Stir corn flour mixture into slow cooker along with cream, bell pepper, undrained chiles, and cumin; cover and cook on low for 1-2 hours or until chowder is thickened.

Using Dairy Products in Soups

When a soup recipe calls for milk or cream, be sure that you don't let the mixture boil after the dairy products are added. The casein protein in the milk can denature and cause curdling, which is undesirable. Just let the soup simmer briefly to heat through and be sure to stir the soup constantly.

White Chicken Chili

 Serves 4

$ Total Cost: $6.98

Calories: 430.26

Fat: 15.93 grams

Protein: 36.94 grams

Cholesterol: 73.43 mg

Sodium: 902.43 mg

1½ boneless, skinless chicken breasts

3 tablespoons flour

½ teaspoon garlic salt

2 tablespoons vegetable oil

1 onion, chopped

2 cups Chicken Stock (page 234)

2 cups water

1 (15-ounce) can pinto beans

1 (4-ounce) can diced green chiles

1 cup shredded Swiss cheese

This rich chili is delicious garnished with some chopped avocado and cold sour cream.

1. Cut chicken into pieces and coat with flour and garlic salt. Heat vegetable oil in large saucepan and cook chicken until lightly browned, about 4 minutes. Remove to 4-quart slow cooker.
2. Add onion to saucepan; cook and stir until crisp-tender. Add stock and water and bring to a simmer, scraping up drippings. Add to slow cooker along with drained beans and chiles.
3. Cover slow cooker and cook for 7–8 hours or until chicken is tender. Add cheese; stir until melted and serve.

Lentil and Chicken Chili

Serves 6

$ Total Cost: $6.18
Calories: 400.26
Fat: 5.78 grams
Protein: 16.84 grams
Cholesterol: 53.78 mg
Sodium: 565.49 mg

1 onion, chopped

3 cloves garlic, minced

2 carrots, sliced

1 tablespoon chili powder

½ teaspoon salt

⅛ teaspoon cayenne pepper

1½ cups dried lentils

½ cup brown rice

½ pound boneless, skinless chicken breasts, cubed

1 (6-ounce) can tomato paste

3 cups Chicken Stock (page 234)

2 cups water

This rich chili uses lentils instead of beans and adds brown rice.

1. Combine onion, garlic, and carrots in bottom of 4 to 5-quart slow cooker. Add chili powder, salt, and pepper.
2. Top with lentils, rice, and chicken. In small bowl, combine tomato paste with 1 cup Stock; stir until tomato paste dissolves. Add to Crock-Pot along with remaining Stock and water.
3. Cover and cook on low for 7–9 hours or until lentils and rice are tender and chicken is thoroughly cooked. Serve with sour cream and salsa, if desired.

Tomato Paste

Tomato paste is a very concentrated mixture of tomatoes and water that has been cooked until it's very thick. It adds a richness to soups, sauces, and stews that you can't get by just cooking down tomatoes. Look for low-salt varieties, since it can be quite salty. You can also find flavored varieties with onion, garlic, and herbs.

Buffalo Chicken Chowder

 Serves 6

$ Total Cost: $6.63

Calories: 420.52

Fat: 19.34 grams

Protein: 22.39 grams

Cholesterol: 69.24 mg

Sodium: 765.41 mg

2 boneless, skinless chicken breasts, cubed

2 tablespoons flour

½ teaspoon salt

⅛ teaspoon cayenne pepper

1 tablespoon olive oil

1 tablespoon butter

1 onion, chopped

4 cloves garlic, minced

¾ cup sliced celery, divided

3 carrots, sliced

4 cups Chicken Stock (page 234)

1 (13-ounce) can evaporated milk

½ cup shredded low-fat Swiss cheese

¼ cup crumbled blue cheese

¼ teaspoon hot pepper sauce

¾ cup chopped tomatoes

¼ cup blue cheese dressing

Flavored like hot and spicy Buffalo chicken wings, this delicious soup is rich and creamy. Yum.

1. Toss chicken with flour, salt, and pepper. Heat oil in large saucepan over medium heat. Add chicken; cook and stir until chicken is light brown; remove from pan.
2. Add butter to pan and melt. Add onion and garlic, cook and stir, scraping up drippings, until vegetables are crisp-tender, about 4 minutes. Place in 4-quart slow cooker with chicken.
3. Add ½ cup celery, carrots, and Stock. Cover and cook on low for 7–8 hours or until chicken is tender.
4. Stir in milk, Swiss cheese, blue cheese, and hot pepper sauce. Cover and cook on low for 30–40 minutes or until cheese is melted and soup is blended.
5. In small bowl, combine tomatoes, ¼ cup celery, and dressing and stir well. Ladle soup into warmed bowls and top with tomato mixture; serve immediately.

Ham Chowder

 Serves 6

Total Cost: $6.39
Calories: 317.88
Fat: 6.99 grams
Protein: 15.39 grams
Cholesterol: 34.29 mg
Sodium: 840.32 mg

1 tablespoon olive oil	4 potatoes, diced
1 onion, diced	3 sliced carrots
2 cloves garlic, minced	1 cup frozen corn
½ teaspoon salt	1 cup cubed ham
⅛ teaspoon white pepper	4 cups Chicken Stock (page 234)
½ teaspoon dried thyme leaves	2 cups water

Chowders are usually made with lots of cheese and cream. But pureeing some vegetables can create almost the same texture.

1. In medium saucepan, heat olive oil over medium heat. Cook onion and garlic, stirring frequently, until crisp-tender, about 5 minutes. Place in 5-quart slow cooker. Add remaining ingredients. Cover and cook on low 8–10 hours, or until vegetables are tender.
2. Using a potato masher or immersion blender, mash or blend some of the vegetables in the soup, leaving others whole. Stir to blend, and serve immediately.

Dried Herbs

Dried herbs are much less expensive than fresh, unless you grow your own. Even if you don't have a garden, you can grow herbs in small pots on a back step or even on your kitchen windowsill. You can then dry them yourself; just rinse, dry, and hang upside down in a cool dry place until the leaves crumble. Crumble, place in small pots, seal, and store in a cool place.

CHAPTER 15

DESSERT

303 Chocolate Marshmallow Dip

304 Pumpkin Bread Pudding

305 Lemon Apple Rice Pudding

306 Baked Stuffed Apples

307 Caramel Peanut Fondue

308 Curried Fruit Bake

309 Poached Pears in Red Wine

310 Caramel Marshmallow Fondue

311 Fruit Pudding

312 Chocolate Coconut Peanut Clusters

313 Strawberry Rhubarb Sauce

314 Black and White Fondue

315 Chocolate-Caramel Fondue

316 Butterscotch Pears

317 Cranberry Pudding Cake

318 Caramel Apple Crisp

319 Cherry Cobbler

320 Dried Cherry Bread Pudding

321 Peanut Butter Fondue

322 Toffee Peach Crisp

323 Caramel Chocolate Cake

324 Apricot Rice Pudding

Chocolate Marshmallow Dip

 Serves 6

💲 Total Cost: $6.59

🥄 Calories: 432.29

Fat: 14.94 grams

Protein: 10.32 grams

Cholesterol: 24.38 mg

Sodium: 241.23 mg

1 (14-ounce) can sweetened condensed milk

1 (12-ounce) package semi-sweet chocolate chips

2 (1-ounce) squares unsweetened baking chocolate, chopped

1 (7-ounce) jar marshmallow crème

Sugar cookies, graham crackers, gingersnaps, angel food cake

Sweetened condensed milk is the creamy basis for this velvety dip. Use your imagination when choosing dippers.

1. In 2-quart slow cooker, combine milk, chocolate chips, and baking chocolate. Cover and cook on low for 2 hours, then stir.
2. Cover and cook on low for another 1–2 hours, as necessary, until chocolate melts and mixture is smooth.
3. Stir in marshmallow crème to blend. Serve immediately with sugar cookies, graham crackers, gingersnaps, or angel food cake for dipping.

Pumpkin Bread Pudding

Serves 10

3 eggs

½ cup sugar

½ cup brown sugar

1 teaspoon cinnamon

½ teaspoon ginger

1 cup canned pumpkin

1 cup milk

1 (14-ounce) can evaporated milk

2 teaspoons vanilla

2 tablespoons butter, melted

8 slices French bread, cubed

1 cup chopped pecans

Bread pudding is a classic comfort food. Adding pumpkin to the recipe gives it a nice boost of flavor (and Vitamin A).

1. In medium bowl, combine eggs, sugars, cinnamon, and ginger until smooth. Then beat in pumpkin, milk, evaporated milk, and vanilla until blended.
2. Generously butter the crockery insert of a 3½-quart slow cooker. Cover bottom with half of the bread cubes and drizzle with butter. Pour half of the pumpkin mixture over all. Top with half of the pecans, then remaining bread, pecans, and pumpkin mixture.
3. Cover Crock-Pot and cook on high for 2 hours, without lifting lid, until set and puffed. Serve warm.

Canned Pumpkin

When a recipe calls for canned pumpkin, be sure that you buy and use what is called "solid pack" pumpkin. If you buy canned pumpkin pie pudding, the recipe will fail because that ingredient contains sugar, emulsifiers, and liquids in addition to pumpkin. If you're feeling ambitious, you could cook and purée a fresh pumpkin and use that.

The $7 a Meal Slow Cooker Cookbook

Lemon Apple Rice Pudding

Serves 6

$ Total Cost: $4.93
Calories: 300.48
Fat: 9.94 grams
Protein: 8.25 grams
Cholesterol: 97.06 mg
Sodium: 225.09 mg

3 cups cooked long grain rice

½ (14-ounce) can sweetened condensed milk

¾ cup milk

2 eggs

¼ teaspoon salt

2 apples, peeled and diced

1 teaspoon lemon zest

3 tablespoons lemon juice

2 tablespoons butter, melted

Rice pudding is one of the ultimate comfort foods. Add apples and lemon and it becomes a trendy dessert that's good for you too.

1. Spray inside of a 3½-quart Crock-Pot with nonstick cooking spray. Combine all ingredients and stir until combined.
2. Cover and cook on low for 6–7 hours or until mixture is thick and apples are tender. Stir at the 1 hour and 4 hour mark during cooking time. Serve warm.

Baked Stuffed Apples

 Serves 4

 Total Cost: $6.11

Calories: 321.16

Fat: 10.61 grams

Protein: 2.58 grams

Cholesterol: 15.26 mg

Sodium: 50.95 mg

4 whole medium apples

2 tablespoons lemon juice, divided

¼ cup brown sugar

2 tablespoons butter

2 tablespoons honey

¼ cup raisins

¼ cup chopped walnuts

½ teaspoon cinnamon

½ cup water

¼ cup sugar

Apples are so good for you! And this recipe turns them into an indulgent, yet healthy dessert packed full of flavor.

1. Using a sharp knife or apple corer, cut out the core of each apple from the top. Do not cut all the way through the apple. Peel the top-quarter of each apple to help prevent splitting as it cooks. Sprinkle the prepared apples with 1 tablespoon lemon juice.

2. In small bowl, combine brown sugar, butter, honey, and cinnamon and mix well. Stir in raisins and walnuts. Stuff the apple centers with this mixture. Place apples in a 3 to 4-quart Crock-Pot so they fit snugly.

3. In heavy saucepan, combine water, sugar, and 1 tablespoon lemon juice and bring to a boil, stirring occasionally. Pour this mixture over the apples.

4. Cover and cook on low for 6–8 hours or until apples are tender when pierced with a knife. Let the apples cool for 30 minutes, spooning pan juices over the apples as they cool. Serve warm.

Apples For Baking

You do have to carefully choose the apples you use in baking recipes. Some apples, including Red Delicious, Fuji, and Gala, break down too much when cooked. The apples which hold their shape in baking include Granny Smith, Golden Delicious, Winesap, and Jonagold. McIntosh apples are best for making applesauce or puddings.

The $7 a Meal Slow Cooker Cookbook

Caramel Peanut Fondue

 Serves 8

½ cup butter

½ cup corn syrup

1 cup brown sugar

½ cup peanut butter

1 (14-ounce) can sweetened condensed milk

4 apples, sliced

You can also use this dip as an ice cream topping, or as part of a banana split sundae.

1. In 2-quart slow cooker, combine butter, corn syrup, and brown sugar; stir well. Cover and cook on high for 2–3 hours, stirring occasionally, until mixture blends and sugar dissolves.
2. Uncover and cook on high for 1–2 hours or until mixture starts to simmer. Add peanut butter and milk. Cover and cook on low for 3–4 hours or until mixture is blended and thickened. Serve with apples.

Curried Fruit Bake

 Serves 8

$ Total Cost: $5.68
Calories: 353.92
Fat: 12.85 grams
Protein: 4.29 grams
Cholesterol: 5.90 mg
Sodium: 251.24 mg

1 cup chopped dates

1 cup chopped prunes

1 (15-ounce) can apricots, chopped

1 (8-ounce) can pineapple tidbits, drained

½ cup brown sugar

2 teaspoons curry powder

2 cups granola

This is like a sophisticated fruit crisp. The granola keeps its crunch in the slow cooker and adds great texture and flavor to the dish.

1. Combine all ingredients except granola in 2-quart slow cooker. Cover and cook on low for 4–5 hours or until sugar dissolves.
2. Sprinkle with granola, and cook on high, uncovered, for 1–2 hours or until mixture thickens. Serve with ice cream or whipped cream.

Granola

There are hundreds of types of granola available on the market. The least expensive is usually the kind you buy in bulk from food co-ops. For slow cooker dishes, look for granola that is very crunchy and not soft or sticky. The low heat and moisture-rich environment will soften crunchy granola to the perfect texture.

Poached Pears in Red Wine

Serves 6

$ Total Cost: $5.83
Calories: 215.48
Fat: 1.08 grams
Protein: 3.29 grams
Cholesterol: 0.0 mg
Sodium: 143.29 mg

2½ cups dry red wine

½ cup orange juice

1 cup sugar

4 large pears

1 cinnamon stick

¼ teaspoon salt

Poached pears are a classic dish that can be served in many ways. Serve the pears by themselves or over ice cream or pound cake.

1. In 3-quart slow cooker, combine wine, orange juice, sugar, cinnamon stick, and salt. Cover and cook on low for 2–3 hours or until sugar dissolves.
2. Cut pears in half, remove core, leaving stem attached to one half. Add to the wine mixture. Cover and cook on low for 5–6 hours, spooning the sauce over the pears twice during cooking time. Remove cinnamon stick and pears.
3. Place pears on serving dish and pour 1 cup wine mixture over. Let cool, then serve.

Caramel Marshmallow Fondue

Serves 8

$ Total Cost: $3.28
Calories: 294.32
Fat: 7.90 grams
Protein: 4.39 grams
Cholesterol: 45.87 mg
Sodium: 254.58 mg

1 (14-ounce) package
  caramels

½ cup cream

1 cup miniature
  marshmallows

1 tablespoon rum, if desired

This unusual fondue is very sweet, so it should be served with tart fruits like apples, pears, and pineapple.

1. Unwrap caramels. Combine with cream in a 2 or 3-quart slow cooker. Cover and cook on low for 2–3 hours, stirring twice during cooking time, until the caramels are melted.
2. Stir in marshmallows and rum, if using. Cover and cook on low for 1 hour longer, stirring twice during cooking time, until mixture is smooth. Serve immediately.

Fondue

Fondue can be served as-is, with the slow cooker being the serving container, or you can cool the mixture and serve it as a great sauce over ice cream or as part of a sundae bar. For dippers, use lots of fresh fruit, cubed pound or angel food cake, and sturdy cookies like chocolate chip or pirouette.

The $7 a Meal Slow Cooker Cookbook

Fruit Pudding

 Serves 6

$ Total Cost: $5.29

Calories: 325.94

Fat: 12.94 grams

Protein: 4.36 grams

Cholesterol: 120.43 mg

Sodium: 322.17 mg

1 (15-ounce) can fruit cocktail

1 (15-ounce) can sliced peaches

1½ cups sugar

3 eggs

½ cup butter, melted

½ cup light cream

1 teaspoon vanilla

½ teaspoon salt

8 slices white bread

This comforting and old fashioned pudding should be served with Hard Sauce (page 322) or vanilla ice cream. Top with some toasted nuts for crunch.

1. Drain fruit cocktail and peaches, reserving ¼ cup juice from peaches. Combine in large bowl and mash some of the fruit with a potato masher.
2. Add sugar, eggs, butter, cream, vanilla, and salt and mix well. Pour into 4-quart slow cooker.
3. Toast the bread and crumble. Stir into fruit mixture. Cover and cook on high for 3–4 hours until pudding is set.

Chocolate Coconut Peanut Clusters

Yields 24 candies

Total Cost: $4.33
Calories: 143.95
Fat: 4.39 grams
Protein: 1.29 grams
Cholesterol: 0.0 mg
Sodium: 143.58 mg

1 pound candy coating, chopped

2 cups semisweet chocolate chips

1 square baking chocolate, chopped

1 teaspoon vanilla

1 cup coconut

2 cups roasted peanuts

Melting chocolate in the Crock-Pot is fun and easy, and it's a great way to make sure it doesn't burn.

1. Combine candy coating, chips, and chocolate in a 2-quart slow cooker. Cover and cook on low until melted, about 3–4 hours, stirring every hour.
2. Turn off heat and stir in vanilla, coconut, and peanuts. Drop by teaspoons onto waxed paper. Let stand until set.

Candy

Homemade candy, especially when made with melted chocolate, sometimes has to have a little bit of encouragement for it to set. Chill the candies in the fridge for about an hour until they are firm to the touch. The chocolate should be crystallized by then so they will be fairly firm at room temperature.

Strawberry Rhubarb Sauce

Serves 8

4 cups chopped rhubarb

¾ cup sugar

½ cup white grape juice

1 cinnamon stick

1 teaspoon vanilla

⅛ teaspoon salt

1 cup chopped strawberries

This excellent sauce can be served on everything from ice cream to pound cake to your morning oatmeal.

1. In 2-quart slow cooker, combine rhubarb, sugar, grape juice, cinnamon stick, vanilla, and salt. Cover and cook on low for 5–6 hours or until rhubarb is soft.
2. Remove cinnamon stick and stir in strawberries. Cover and cook on low for 1 hour. Slightly mash some of the fruit, leaving some whole. Serve immediately or cover and refrigerate up to 3 days.

Black and White Fondue

 Serves 6

$ Total Cost: $5.63
Calories: 329.12
Fat: 12.96 grams
Protein: 4.36 grams
Cholesterol: 14.96 mg
Sodium: 235.23 mg

1 (14-ounce) can sweetened condensed milk

1 (12-ounce) package semi-sweet chocolate chips

1 (1-ounce) square unsweetened baking chocolate, chopped

¼ cup cocoa powder

2 tablespoons honey

2 teaspoons vanilla

1 (8-ounce) bar white chocolate with almonds, chopped

Fondue is such a wonderful communal dessert. Strawberries are the best choice for dipping into this creamy and sweet mixture.

1. In 2-quart slow cooker, combine condensed milk, semisweet chocolate, baking chocolate, cocoa, and honey; mix well. Cover and cook on low for 1–2 hours or until chocolate is melted and mixture is smooth. Stir well and add vanilla.
2. Add chopped candy bar. Stir just to combine, then cook on low for 10 minutes. Do not stir; serve immediately with skewered strawberries.

White Chocolate
White chocolate isn't true chocolate because it doesn't contain any chocolate liquor. There are some candy coatings which masquerade as white chocolate, but they do not contain any cocoa butter, which is the main ingredient in true white chocolate. Make sure that you carefully read labels in the supermarket.

Chocolate-Caramel Fondue

 Serves 8

💲 Total Cost: $7.00

🥄 Calories: 385.56

Fat: 15.96 grams

Protein: 4.39 grams

Cholesterol: 12.63 mg

Sodium: 243.91 mg

1 (12-ounce) package semi-sweet chocolate chips

1 cup milk chocolate chips

2 (1-ounce) squares baking chocolate, chopped

1 (13-ounce) can dulce de leche sweetened condensed milk

10 caramels, unwrapped and chopped

Serve this dip with cookies, pieces of pound and angel food cake, and fresh fruits such as strawberries, pineapple, and apple slices.

1. In 2-quart slow cooker, combine semisweet chocolate chips with milk chocolate chips, chopped chocolate, and sweetened condensed milk. Stir to combine.
2. Cover and cook on low for 1 to 1½ hours or until chocolate is melted and mixture is smooth. Stir in caramels; cover and cook on low for another 30 minutes to melt caramels. Serve immediately.

Butterscotch Pears

Serves 8

$ Total Cost: $6.79
Calories: 312.24
Fat: 7.49 grams
Protein: 2.91 grams
Cholesterol: 12.38 mg
Sodium: 215.09 mg

4 large, firm pears

1 tablespoon lemon juice

¼ cup dark brown sugar

3 tablespoons butter, softened

2 tablespoons flour

½ teaspoon cinnamon

¼ teaspoon salt

½ cup chopped pecans

½ cup pear nectar

2 tablespoons honey

This delicious combination can be served alone, with sweetened whipped cream, or as a topping for ice cream or angel food cake.

1. Cut pears in half and remove core; do not peel. Brush pears with lemon juice. In medium bowl, combine brown sugar, butter, flour, cinnamon, and salt; mix well. Stir in pecans.
2. Fill the pear halves with the brown sugar mixture, mounding the filling. Place, filling side up, in 3½-quart slow cooker; layer the pears. In small bowl, combine nectar and honey; stir to blend. Pour around pears.
3. Cover and cook on high for 2–3 hours or until pears are tender. Serve immediately.

Slow Cooker Fruit

Some fruits cook very well in the slow cooker. Harder fruits like apples, pears, and pineapple are naturals. Canned and fresh peaches also work well, but fresh peaches tend to become too mushy. The fruits do not cook for a long time; generally only a few hours, because they break down quickly.

The $7 a Meal Slow Cooker Cookbook

Cranberry Pudding Cake

Serves 10

Total Cost: $7.00
Calories: 456.39
Fat: 15.94 grams
Protein: 9.83 grams
Cholesterol: 79.54 mg
Sodium: 452.78 mg

1 (16-ounce) package pound cake mix

1 (4-ounce) package French vanilla pudding mix

1½ cups sour cream

3 eggs, beaten

¾ cup vegetable oil

½ cup water

¼ cup cranberry juice

½ cup fresh cranberries, chopped

½ cup dried cranberries, chopped

½ cup white chocolate chips

Cranberries and white chocolate complement each other beautifully in this easy and delicious slow cooker cake.

1. Spray a 4-quart slow cooker with nonstick baking spray containing flour. In large bowl, combine cake mix, pudding mix, sour cream, eggs, oil, water, and cranberry juice. Beat with electric mixer until combined, then scrape sides and beat for 2 minutes longer.

2. Fold in the cranberries, dried cranberries, and white chocolate chips. Pour batter into prepared slow cooker, cover, and cook on low for 6–7 hours or until the cake begins to pull away from sides of pan.

3. To serve, scoop cake out of slow cooker and top with ice cream or whipped cream.

Caramel Apple Crisp

Serves 8

¼ cup butter

½ cup chopped pecans

1 cup rolled oats

½ cup brown sugar

1 teaspoon cinnamon

⅛ teaspoon cardamom

½ teaspoon salt

2 cups granola cereal

4 cups peeled apple slices

14 unwrapped caramels, chopped

3 tablespoons flour

¼ cup apple juice

Caramels melt together with apples in this delicious recipe, and the topping melts into a candy-like mixture. Serve with sweetened whipped cream or vanilla ice cream. Yum!

1. Spray a 3-quart slow cooker with nonstick cooking spray and set aside. In large skillet, melt butter. Add pecans and rolled oats; cook and stir until toasted and fragrant. Stir in brown sugar, cinnamon, cardamom, and salt.
2. Add granola cereal; stir and remove from heat. Place apple slices and chopped caramels in prepared slow cooker. Sprinkle with flour and top with apple juice. Top with granola mixture.
3. Cover and cook on low for 6–7 hours or until apples are tender and topping is set. Serve with ice cream or whipped cream.

Fruit Crisps

Fruit crisps are made of fruit cooked with sugar and butter, topped with a crumbly topping. In the slow cooker, the toppings are usually made of granola or chopped nuts so it retains some texture in the moist cooking environment. You can also top the finished dish with more chopped toasted nuts if you'd like.

Cherry Cobbler

 Serves 6

$ Total Cost: $6.49

Calories: 375.94

Fat: 14.29 grams

Protein: 10.94 grams

Cholesterol: 107.43 mg

Sodium: 362.93 mg

1 (15-ounce) can sour pie cherries

¾ cup sugar

3 tablespoons flour

1 cup reserved cherry juice

6 tablespoons butter

1 cup rolled oats

½ cup granola

¾ cup brown sugar

½ teaspoon salt

½ teaspoon cinnamon

1 cup flour

½ teaspoon baking soda

This excellent cobbler combines sour cherries with a candy-like topping. This is delicious served with vanilla ice cream or sweetened whipped cream.

1. Drain cherries, reserving juice. In large saucepan, combine sugar and flour; mix with wire whisk. Add reserved cherry juice and stir. Cook over medium heat until mixture thickens and boils. Stir in cherries and remove from heat.
2. Spray a 2-quart slow cooker with nonstick cooking spray. Place cherry mixture in bottom of slow cooker.
3. In large skillet, melt butter over medium heat. Add oats; cook and stir until fragrant and lightly toasted. Remove from heat and add granola, brown sugar, salt, and cinnamon; mix well. Stir in flour and baking soda until crumbly.
4. Sprinkle skillet mixture over cherry mixture in slow cooker. Cover and cook on low for 5–6 hours. Serve immediately with ice cream or whipped cream.

Dried Cherry Bread Pudding

Serves 6

$ Total Cost: $6.89
Calories: 429.21
Fat: 15.95 grams
Protein: 9.87 grams
Cholesterol: 20.52 mg
Sodium: 293.65 mg

5 cups French bread cubes

3 eggs, beaten

1 cup heavy cream

½ cup whole milk

⅔ cup sugar

3 tablespoons butter, melted

1 teaspoon vanilla

¼ teaspoon salt

1 cup dried cherries, chopped

¾ cup chopped pecans

½ cup caramel ice cream topping

Dried cherries are tart and delicious. It's best to chop them and examine them carefully before stirring into the topping, because they can still contain pits.

1. Heat oven to 300°F. Place bread cubes on cookie sheet. Toast in the oven for 30–40 minutes or until dry to the touch. Place in 3-quart slow cooker along with cherries and pecans; mix gently.

2. In large bowl, combine eggs, cream, milk, sugar, butter, vanilla, and salt; beat until combined. Pour into slow cooker. Let stand for 15 minutes, pushing down on bread mixture occasionally so it absorbs the sauce.

3. Cover and cook on high for 1 hour, then reduce heat to low and cook for 5–6 hours longer until pudding is fluffy and set. Spoon into dessert bowls and top with a drizzle of caramel ice cream topping

Dried Fruit

Dried fruit is more expensive than fresh fruit, but the flavor is very concentrated so you don't need as much. Look for dried fruit in food co-ops and natural food stores to save a little money. These fruits are perishable and have expiration dates, so follow them closely.

Peanut Butter Fondue

 Serves 6

💲 Total Cost: $6.98
🥄 Calories: 435.21
Fat: 17.94 grams
Protein: 11.84 grams
Cholesterol: 42.54 mg
Sodium: 432.11 mg

1 cup peanut butter

1 (14-ounce) can sweetened condensed milk

1 (13-ounce) can evaporated milk

1 cup peanut butter flavored chips

¼ cup butter

Sliced apples

Marshmallows

½ cup chopped peanuts

If the fondue is too thick, you can stir in more evaporated milk. This can also be served as a sauce over ice cream or pudding.

1. In 2-quart slow cooker, combine peanut butter, both kinds of milk, chips, and butter; mix well. Cover and cook on low for 3–4 hours or until mixture is smooth, stirring once during cooking time.
2. Arrange dippers on a platter around the fondue, and provide forks, skewers, or toothpicks. Dip fruits and marshmallows into the fondue and roll into peanuts.

Toffee Peach Crisp

Serves 6

$ Total Cost: $6.87

Calories: 392.54

Fat: 16.38 grams

Protein: 10.96 grams

Cholesterol: 20.54 mg

Sodium: 259.38 mg

6 peaches, peeled and sliced

1 tablespoon lemon juice

½ teaspoon cinnamon

¼ cup caramel ice cream topping

1 cup rolled oats

⅔ cup brown sugar

½ cup flour

½ teaspoon salt

½ teaspoon cinnamon

¼ cup butter, melted

1 cup granola

½ cup crushed toffee

Peaches and toffee are a wonderful combination. The toffee melts in the topping, adding a sweet burst of flavor, while the peaches become soft and tender.

1. Spray 3-quart slow cooker with nonstick cooking spray. Place peaches, lemon juice, and cinnamon in slow cooker and mix. Drizzle with caramel ice cream topping.
2. In large bowl, combine oatmeal, brown sugar, flour, salt, and cinnamon; mix well. Add melted butter; stir until crumbly. Stir in granola and toffee.
3. Sprinkle over peach mixture in slow cooker. Cover and cook on low for 4–5 hours or until peaches are tender and topping is hot. Serve with ice cream or sweetened whipped cream.

Hard Sauce

Hard sauce is simply a mixture of butter, sugar, and flavorings that is beaten until fluffy. It looks like frosting. It is served on warm desserts, where it melts into a creamy and sweet sauce. To make it, beat ½ cup softened butter with 1½ cups powdered sugar until smooth. Stir in 2 teaspoons vanilla and 1–2 tablespoons rum, if desired.

Caramel Chocolate Cake

 Serves 10

$ Total Cost: $5.32
Calories: 425.87
Fat: 15.32 grams
Protein: 5.39 grams
Cholesterol: 74.92 mg
Sodium: 364.91 mg

1 (3-ounce) package cream
    cheese, cubed

½ cup milk

1 cup sour cream

¼ cup cocoa

1 egg

2 (8.2-ounce) packages
    chocolate chip muffin mix

2 tablespoons butter

½ cup brown sugar

½ cup caramel ice cream
    topping

½ cup water

A cake baked in the slow cooker! This one has the best combination of textures and flavors. Serve warm with some ice cream on top.

1. In small microwave-safe bowl, combine cream cheese and milk. Microwave on 50 percent power for 1 minute; remove and stir. Continue microwaving for 30-second intervals until cream cheese melts; stir with wire whisk to blend.
2. Place in large bowl; stir in sour cream, cocoa powder, and egg. Mix well. Add both packages muffin mix and stir just until combined.
3. Spray a 3½-quart slow cooker with nonstick baking spray containing flour. Spread batter evenly in slow cooker.
4. In small saucepan, combine butter, brown sugar, ice cream topping, and water; heat to boiling, stirring until blended. Carefully pour over batter in slow cooker.
5. Cook on high for 2½ to 3 hours or until cake springs back when lightly touched. Uncover, turn off slow cooker, top loosely with foil, and let stand for 30 minutes.
6. Gently run a sharp knife around the edges of the cake and invert over serving plate until cake drops out. If any sauce remains in slow cooker, spoon over cake. Cool for 30–45 minutes before serving.

Apricot Rice Pudding

Serves 6

1 cup medium grain white rice

1 cup sugar

¼ cup butter

¼ teaspoon salt

⅛ teaspoon cardamom

⅛ teaspoon nutmeg

2 cups apricot nectar

1 cup light cream

1 cup milk

2 teaspoons vanilla

½ cup finely chopped dried apricots

1 cup chopped canned apricots in juice, drained

Rice pudding is wonderful comfort food. When flavored with apricot nectar, cardamom, and nutmeg, it becomes a gourmet dessert.

1. Combine all ingredients except canned apricots in 2-quart slow cooker. Cover and cook on low for 2 hours, then remove lid and stir.
2. Cover and continue cooking on low for 2–3 hours longer, until rice is tender and pudding is desired thickness, stirring every 30 minutes. Stir in canned apricots, cover, and cook for another 30 minutes. Serve warm or cold.

Rice Pudding

White rice is the perfect slow cooker rice pudding ingredient. It releases lots of starch in the low heat, high moisture environment of the appliance, and that makes the rice pudding creamy and rich. It is important to stir occasionally as the rice cooks so it doesn't sink to the bottom and form a solid layer.

APPENDIX A
GLOSSARY

Al dente: An Italian phrase meaning "to the tooth" that describes pasta when it is properly cooked.

Angel food cake: A cake made of mostly egg whites, sugar, and flour. It is usually fat-free.

Applesauce: A sauce made of cooked or uncooked apples, usually flavored with sugar and spices. Used as a fat substitute in low-fat baking.

Arborio rice: A short-grain Italian rice used to make risotto. It has more starch that makes the sauce in the finished product creamy.

Aroma: A volatile, or airborne, compound which reacts with the body's olfactory system to produce a sense of smell.

Bake: To cook in an oven using dry heat. Baked goods include bread, casseroles, pastries, cookies, and cakes.

Barley: A cereal grain that is fat-free and contains a large amount of fiber and B vitamins. Barley is sold as whole grains, flakes, and flour.

Baste: To cover a food with liquid as it cooks. Basting helps preserve moisture and adds flavor.

Braise: To cook with wet heat. Braised food is usually browned, then cooked in a closed environment with water or other liquid.

Brown: In food, a reaction to heat that causes sugar and protein molecules to combine, creating a brown color on the surface.

Butter: A by-product of milk, butter is concentrated milk fat produced by agitating heavy cream. It is used in cooking and baking.

Cake flour: Flour made of low-protein wheat. The flour has a higher percentage of starch and less gluten, which results in a finer crumb and more tender texture.

Carbohydrate: One of the three main compounds which make up food, carbohydrates are chains of simple sugars. One gram of carbohydrates provides four calories.

Cheese: A dairy food made by coagulating milk using acids and enzymes. Cheese can be made from the milk of cows, sheep, and goats.

Chutney: A thick, low-fat sauce, usually sweet, made from fruits or vegetables and spices. Chutney is an accompaniment to Indian foods.

Cocoa: Cocoa is a powder made from the dried seed of the cacao tree. It is unsweetened and low in fat, used in cooking and baking.

Condensed milk: Milk which has been cooked to reduce the water content. Usually sweetened with sugar and sold as sweetened condensed milk.

Condiment: A sauce or highly flavored substance used to add flavor, usually after food is cooked. Condiments include pickles, mustard, and ketchup.

Cooking spray: A spray made of oils that is used to grease pans and sauté food with very little fat. Also can be combined with flour for baking purposes.

Cream of tartar: Potassium hydrogen tartrate is an acid salt used to stabilize egg white foams and, when paired with baking soda, creates baking powder.

Crock-Pot: Another name for a slow cooker.

Dijon mustard: A spicy mustard made from a French recipe. Instead of the typical vinegar, a substance called verjuice, made from unripe grapes, is used.

Dredge: To coat in flour, cornmeal, or another dry substance. Meats are usually dredged in flour before being sautéed.

Emulsify: To combine a fat and a liquid, two substances which repel each other. Emulsification can be produced by adding energy to the mixture, or ingredients, called emulsifiers, can be used.

En papillote: To cook wrapped in paper or foil. Foods cooked en papillote are more moist. Used in cooking delicate foods.

Evaporated milk: Milk that has had approximately 60 percent of its water removed. Usually found canned, can be whole, low-fat, or nonfat.

Fat: Compounds made of fatty acids and glycerol which are insoluble in water. Fats are necessary for life, and are found in many foods. One gram of fat provides 9 calories.

Fruit: The part of a plant which produces seeds. Fruits are usually edible, and usually sweet.

Gelatin: A substance used to thicken juices and other liquids, made from animals' connective tissue.

Glaze: A thin coating used to add flavor and improve appearance of foods. Glazes can be savory or sweet.

Grill: A dry heat method of cooking, over charcoal or a strong heat source. Grilling cooks food quickly and adds flavor by caramelization.

Herbs: Deciduous plants, whether annual or perennial, that have edible leaves and provide flavor. Herbs include cilantro, basil, oregano, chives, and parsley.

Honey: A sweet, thick fluid produced by honeybees. Bees make the honey by using nectar from flowers they collect with their tongue.

Infuse: To permeate one substance with another. Extracts are made by infusing alcohol with aromatic substances from beans and berries.

Insert: A heavy container, made of ceramic or stoneware, which fits inside the slow cooker heater and holds the food.

Jalapeño: A medium-sized chili pepper that has moderate heat. Used to add spicy heat to foods.

Julienne: To cut food into small, thin strips, usually about ⅛-inch thick or less.

Leavening: Substances, including baking powder and yeast, that add carbon dioxide to products, making them rise and giving them a fine texture.

Legumes: The dried fruit of plants, legumes develop in a pod. They are usually cooked before serving, and include black-eyed peas, chickpeas, kidney beans, and black beans.

Mayonnaise: An emulsification of egg yolks and vegetable oil. Lower-fat varieties, with gums and stabilizers added, are available.

Meat thermometer: A thermometer that registers the internal temperature of meat when it's cooked.

Monounsaturated fat: A fatty acid that contains one double bond between two carbons. Considered the healthiest of fats. This fat is liquid at room temperature, but usually becomes solid at refrigerator temperatures.

Mustard: A condiment made by combining ground mustard seeds with vinegar, wine, or verjuice. Mustards can be smooth or coarse, depending on the grind of the seeds.

Neufchatel cheese: Technically, a soft cheese from France with an edible rind. Sometimes, low-fat cream cheese is marketed as Neufchatel in the United States.

Olive oil: Oil high in monounsaturated fat, made by pressing olives. Olive oil comes in several types, the finest being cold-pressed extra-virgin.

Pan fry: To fry in a small amount of fat in a hot pan or skillet.

Pepper: The fruit of a flowering vine, dried and used to add spice to foods. Pepper can be black, red, white, green, and pink. Or the firm-fleshed fruits of the pepper plant. Peppers include habanero, jalapeño, bell pepper, and Scotch bonnet.

Pita bread: A low-fat bread made by baking at a very high oven temperature so the carbon dioxide explodes, creating a thin-shelled hollow. Pita breads are usually cut in half and filled with sandwich fillings.

Protein: One of the three compounds that make up life, proteins are made from chains of amino acids. One gram of protein provides 4 calories.

Risotto: A dish made by cooking medium or short-grain rice with liquid or broths, stirring to release the starch from the rice.

Roast: A dry-heat cooking method; food is roasted in the oven at fairly high temperatures. Also refers to a cut of meat which has been roasted.

Roux: A combination of flour and fat, cooked until the starch granules in the flour swell. Used as the base for thickening sauces and soups.

Salt: Sodium chloride, a mineral compound added to foods to help enhance flavors. Also one category of taste bud.

Sauté: To cook food for a short amount of time over fairly high heat, stirring so the food cooks evenly.

Slow Cooker: An appliance which cooks by surrounding food with low, consistent heat.

Spices: Dried fruits, seeds, bark, or roots of plants that are used to season food. Spices include cinnamon, ginger, nutmeg, cardamom, and anise.

Taste: The ability to respond to chemicals in food, through the tongue and nose. There are five tastes the tongue can detect, including sweet, salty, bitter, sour, and umami. Taste is sensed in the brain.

Taste bud: Small papillae, or raised bumps, found on the tongue which contain receptors for the five tastes: sour, salty, sweet, bitter, and umami.

Vegetable: A usually savory edible part of a plant. Vegetables do not contain seeds.

Yogurt: A dairy product made by fermenting milk. Bacterial cultures are added to fresh milk. These bacteria then transform lactose, or milk sugar, to lactic acid, thickening the product.

APPENDIX B
SUGGESTED MENUS

When planning the menu, cost is an important factor, but nutrition, taste, and satisfaction are also important. Be sure to balance your meals by selecting foods that are nutrient dense and by building the most colorful plate possible.

THREE-COURSE LUNCH
Chicken Cheese Pitas
Autumn Soup
Caramel Chocolate Cake

DINNER FOR THE BOSS
Suave Cooked Salsa
Broccoli Cheese Soup
Beef Carbonnade
Crunchy Sweet Potatoes
Creamed Corn
Butterscotch Pears

BREAKFAST FOR FOUR, FOR TEN
Slow-Cooker Fruity Oatmeal
Egg Muffin Sandwiches
Coffee

CHRISTMAS DINNER
Sweet-and-Sour Mini Sausages
Fork Tender Pot Roast
Crunchy Sweet Potatoes
Creamy Ginger-Pumpkin Soup
Dried Cherry Bread Pudding

SUNDAY BRUNCH
Apple Walnut Strata
Sausage Rolls
Slow Cooker Scrambled Eggs
Coffee

PICNIC IN THE PARK
Apricot Ham Wraps
Potato Salad
Chocolate Coconut Peanut Clusters

SPECIAL BIRTHDAY CELEBRATION

The Dip Olé!
Three-Cheese Dip
Tangy Apricot Cube Steaks
Garlicky Green Beans
Pumpkin Bread Pudding
Wild Rice Salad

KID'S BIRTHDAY PARTY

Chili Mac
Orange Glazed Carrots
Tater Tot Casserole
Peanut Butter Fondue
Chocolate Marshmallow Dip

COZY NIGHT WITH FRIENDS

Honey Pineapple Chicken Wings
Teriyaki Pork Chops
Curried Rice
Coriander Carrots
Cherry Cobbler

NIGHT WITH FAMILY

Apple Stuffed Chicken Rolls
Curried Rice
Cheesy Carrots
Apricot Rice Pudding

FAMILY DINNER FOR TEN

Porcupine Meatballs
Cashew Rice Pilaf
Buttermilk Mashed Potatoes
Lemon Apple Rice Pudding

APPETIZER PARTY

Sweet 'n Crisp Curried Nuts
Buffalo Wings
Onion Chutney
Slow Cooker Caponata
Spicy Empanadas
Cheesy Taco Dip
Peanut Caramel Corn

WHEN THE CUPBOARD'S BARE

Potato Frittata
Sweet and Spicy Carrots
Curried Fruit Bake

INDEX

A

Alfredo sauce, 193
Apples, 16, 33, 35, 39, 41, 41, 56,
    85, 100, 110, 117, 122, 172,
    184, 199, 244, 305, 306, 307,
    318
    chutney, 142, 172
    pie filling, 36
Apricot, 220, 308, 324
    nectar, 131, 324
    preserves, 73, 88, 195, 220

B

Bacon, 38, 43, 47, 79, 94, 105,
    161, 189, 232, 240, 262, 286,
    292
Barbecue sauce, 83, 97, 133, 141,
    222
Barley, 268, 290
Beans, 11, 15, 19, 27, 72, 74, 77,
    80, 94, 128, 134, 152, 153, 155,
    163, 168, 169, 179, 181, 185,
    187, 189, 190, 192, 210, 224,
    223, 231, 235, 236, 245, 248,
    258, 267, 277, 278, 279, 280,
    284, 289, 291, 294, 298
Beef, 26, 58, 59, 60, 61, 62, 63, 64,
    65, 66, 67, 68, 69, 70, 71, 72,
    73, 75, 78, 79, 80, 211, 213,
    216, 217, 218, 221, 222,

Beef—*continued*
    223, 233, 256, 261, 264, 276,
    280, 281, 283, 289, 290, 291,
    293, 296,
    stock, 60, 62, 70, 71, 211, 219,
    242, 248, 255, 256, 276,
    278, 280, 283, 290, 296
Beer, 189, 253
Beets, 240
Biscuit mix, 160
Blueberries, 33
Bratwurst, 92
Bread, 35, 39, 46, 54, 112, 115,
    214, 217, 242, 244, 255, 304,
    311, 329
Broccoli, 60, 82, 119, 249
Buns, 218, 219, 221, 222, 223,
    224, 227
Buttermilk, 186

C

Cabbage, 26, 87, 92, 245, 259, 278
Cake mix, pound, 317
Caramels, 310, 315, 318
Carrots, 118, 130, 134, 135, 157,
    161, 178, 188, 191, 195, 197,
    203, 206, 276, 278, 283
Cashews, 200
Celery, 146, 152, 161, 181, 222
Cauliflower, 282
Cheese, 11, 14, 17, 18, 19, 26, 27,
    28, 30, 42, 45, 46, 47, 48, 49,
    50, 54, 86, 91, 99, 105, 107,
    108, 110, 113, 115, 118, 121,
    146, 153, 154, 163, 165, 166,
    170, 172, 173, 174, 175, 177,

Cheese—*continued*
    182, 193, 198, 203, 204, 205,
    207, 213, 214, 217, 225, 227,
    228, 242, 249, 253, 255, 274,
    295, 300, 323
Chicken, 54, 103, 104, 105, 106,
    107, 108, 109, 110, 111, 112,
    113, 114, 115, 116, 117, 118,
    119, 120, 121, 122, 123, 125,
    126, 127, 128, 129, 130, 131,
    132, 133, 134, 135, 136, 137,
    138, 139, 140, 141, 142, 226,
    231, 234, 239, 251, 252, 258,
    259, 263, 265, 271, 277, 281,
    298, 299, 300
    stock, 82, 94, 101, 114, 117,
    123, 130, 131, 134, 136,
    142, 147, 149, 157, 159,
    160, 161, 231, 232, 236,
    239, 240, 242, 244, 246,
    247, 249, 250, 251, 252,
    253, 277, 282, 286, 287,
    288, 292, 295, 297, 299, 301
Chickpeas, 166, 172, 174, 175, 180
Chiles, 126, 153, 170, 189, 194,
    215, 238, 296, 298
Chili, 215, 274
Chocolate, 303, 312, 314, 315
Clams, 158, 161
Coconut, 202, 312
Cooking
    flexibility, 5
    time, 4-5
Coriander, 191
Corn, 49, 53, 130, 152, 182, 187,
    194, 204, 235, 251, 258, 268,
    272, 274, 277, 279, 292, 297

Corn—*continued*
  cereal, 30
  chips, 261
Cornmeal, 52, 175
Coupons, 6
Couscous, 174
Crab. *See* Surimi
Cranberries, 317
Cream, 117, 150, 161, 165
Curry, 23, 29, 111, 131, 142, 147, 150, 172, 196, 199, 252, 308

D

Dumplings, 235

E

Edamame, 164
Eggplant, 13, 24, 177
Egg(s), 40, 42, 45, 47, 50, 53, 55, 115, 194, 311
  noodles, 70, 239, 254
Elbow macaroni, 77
Enchilada sauce, 108, 223, 225, 254
English muffins, 47

F

Fish, 144, 145, 153, 156
Fruit cocktail, 311

G

Garlic, 20, 22, 59, 67, 132, 181, 188, 192, 198, 205
Gemelli pasta, 146
Ginger, 156, 190, 208, 226, 250

Grapes, 146, 265, 271
Granola, 51, 202, 308, 318, 319, 322
Grits, 154

H

Ham, 53, 54, 99, 220, 229, 260, 273, 301
Hominy, 238
Honey, 22
Hot pepper sauce, 198, 300

K

Kaiser rolls, 216
Kielbasa, 248

L

Lasagna noodles, 86, 121, 173
Lemon, 138, 305
Lentils, 285, 299
Lettuce, 212, 213, 223, 225, 226, 258, 261, 274
Linguine, 158

M

Marshmallows, 303, 310
Meal planning, 4
Meatballs, 74, 76
Meatless crumbles, 214
Money saving tips, 2-3
Muffin mix, 80, 194, 323
Mushroom, 119, 133, 167, 173, 177, 178, 213, 214, 283
Mustard, 98, 116

O

Oatmeal, 37
Oats, 41, 318, 319, 322
Onion, 11, 13, 15, 16, 17, 21, 31, 55, 67, 85, 118, 126, 130, 132, 144, 211, 224, 242, 255, 269
Orange
  juice, 156, 188, 195
  marmalade, 156
Organization, 5-6

P

Paprika, 136
Parsnip, 197
Pasta, 281
  sauce, 63
Peaches, 36, 311, 322
Peanut(s), 29, 30, 32, 132, 307, 312
  butter, 125, 226, 321
Pear, 51, 172, 309
Peas, 201, 206, 276, 316
  split, 243
Peppers, 11, 31, 71, 93, 96, 103, 107, 108, 113, 126, 129, 153, 154, 163, 168, 175, 176, 177, 179, 180, 185, 210, 211, 216, 220, 225, 229, 264, 267, 272, 277, 284, 291
Pineapple, 12, 22, 36, 66, 111, 144, 308
Pineapple-orange juice, 208
Pita bread, 45, 210, 212, 213, 228
Pizza dough, 120
Popcorn, 32, 253

Pork, 82, 83, 84, 85, 87, 88, 89, 90, 91, 93, 96, 98, 222, 238, 254
and beans, canned, 74, 79, 84
Potatoes, 23, 40, 49, 55, 78, 99, 128, 133, 145, 148, 161, 165, 170, 171, 186, 193, 197, 198, 205, 229, 243, 246, 247, 260, 262, 264, 266, 268, 269, 272, 276, 278, 283, 286, 293, 295, 301
Pudding mix, 317
Pumpkin, 250, 304

R

Raisins, 90, 112, 117, 271
Red snapper, 149, 152, 266
Rhubarb, 313
Rice, 71, 76, 82, 114, 123, 131, 135, 140, 144, 147, 148, 151, 155, 157, 159, 166, 167, 176, 179, 182, 187, 196, 200, 201, 231, 267, 270, 279, 299, 305, 324
wild, 101, 164, 200, 265, 270, 273, 282, 288
Rutabaga, 197

S

Salmon, 147, 151, 157, 292
Salsa, 18, 19, 27, 58, 61, 113, 132, 153, 187, 189, 194, 225, 258, 264, 280
Sausage, 12, 44, 46, 48, 52, 69, 86, 95, 100, 228, 262, 286, 294
Shell pasta, 245
Shopping, 7

Shrimp, 17, 145, 148, 154, 266
Slow cooker, 2
best foods, 3-4
care of, 6-7
safety, 8-9
Soup, canned, 103, 105, 109, 110, 114, 116, 118, 119, 120, 133, 146, 160, 207, 249, 251, 279, 293
Spaghetti, 63, 95, 171, 178
sauce, 121, 177
Spinach, 42, 121, 159, 240, 258
Squash, 173, 174, 177, 199, 224, 235, 244, 267
Strawberries, 313
Surimi, 159
Sweet potatoes, 43, 100, 156, 160, 184, 193, 202, 208, 247, 260

T

Taco
sauce, 71, 77, 93, 94, 97, 211, 216, 261
shells, 113, 148, 170
Tater Tots, 207
Toffee, 322
Tomato(es), 11, 13, 17, 28, 31, 75, 95, 109, 139, 155, 158, 168, 169, 170, 176, 178, 213, 217, 231, 232, 245, 254, 273, 277, 284, 289, 291, 294
juice, 163, 176, 179, 221, 227, 281
sauce, 64, 68, 71, 76, 86, 103, 113, 123, 139, 134, 140, 154, 163, 175, 210, 213, 218, 280, 284, 285, 291, 294

Tortilla(s), 58, 59, 61, 91, 103, 163, 215, 223, 225, 229, 241
chips, 27, 69, 108, 109, 274
Tuna, 146, 150, 160
Turkey, 227, 288

V

Vegetable broth, 155, 164, 166, 167, 168, 172, 173, 174, 175, 176, 180, 182, 196, 235, 245, 279, 285
Vegetarian burgers, 23

W

Waffles, 38
Walnuts, 29, 30, 35, 37, 51
Waste, 7-8
Wheat, 130, 180
Wine, 139, 309
Wonton wrappers, 23

Y

Yogurt, 136, 142

Z

Zucchini, 224, 245